The Norfolk Guid
Wilhelmine Harro

GW00381300

Norfolk is changing faster than most counties; in
growth between 1976–1986 was 8%, which is si:
average. This is reflected in the number of new
buildings; the influx of new business people equalled by the proliferation of
'second homes' – people who originally came to Norfolk for holidays and
then on retirement decided to settle here.

Planning has in general managed to keep pace better than in many other
parts of England; the listing of buildings has been brought up to date, and
several historic centres of market towns, such as Holt, Harleston, Stoke
Ferry, Downham Market and Fakenham have been by-passed. Huge
supermarkets have sprung up on the outskirts of Norwich and many of the
small towns; and the village shop has almost disappeared, as has the post
office, the school, the pub, the railway station; and many a parish church is
threatened with closure too, which all seems paradoxical with the increasing population.

But there is still much to see; there are 659 churches which can be visited;
4 National Trust properties, Blickling, Felbrigg, Oxburgh and Sheringham, as well as stretches of coastline with bird sanctuaries; several great
private houses, such as Holkham and Houghton; sandy beaches and cliffs
where rare birds nest, pretty villages, woodlands, and interesting farm land
with fine barns and houses.

There are good museums and picture galleries in Norwich, and many
small and very attractive local ones, as at Cromer and Glandford.

There are first-rate theatres in Norwich and a thriving cinema in Cromer,
and there are often concerts in the wonderful settings of the parish churches.

It is a fascinating county from every angle.

Wilhelmine Harrod was born in Norfolk and has lived there for much of her
life; for the last 25 years in a beautiful Georgian Old Rectory in North
Norfolk. She is the widow of the distinguished Oxford economist, Roy
Harrod, who also came from a Norfolk family.

Lady Harrod has been involved in Conservation all her life; at one time
Secretary of the Georgian Group; on the Committee of the Oxford Preser-
vation Trust; a Trustee of the Historic Churches Preservation Trust;
Chairman for many years of the Norfolk Society (the Norfolk branch of the
Council for the Protection of Rural England); and a member of the Regional
Committee of the Norfolk Trust.

She is the Founder-President of the very successful Norfolk Churches
Trust. She has two sons.

THE
NORFOLK
GUIDE

Wilhelmine Harrod

The Alastair Press

Published by
The Alastair Press
2 Hatter Street
Bury St Edmunds
Suffolk

This edition published 1988
First published in 1958
by Faber and Faber Ltd
under the title of
"A Shell Guide – Norfolk"
Second edition 1964
Third edition 1966
Fourth edition 1982

ISBN 1 870567 35 8 Hardback
ISBN 1 870567 30 7 Paperback

Cover illustration: 'Salthouse from the Heath' by
Ruth Batchelor

Title page: The famous gingerbread rocks at
Hunstanton
Frontispiece: Sarah Hare, who died in 1744 ordered
this wax effigy of herself. It is in Stow Bardolph
church.
Endpapers (hardback only): Specimens of the
Architectural Antiquities of Norfolk by John Sell
Cotman

Acknowledgements

The first Shell Guide to Norfolk, which appeared
in 1958, was written jointly by myself and Charles
Linnell, who was then rector of Letheringsett. He
was very knowledgeable about everything in
Norfolk, where he had spent his whole life, and
his death at the age of 49 in 1964 was a sad loss.

For this edition there are many new entries: on
the churches and the city of Norwich by Simon
Cotton; on King's Lynn by Michael Begley; and
on the houses by Michael Sayer, with valuable
advice from Tony Baggs. Without their very hard
work and superior knowledge this edition would
never have appeared.

Preface

Norfolk was once almost an island – "cut off by
the North Sea and the Great Eastern Railway" –
but no longer; inter-city trains, dual carriage-
ways, and Norwich Airport make life easier for
the increasing numbers of the "executive" class
who discovered that property was cheap in East
Anglia, and moved in. Life here has changed to
accommodate them. Old cottages – two at a time
– are turned into smart homes, or old barns into
luxurious residences (this has not happened to
the redundant churches yet, though there are
rumblings of that too).

Most people use the new huge supermarkets
now, and the village shop and post office has to
close, and old people without cars – and there are
still a few – have to get someone else to fetch their
pensions and their groceries, and they miss the
community life of their own shop.

The incomers have brought advantages too.
Until lately there were only one or two good
restaurants in the county; now there are many
excellent and attractive eating places, and shops
and supermarkets are full of exotic foods as well
as local specialities like crabs and mussels, and
samphire from the marshes. There is even a local
oyster fishery at Morston. Local characteristics
that once were taken for granted are now
exploited; and the many new museums, picture
galleries and potteries show a new sophistication.
There are literally hundreds of "antique" shops,
and many useful second-hand bookshops in the
villages as well as the towns.

The landscape is changing too, with the new
houses and the tidy gardens full of conifers
and heather; the dear old gnomes have almost
vanished now and are much missed. With the
decline of agriculture, tourism is to be the main
Norfolk industry, and there is a rash of red-brown
signs pointing to some place of cultural interest –
a windmill, a stately home, a country park. The

great gales of October 1987 devastated woodlands, parks and gardens; efforts are being made to tidy up and replant but many places will look wounded for many years to come. There is much concern for ecology now, and new sites of special scientific interest; more protection for wild flowers and butterflies and the flora and fauna almost banished by the intensive farming of recent years.

Inevitably there have been other changes since this edition first appeared in 1982. The National Trust has acquired two more bits of coast, and has bought the very important Sheringham Park and Hall, the favourite work of Humphry Repton and his son. The Redundant Churches Fund has assumed responsibility for Thurgarton Church and allows several services a year in its now well-cared for interior. There are no longer any monks at Dunton or Snetterton but both have very well-attended "occasional" services. There are changes in the Norwich city churches too; St Gregory's is an Art Centre, with emphasis on music; St John De Sepulchre and St John Maddermarket are now used by local Orthodox groups; St Michael at Pleas has become a sort of Portobello Road with market stalls in the nave and a café in the sanctuary; St Michael (St Miles) Coslany is a centre for the martial arts; St Clement's, though officially "redundant", is still open for worship and private prayer, and is wholly maintained by the faith and effort of a Norwich bus driver, who is also a Methodist minister. The Rev. Jack Burton is incidentally a poet, and the author of "A City of Churches", the best and most evocative account of all the 52 churches which once made Norwich a fine city.

Other city churches are now threatened with closure, as are several in the county. The famous collection of medieval churches in Norfolk, with their fine furnishings, is being sadly diminished; they have been one of the main attractions of the county for hundreds of years; soon they will be, at best, just a feature in the landscape, and some may even disappear totally. The non-conformist chapel at Lamas is now a house, and its grave yard a garden; Anna Sewell's grave is embedded in the outside wall.

Among success stories, Gunton Hall has been restored and the very attractive out-buildings turned into houses, and the park and gardens are being revived. The little Adam church, in the care of the Redundant Churches Fund, is used often. Melton Constable Hall is in need of the same treatment before it deteriorates irretrievably. The Grange at Thornage is now a Camphill Village Trust home, and at Walcot the old barns and cottages are being converted to holiday homes convenient for disabled people, with a new lake and attractive planting. Several other big houses are now homes for the elderly, as at Letheringsett Hall and Swanton Novers.

In the field of industrial archaeology much progress has been made at the Fakenham Gas Works, built in 1846 and disused since the coming of North Sea Gas in 1965. The gas holder and much of the complicated machinery have been restored and The Fakenham Museum of Gas and Local History is housed in an out-building. In Gunton Park near Hanworth the water powered saw mill is being made to work again. In Norwich there has been a splendid revival of the Victorian Plantation Garden, in the shadow of the Roman Catholic Cathedral. Other buildings, for example the Soane lodges at Langley Park, have been restored.

On the whole, the good just about balances the bad; but only constant vigilance and, when necessary, stiff resistance, will ensure that we retain some of the character of this once remote county.

Wilhelmine Harrod, Holt, 9th March 1988

Illustrations

Note: Captions to the photographs include place names in **bold type**. These refer to entries in the gazetteer, pages 35–188.

Sall church – St. Peter and St. Paul, 15th century

The barn at **Dersingham** – 1671

Hempstead-by-Holt, reed-thatching the roof

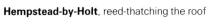

Carrstone house, **Stow Bridge** station

Chalk barn at **Thornham** near the Wash

Sheringham crab boats – sharp both ends to enable them
to land on the local beaches in rough weather

Greenhouse in village of Upper **Sheringham**

Introduction

Norfolk is not flat, a fact that surprises countless visitors who believe the whole county to be a continuation of The Fens. Although the highest points are only just over 300 feet above sea-level, there is tremendous variety in the landscapes. In the north, near Holt, and again in the west, around Hillington and Harpley, the county is undulating, and the best view of Norwich is from the heights of Mousehold Heath.

Perhaps the most characteristic feature is the wide sky, inspiration for countless artists. The atmosphere is brilliantly clear, the air bracing and the winds keen, sometimes bitterly piercing. Along the coast and in places inland the trees are twisted and bent by the force of the gales.

In some respects Norfolk is an island—it used to be said that it was cut off to the north and east by the sea, and to the south and west by the London & North Eastern Railway; certainly there are pronounced local peculiarities, notably the dialect. Historically, Norfolk has been independent; the traditional suspicion of 'foreigners' may have its roots in the days of the Danish invasions. In mediaeval days it was the most heavily populated county and a leading area in the woollen industry.

Although man appeared here in the Palaeolithic Age, some 400,000–500,000 years ago, the only evidence of this settlement is found in the form of his primitive flint tools; Palaeolithic settlements generally appear to have coincided with the river valleys. The first real sites to be considered are the Neolithic flint mines (c. 2000 B.C.), the most celebrated of which are Grimes Graves at Weeting near Brandon, where nearly 400 shafts have been located. The mines vary from open pits to shafts 30 feet deep with galleries radiating from them. Red deer antlers were used as picks. Other settlements of the period have been found at Edingthorpe, Whitlingham, in the Harpley–Rudham area, and Ditchingham—fairly well dispersed throughout the county—but none as impressive as Weeting, which has been described as the most exciting archaeological monument in eastern England. Although there is little to be seen on the ground, the late-Neolithic henge ('Woodhenge') at Arminghall is of considerable importance. This was a temple consisting of a central sanctuary surrounded by two ditches separated by a bank, accessible by a causeway. In the sanctuary eight oak posts were sunk into the ground in the form of a horseshoe.

The transition from the Neolithic to the Bronze Age occurred about 1700 B.C. and the most substantial remains of the period are in west Norfolk. This is due to the Wessex culture moving up the Icknield Way. Cell and disc barrows exist at Great Bircham, Weasenham and Rudham—all in the same area —Rushford and Salthouse. These barrows were probably mainly erected by the Urn folk of Wessex descent to contain cremations. They were used by successive generations and often occur in groups. Most barrows are close to the Icknield Way but there are others on the north Norfolk coast and in the Yare and Wensum valleys, and it seems that Norfolk first acquired a settled population (based on agriculture) about this time.

The Iron Age began about 500 B.C. and although there are fewer archaeological relics (owing to the greater chemical re-activity of iron), it has left much more sub-stantial sites above ground than the previous periods. This seems to be partly due to inva-sions around 250 B.C. which led to the con-struction of several hill forts, as at Nar-borough, Tasburgh and South Creake. A second series was built about the time of Christ: Thetford, Warham, Holkham and Wighton. Undoubtedly the most impressive of these is the Warham site, known confus-ingly as the 'Danish Camp', which overlooks the River Stiffkey and still retains some of its ramparts. The purpose of these forts may have been to guard the territory of the Iceni against the Belgae, but shortly after their construction the Romans moved into East Anglia and the whole situation changed, particularly after the Iceni rising (A.D. 60). It was to guard against a repetition of this that the signal station at Thornham was built; signals could be sent to the Ninth Legion at Lincoln at need.

The Roman administrative capital was Venta Icenorum (Caistor St Edmund), just south of Norwich, where substantial remains survive; an earthen rampart (a later Roman addition) and ditch enclose an area of some 40 acres just to the east of the Tas. The town grew from an assembly of small wattle-and-daub huts to masonry buildings. Venta was linked to Camulodunum (Colchester) by road—the present A140—whilst other roads built, or taken over, by the Romans include Peddars Way, which runs across the county from Holme to the Suffolk border. Substantial parts of this can easily be followed—particularly a stretch of 10 miles north of Castle Acre, the first four miles of which coincide with the course of the present road. Other roads led from The Fens through Denver and Fincham and past Elmham and Reepham to the east coast, up from Ixworth through to Attleborough and from Thetford to Bunwell (and Caistor). The last two of these crossed at Eccles, site of an as yet uncovered Roman settlement. Another road led inland from Holkham to Peddars Way at North Pickenham; whilst others remain to be discovered. One almost certainly led north from Venta towards Cromer through Stratton Strawless (like Long Stratton and Stradsett, the name indi-cates a Roman road). A number of settlements were located on these roads, and some have been excavated.

Some fifty years after the building of Venta Icenorum, the Roman town of Caister-by-Yarmouth was constructed to serve the port there (Caister was then on the sea and Yarmouth did not exist); substantial remains, including part of the flint wall (A.D. 150), survive. A number of contemporary villa sites have been located, principally in west Norfolk: e.g. West Newton, Appleton, Gayton Thorpe and Grimston.

Towards the end of the 3rd century, the Romans found it necessary to build fort-resses to combat Saxon pirates; one of these is in Norfolk at Brancaster. It is now about a mile inland from the sea and little remains to interest the visitor, but the big 3rd-century fort at Burgh Castle, on the Suffolk side of Breydon Water, retains its 15-foot-high walls on three sides—a most impressive sight.

The main features of the subsequent Saxon period are twofold. Firstly, the sub-stantial remains, possibly 8th century, of the Saxon cathedral at North Elmham, the seat of the bishop until the see was transferred to Thetford in 1075. It owes its survival to the fact that Bishop Despencer made it into a fortified manor in 1387. Then there are the 'ditches'—Launditch near Mileham, Fossditch near Weeting, and Devil's Dyke (Bichomditch) near Beechamwell. These earthworks—like others elsewhere in East Anglia—seem to have been constructed to control traffic on the most important roads, probably c. A.D. 400–500. They were several miles long and often begin and end at rivers.

Two Norman castle keeps exist—Norwich and Castle Rising. Both are considerable earthworks. At Castle Acre, once just as large, much survives, and is now being excavated. The Normans were able to subdue the native population only by virtue of military strength and it was to this end that the castles were built. Motte-and-bailey castles exist in fragmentary form at New Buckenham (the best), Old Buckenham, Thetford (very high motte), Bessingham, Wormegay, Mileham, Horsford and Swanton Morley, and ringwork at New Buckenham. Somewhat later are the very substantial city walls of Norwich (Lynn and Yarmouth were walled, too) of about 1300. The latest 'castles' are best exemplified by Baconsthorpe, Weeting and Caister, the latter with its Fastolf connections particularly splendid.

Of the few big Norman abbey churches, the naves of the two Benedictine houses, Binham and Wymondham, survive as parish churches. Of the two Cluniac houses, the magnificent west front of Castle Acre still stands and, although not so striking, much remains at Thetford. Apart from these, there are important remains of the Benedictine priory at Horsham, North Creake, Pentney and Coxford (Augustinian), Greyfriars, Lynn and Walsingham (Franciscan), and the imposing east wall of the Augustinian house at Walsingham. Also remains of the famous priory at Bromholm and the medieval shrine at Walsingham.

The villages

Domesday Book shows that East Anglia was the most heavily settled part of England in the 11th century, and a number of the settlements in existence then, or later, have now vanished. These are known as lost or deserted mediaeval villages; there are more of them (150) in Norfolk than in almost any other county.

Villages have been abandoned continually during the last several hundred years; the popular idea that the Black Death was the sole cause is unfounded. The Black Death was generally a cause of depopulation, rather than desertion, of a community, and most settlements diminished over a period, often of several hundred years, rather than 'overnight'. It seems that even before 1349 villages were in the process of being given up, and this probably indicates that these were settlements in areas of relatively poor soil—for example, Breckland which had been over-colonized. Another reason, particularly in the 18th century, was the creation of large parks around houses and the opening of uncluttered vistas. Houghton is an excellent example of this, some others being Holkham, Felbrigg, Didlington and Gunton. However, many of these settlements were in decline before their enforced removal. Also, although Norfolk soil was not as suitable for sheep as, say, the East Midlands, landlords do seem to have caused depopulation by over-grazing on the common lands and depriving the villages of their land. This appears to have been the case at Sturston, Bawsey, Leziate, Mintlyn, Narford and elsewhere. Another cause was encroachment of the sea, as at Eccles and Shipden.

Each settlement would, in ancient times, have had its own church; it seems to have been the aim of the Saxons and Normans to provide a church in each manor—the cause of that familiar Norfolk phenomenon, two or more churches close together, sometimes actually in the same churchyard, as, for example, at Reepham, Antingham and South Walsham. Often it is a solitary church that provides the evidence for a deserted village. It may be a ruin (Egmere, Burgh Parva) or intact (West Harling, Beeston St Lawrence), although it should be remembered that a church may have been built on an isolated site because that was a pre-Christian place of worship, as at Barmer or Keswick. Sometimes the church will be accompanied by a farm or Hall (Threxton, Frenze) or a few cottages (Pensthorpe, Oxwick). Perhaps the evidence is less obvious—a hollow way in the fields that was the old village street, as at Shotesham St Mary or Pensthorpe, or the fishponds (meat was forbidden throughout Lent) at Egmere.

The church was the most substantial building in all these villages and it is interesting to trace its fate. In a number of cases, the church has survived the loss of its village and continues in regular use, such as Bradeston, Beeston St Lawrence and Waterden, amongst others. Often, though, there has been a gradual decline. Houghton-on-the-Hill has probably consisted of no more than a farm, a church and the odd few cottages for several hundred years. A faculty was given to replace the original chancel with a very short one in 1760, but though it also had the usual Victorian restoration (1895), the little Saxon church was abandoned after the last war. At Hargham, the village was depopulated in the 17th century and the church tower fell about 1750. A faculty was given in 1753 to take down part of the church; the chancel and the eastern half of the nave were restored and were regularly used up to a few years ago. At Roudham, however, a man was working on the tower about 1735 and incautiously let

ashes fall from his pipe onto the thatched roof. The diminished community did not see fit to repair the church and it has been a ruin ever since. These are relatively recent examples; many churches fell into disuse in the 15th and 16th centuries and were in some cases appropriated to secular purposes as with Wallington, turned into a barn by Sir Francis Gawdy at the end of the 16th century. Others ruined by then include Egmere, Godwick and Quarles.

The creation of deserted villages has gone on up to the present day, with the formation of the Stanford Military Training Area, when Lynford, Langford, West Tofts, Tottington and Stanford were taken over by the army. On the other hand, Earlham, where the Hall and church had only the odd house for company for many years, has become a thriving suburb of Norwich and site of the University of East Anglia, and this metamorphosis may happen in other places as the population of Norfolk continues to increase and village character changes. More and more, and not only around the bigger towns, the villages are becoming dormitories or places where townspeople have holiday homes to which they eventually retire. Village life has been steadily eroded in the last two decades. Almost all the small village schools are closed and children are bussed to a larger one; the breweries close the small village pubs, the few that are left sell Real Ale and are privately owned; the branch lines have almost all been scrapped and the railway stations turned into trendy homes, antique shops or museums; many village post offices have gone and the old people have to ask friends to collect their pensions in the nearest town; Nonconformist chapels stand derelict or become private houses; and finally, the parish church is closed too, thereby ending what is often nearly a thousand years of continuing history and community life. Every one of these closures has been fought against, without success. Even those who never darken its doors like to know that the church is there, especially when the rest of the rural community life is being dismembered so quickly and so brutally. From 1968 when the Pastoral Measure sought to 'rationalize' the parish system, churches have been in graver danger than at any time in their history; even graver than at the Reformation or the Commonwealth. East Anglia, with its vast number of churches, its small quota of clergy and its low average income, is particularly vulnerable; in the diocese of Lincoln a church (Salmonby) has been demolished; in the diocese of Chelmsford a church (Langdon Hills) was 'converted' into a dwelling house (kitchen in the sanctuary, font retained as an ornament) and in the city of Norwich, St James, Pockthorpe, has become a puppet theatre. But the county of Norfolk, with over 600 mediaeval churches, can be proud of the fact that only 29 have been closed so far. There might have been more; many others were seen by the authorities as potentially redundant, but strong local feeling, encouraged by the Norfolk Churches Trust, has managed to stem the tide, perhaps even to turn it. As the Poet Laureate, Sir John Betjeman, has said, 'Norfolk would not be Norfolk without a church tower on the horizon or round a corner up a lane. We cannot spare a single Norfolk church. When a church has been pulled down, the country seems empty or is like a necklace with a jewel missing!' (*Norfolk Country Churches and the Future*, 1971). And though Alexander Solzhenitsyn is writing about central Russia, it could as well be Norfolk when he says, 'Travelling along the country roads ... you begin to understand why the countryside has such a soothing effect. It is because of its churches. They rise over ridge

and hillside; from far away they greet each other; from distant unseen villages they rise towards the same sky. But as soon as you enter a village you realise that the churches which welcome you from afar are no longer living. In one church machine tools are humming away; another stands silent, simply locked up. Our ancestors put their best into these stones and these belfries—all their knowledge and all their faith.' (*Stories and Prose Poems*, Penguin Books, 1973). In general, this is how people in Norfolk feel; luckily, since 1977 the Government has felt it too, and the Department of the Environment now gives very generous grants to parish churches, and they have been particularly good to Norfolk where the need is so great.

The churches

You cannot go far in Norfolk without seeing a mediaeval church. Just as the landscape varies, so do the churches; in the south-east, prosperous at the time of Domesday, one expects small, round-towered buildings; just as in the rich marshland and north-east of the county they are frequently large and airy, with a big 14th- or 15th-century tower. The landscape is dotted with them; in some parts they are like a fleet of ships riding the waves. They have survived storms before and will go on doing so.

Norfolk was one of the first parts of Britain to hear the Gospel and if there are none of the vast Saxon churches found elsewhere, like Brixworth in Northamptonshire, there are some hundred with evidence of 11th-century, or earlier, work, not to mention the substantial remains of the Saxon cathedral at North Elmham, the only one in England left so nearly intact. Many of these early churches may have been of wood, but builders also used the local pebbles, flint and carrstone. So it was that one of the great

15

East Walton

East Lexham

Norfolk hallmarks, the round tower, came about, for they required no stone quoins; there are about 120 of these towers in existence (and evidence for more) of which about a quarter are Saxon.

The coming of the Normans led to a fresh impetus, and many churches have work of this period; there are some 70 Norman doorways, for example, sometimes with tremendous carving like Hales, Larling and Heckingham. Stone became available, mostly waterborne, from as far as Caen in Normandy, although it was only used in quantity in the grander churches like Wymondham Abbey, Norwich Cathedral and St Margaret's, Lynn. As the prosperity of the area grew, so did the churches; some of the Norman parish churches of the late 12th century, such as Tilney All Saints and Walsoken, exemplify this. In the following century West Walton is *facile princeps*, although there are other fine examples such as

Thorpe-next-Haddiscoe

Merton

Binham Abbey, but the 14th and 15th centuries saw tremendous building and rebuilding as even small villages vied with their neighbours in erecting wide naves and soaring towers. The Decorated period gave us examples like Cley, Elsing, Harpley, Hingham, Great Walsingham, Beeston-next-Mileham, and the succeeding century went further with Salle, Cawston, Swanton Morley, Walpole St Peter and Terrington St Clement, with coastal churches such as Salthouse, Cromer and Blakeney, and particularly the Norwich churches, which reflect the prosperity of the region. Norfolk is not a county of spires, stone being something of a luxury; Methwold and Snettisham are the finest of a group in west Norfolk (where stone was most accessible), but there are a number of lead-covered spirelets, the finest being East Harling and Shipdham. As if by compensation, the towers frequently top 100 feet, with Cromer the tallest.

Bessingham

West Lexham

Quite apart from the actual fabric, the churches are rich in mediaeval fittings; the fine timber roofs as at South Creake, Salle, Cawston, Necton and elsewhere, although later 'restoration' has been responsible for the loss of many, so that Norfolk is not quite so richly endowed as Suffolk. Fonts range from the Norman, with a particularly famous group in West Norfolk at Toftrees, Shernborne, Burnham Deepdale, and elsewhere, through the so-called East Anglian 15th-century font with lions round the stem and the Evangelists and angels on the bowl, to the culmination, the Seven-Sacrament font, of which Norfolk has some 25 of the 40 known, particularly fine examples being at Sloley and East Dereham, with Gt Witchingham retaining much of its original colouring. There are fine 14th- and 15th-century benches, sometimes filling the church, as at Wiggenhall St Mary and Wiggenhall St Germans, with figures in niches at the end.

Runhall **Edgefield** old church **Gayton Thorpe**

and often delightful carving on the armrests. Then there are the dozen brass eagle lecterns (such as Norwich St Giles, 1493, and Wiggenhall St Mary, 1518), and the fine stained glass, products of the Norwich School of glass-painting, which may be seen at its best at East Harling, Norwich St Peter Mancroft and North Tuddenham (not to mention the imported continental 16th-century glass as at Erpingham and Warham St Mary). Then too, there are wall paintings which still come to light (Little Witchingham, Heydon and the 13th-century Adoration of the Magi at Shelfhanger have all been uncovered in the last decade), such as the St George at Fritton and Norwich St Gregory, the Life of St Christopher at Hemblington, the Jesse Tree at Weston Longville, and the Three Quick and the Three Dead (the three Kings out hunting, meeting three skeletons who assured them, 'as you are, so once were we') and Seven Works of Mercy at Wickhampton.

Tilney All Saints

Redenhall

But it is probably the rood screens which are Norfolk's greatest possession, for there are over 200, in part or complete, and many of these still retain their figure painting, the three finest undoubtedly being Barton Turf, Attleborough and Ranworth, although there are many other fine ones, whether with figures of saints and apostles or sometimes with whole scenes, notably the vivid St George at Wellingham; even those which have lost their painting are often exquisitely carved.

One can but marvel at this richness, particularly when the succeeding five centuries have taken their toll, through misplaced zeal, greed and neglect. But even now an impression of the grandeur can be realized through visiting churches like South Creake or Salle.

The period after the Reformation left few positive marks, although the singlemindedness of Bishop Wren of Norwich in following the policy of Laud has left a large number of

Jacobean and Stuart fittings, especially pulpits and altar rails which may be enjoyed to the full at Thompson, Tibenham and Wilby. However, the following twenty years saw a removal of many of these, and their predecessors, although it should be remembered that the Cromwell who caused most damage to the churches was Thomas, not Oliver.

After nearly 200 years of Reformation, Rebellion, Restoration, etc., it is no wonder that church affairs slept in the 18th century. Few churches were built—North Runcton, 1714, Yarmouth St George's, 1713, Gunton (Adam), 1769, Sisland, 1761, and Thorpe Market, 1795—which range from classical to Gothick; but several mediaeval churches retain to this day their fittings of that leisured age, whether just the box pews (Worstead, Terrington St John) or a complete set including pulpit and altar rails (Warham St Mary, Thurning, Bylaugh).

The Industrial Revolution left Norfolk fairly untouched, although a few Norman and Gothic-revival churches were built for the growing suburbs of Norwich and Yarmouth; on the other hand, many buildings were restored, often alas badly, although it must be remembered that without the much-maligned efforts of the Victorians, many of these buildings would by now be in ruins. An example of the work of Pugin is at West Tofts, which is closed, and can only be seen by arrangement, as it is in the Military Training Area. Another is the Roman Catholic Chapel in the grounds of Oxburgh Hall.

Within the last decade groups of parishes have been formed in rural areas, with perhaps as many as a dozen churches being served by a team of three or four clergy. This has undoubtedly been a mixed blessing; old insularities have been broken down but often the parishes concerned have lost much of their individual character and their local loyalties. Despite the plethora of churches, few have yet been made officially redundant, but some have been neglected to the verge of ruin, and the future of the disused Norwich City churches gives grounds for concern, although attempts are being made to find alternative uses for them.

It is probable that more churches will be proposed for redundancy, but it is to be hoped that as many as possible of these magnificent buildings will continue to serve their original purpose as focal points of the community (and, in a small village, often the only one left) and buildings dedicated to the glory of God.

Until 1979 when General Synod, at the instigation of a Norfolk Archdeacon, reconsidered this clause, the Pastoral Measure 1968 decreed that churches could be (and some were) demolished (without planning permission from which they were exempt) unless an alternative use could be found for them, although if they are of outstanding architectural or historical interest, they can be vested in the Redundant Churches Fund which will maintain the fabric and allow occasional services. The Norfolk Churches Trust, a voluntary body registered as a charity but with no endowments, does its best to accept churches which are in danger of ruination or conversion to an unsuitable use. They have at present Dunton St Peter and Snetterton All Saints, where small religious communities are established, living in the church and using the chancel for their daily offices; Barmer All Saints, West Rudham St Peter, Cockthorpe All Saints, Frenze St Andrew, Hargham All Saints, Rackheath All Saints and Morton-on-the-Hill St Margaret are all maintained by the Trust with local help and used for occasional services. At Tivetshall St Mary the ruins have been 'stabilized' by the joint efforts of the Norfolk

Churches Trust and the local authorities (particularly Norfolk County Council), who work closely with the Trust. The Redundant Churches Fund, a statutory body with money from the Government, the Church Commissioners and the sale of redundant church sites, maintains North Barningham St Peter, Barton Bendish St Mary, Buckenham Ferry St Nicholas, Coston St Michael, Feltwell St Nicholas, Gunton St Andrew, Hale St Margaret, West Harling All Saints, Islington St Mary, Brandiston St Nicholas, East Ruston St Mary and Moulton St Mary, and in these also there can be occasional services.

The Friends of Friendless Churches, a charitable organization doing just what its name implies, based in London but acting nationally, has helped many Norfolk churches and has assumed responsibility for Corpusty St Peter. There are four or five other 'redundant' churches, not counting the Norwich City ones, whose future is uncertain. These include Crownthorpe St James (almost a ruin), Panxworth, Thetford St Mary and Thurgarton All Saints. The pity is that any of these churches ever passed out of the parish system; they present a far greater problem to the Church as a whole when they are closed than when they remain in use. Had state aid come sooner than 1977, it is probable that there would be many fewer redundancies and closures. Norfolk is proud of its churches and believes that from every point of view, even the material one of tourist attraction, they should be maintained *as churches*; stripped of their function, their furnishings and their historical evidence (monuments, etc.) they lose everything except their landscape value, and in the cases of some 'conversions', they lose even that. So far, this has not happened in Norfolk, and it is confidently believed that it never will.

The landscape

The coastal belt has wide marshes along much of the perimeter, particularly north and west. In parts they are drained and cultivated, as in the Marshland and on the Sandringham estate, and the Waveney valley in the south where there are dykes and windmills; others are wild and full of bird watchers like the sanctuaries in north Norfolk at Scolt Head and Blakeney Point. Both here and in Broadland there are rare plants, birds and butterflies (some species, formerly extinct, have been re-established). One excellent way of realizing the variety in Norfolk is to visit the room of dioramas in the Castle Museum in Norwich and see the displays of wildlife in their habitats. The coastal fringe is occasionally interrupted by cliffs, as at Hunstanton and Cromer; those in the Weybourne and Sidestrand belt suffer particularly badly from erosion, caused in part by tidal action. This erosion has occurred further east, too, resulting in the disappearance of villages like Little Waxham and Eccles. In parts the defences against the sea are sand dunes stabilized by planting marram grass or pines; despite this, there has been bad flooding at times, particularly 1953 and 1978 around Wells and Sea Palling and the shores of the Wash. The villages mirror the geological features of the area; in the north-west towards the Wash, buildings are generally of brown carrstone or pink and white chalk. Further east, flints are the main material, with brick for corner quoins. The north Norfolk villages such as Blakeney and Wells have rows of 18th/19th-century houses running down narrow streets to their harbours. The majority of villages along this coast were ports until they succumbed to silt.

North-west Norfolk stands mainly on chalk, with carrstone and red chalk in the

Hunstanton/Snettisham area. The landscape is crossed by long sweeping roads, often straight, and one sees the same neat arrangement in the fields. This contrast to east Norfolk is paralleled in the increased distance between settlements, which tend to be larger. There is a great feeling of space under the wide sky.

Further to the east, the settlements are smaller and closer together, the roads wind more, probably a sign of piecemeal clearance of forest. The principal features, like the Cromer Ridge and the Glaven Valley, are products of Ice-Age glaciers and this undulating country is particularly attractive, with pretty villages like Glandford, Thornage, Hunworth and Stody.

Broadland marks another change; the Broads were created by mediaeval peat-digging. The land is flat but not the uniform flatness of The Fens, for there are subtle variations in level, even as the coast is approached; unlike The Fens, too, there is more woodland. The villages tend to be larger, although the area was never as prosperous as the north-east, and this is reflected in the smaller churches, which usually stand on the highest point, away from any danger of flooding. The original settlements close around them probably spread out as drainage improved.

Inland and south of Norwich the landscape and architecture change again; here there are rivers and lush watery meadows with many willows. Between the valleys of the Yare, Tas and Chet, the landscape is typically flat, as around New Buckenham and Bunwell, or particularly along the A140 between Dickleburgh and Long Stratton. The cottages are built of clay lump, painted pink and white, with very steep-pitched roofs, usually thatched, and sometimes with black-painted weather boarding. Although some villages near Norwich have become

dormitories with mass-produced housing, for example Tasburgh, modern council housing at its best can be seen at places like Loddon and Hales. The parishes here are often very small, like their churches—which, though small, are well cared for; the villages like Gissing, Framingham Earl and Morningthorpe are snug under their big trees. There are fine oaks and ashes in what few hedgerows are left, the atmosphere is calm and dreamy, and one thinks of Crome and Gainsborough, who got it exactly right in the *Poringland Oak* and *Mr and Mrs Andrews*. The Waveney valley and Suffolk border have great wide marshes, bigger churches, and very scattered villages with little staithes along the river and its tributaries, some abandoned and weed-grown, others with an inn and sailing boats, like Burgh St Peter.

Breckland covers a large part of south Norfolk around Thetford and Brandon. The standard work on Breckland, W. G. Clarke's *In Breckland Wilds*, defined it as an area covering some 250 square miles with a northern boundary about Narborough, extending in the west to Feltwell and to Garboldisham and Harling in the east (it extends into north Suffolk, too). It is the least densely populated part of eastern England, but it has not always been so, for the area was crossed by three pre-historic trackways. There are nearly 30 'lost' villages here, settlements which were deserted during the Middle Ages. The soil is light and sandy, and the area was open heathland, for the vast forests of pines, firs and other conifers are plantings by the Forestry Commission only over the past 70 years. Another part of Breckland has become inaccessible for a different reason —the Ministry of Defence took over five villages to make what was then called the Stanford Battle Area in 1942. This is now known as the Military Training Area. How far the depopulation of five villages and difficulty of

The north coastal fringe

(*above*) **Burnham** Overy Staithe

(*below*) **Salthouse**

Thornham (*above*)

Wells-next-the-Sea (*below*)

▷

Broadland

access to four important mediaeval churches is counterbalanced by the preservation of fauna and flora in an area free of pesticides and fertilizer is a moot point. Many of the 18th- and 19th-century houses which stood in their own parks, inside and around the Military Training Area, have vanished, such as West Harling, Buckenham Tofts and Didington. One characteristic feature of Breckland is the meres, large ponds whose water levels vary from full to empty over quite short periods of time, depending on the water level in the chalk. Where Breckland does survive unforested, the heath has an

unspoilt, wholly natural appearance and one would not be surprised to see bustards, though unfortunately the last one was shot in 1838. There are several large villages and towns with fine churches; Swaffham is a splendid Georgian market town, but Thetford has expanded very rapidly as an industrial town, taking London overspill, losing its former identity, but also declining in popularity with the Londoners.

North of Breckland is central Norfolk, an area crossed by the Yare and Wensum, the latter winding its way south-east to Norwich through a particularly attractive valley around Morton and Ringland. Although this is generally a tableland, as with the boulder clay area called 'High' Suffolk, there are subtle gradients with occasional delightful vistas; just as in Suffolk, there are many moats, often abandoned and deserted. There are some large towns like Wymondham, Dereham, Attleborough and Hingham, which have fine houses and churches, but typically there are small villages with moderate-sized churches. Here in the granary of Norfolk, the loss of hedges to create bigger fields has had its effects, both on wildlife and topsoil.

Last of all there is Marshland, the really flat area joining Norfolk to the Fens, with rich black land reclaimed from the sea. Here are great flat fields separated by ditches, with yellow-brick pumping stations, neat brick houses, acres of tulips, hyacinths, strawberries, fruit trees, potatoes and corn, and really huge and magnificent churches, e.g. Terrington St Clement, Walpole St Peter and West Walton. The villages are rather dull, but here and there is an old romantic house like the remains of the ancient home of the Kerviles at Wiggenhall St Mary.

The houses

The great houses of Norfolk are famous—like Raynham, Holkham and Houghton—but often one comes across some superb red-brick Tudor house, as at Wilby or Kirstead. In the absence of local stone (the exceptions being flint and carrstone), many Norfolk houses are built of brick, which was in regular use from the 15th century. One of the earliest examples is Sir John Fastolf's castle at Caister (1432–5), and Lord Scales' gatehouse at Middleton followed soon after. Oxburgh (1482) is, of course, pre-eminent at this date, although the original work at Mannington is of this period, and one regrets the loss of Shelton and the ruination of Baconsthorpe. Elsing, serene in its moat, is partly timbered and its chapel has a nice perpendicular window with the same battlement tracery as in Lyng church, and was built about 1460–70.

The early 16th century is represented by Hunstanton Hall, Great Snoring, Wallington, Denver, Barnham Broom, Great Cressingham and, most spectacular of them all, the Fermors' great house at East Barsham. Later in the century came Fincham, Thorpland, Rainthorpe, Breckles (1583), Gowthorpe, Morley, Flordon, Shimpling, Thelveton, Woodhall in Hilgay, Foulden and the greater seats of Heydon (1581–4), Stiffkey, Channonz in Tibenham (1569, with only one wing left) and the great Paston seat of Oxnead (again only one wing left). What Norfolk lacks is smaller timber-framed manor houses in a number comparable to those surviving in Suffolk, and it is no surprise that of those that do survive, Blo' Norton and Wortwell are right on the border, and Great Ellingham and Saxlingham Nethergate in the south of the county.

From the Jacobean period and just after that date Kirstead (1614) and Wilby, Gillingham, Barningham (1612), Felbrigg (c. 1620), Little Melton and Bawburgh (1634). The two great houses of this time are, however, the mansions of Sir Henry Hobart, the Chief Justice, at Blickling (1616–27) by Robert Lyminge, the principal architect of the Cecils' great house at Hatfield in Hertfordshire, and Sir Roger Townshend's new one at Raynham (1622) which shows the strong influence of Inigo Jones, although the builder employed was William Edge. It was now that the shaped gable made its appearance in Norfolk, and Bawdeswell, Gateley, Hoveton House and Snettisham Old Hall

Breckland: near **Didlington** (*above*); **West Harling** (*below*) ▷

are among the many pleasing examples of this tradition that occur after 1660.

Relatively few of the manor houses of the 16th and early 17th centuries survived as family houses beyond the early 18th century. There was a tendency to replace the earlier Hall with a classical house (Morley is a good example and so is Hardingham, where the Old Hall survives near the church), or to add a wing. The new classicism was followed at Ryston (1669–72), built for himself by Sir Roger Pratt, the amateur architect and designer of Coleshill in Berkshire for his cousin (though not much of his work survives at Ryston), and by another gentleman amateur, William Samwell, in the new wing at Felbrigg (1674–87). In its decoration, this wing is markedly similar to Melton Constable (1664–70) and the tradition was also followed at Ditchingham, Barton Turf and, much later, Honing (1748). One of the best examples of the period is at Narford, built about 1700 (although added to later) for the scholar and antiquarian Andrew Fountaine, with its frescoes by the Venetian, Giovanni Antonio Pellegrini (1708–13).

There was an economic reason, too. Between the 12th century and the Restoration period, the number of gentry at any time was some 400 families. There were some 450 lordships of manors, although latterly often amalgamated. However, the growth in estate size that occurred between the late 17th and early 19th centuries reduced the number of gentry by nearly half, and the old manor houses became tenant farmhouses far more often than they were replaced by new halls. It was by the biggest of these growing estates that the Palladian revival was supported, beginning with Sir Robert Walpole's great house at Houghton (1721) by Colen Campbell. Holkham, begun in 1734, inevitably takes pride of place. Designed for Thomas Coke by Lord Burlington and William Kent, its austere and restrained exterior combined with its palatial rooms make it one of the finest houses in Europe. Matthew Brettingham who completed Holkham, went on to enlarge Langley for the Proctors and Gunton for the Harbords (although his work here was burnt in 1882). In the same style are Kimberley, built by Thomas Prowse for the Wodehouses about 1750 and Wolterton, built for the junior branch of the Walpoles by Thomas Ripley, 1727–41.

Norfolk is, of course, abundant in Georgian houses. Soane is well represented at Shotesham (c. 1785) and Letton (1785–8) and by the music room and the cruciform library at Earsham (1785) and, vicariously, at Burnham Westgate (1783). Wyatt was responsible for a new wing at Gunton (c. 1785). There are rococo interiors at Gateley and Cavick House, Wymondham. It was at this time that the north front of Blickling (1767–79) was built by Thomas Ivory, the architect of the Assembly Rooms in Norwich (1754), and his family, although here the Jacobean style is carefully matched. Lancelot (Capability) Brown laid out the grounds at Holkham (1762) and Ditchingham. The county proliferates, meanwhile, in medium-sized and small Georgian seats like Hilborough (1779), Thornham, Hoveton Hall, Smallburgh, Briningham, Sparham House, and parsonages frequently of comparable size.

Humphry Repton, with his son John Adey Repton, built Sheringham Hall (1812–19) which still retains its well-laid-out grounds and the original Red Book. He was also responsible for landscaping at Catton, Honing (including some alterations to the house in 1792), Hoveton House, Walsingham, and perhaps Bolwick. John Adey Repton remodelled the south front at Barningham (1805) and George Stanley Repton added the arcading on the garden front at Wolterton (1818).

The Gothic revival begins in a very restrained way with Beeston St Lawrence (1786) and continues with Donthorne's work, particularly Cromer Hall (1829), the refronting at Westacre High House (1892) and the stables at Felbrigg (1829), but his Hillington Hall has been demolished. Moving further into the 19th century, Charles Barry jun. is represented by the great ruined mansion of the Lombes at Bylaugh, Blore built Haveringland (1839, now gone) for the Fellowes family, and added a wing to Merton (c. 1830), Salvin built North Runcton Hall (1835, now demolished) and worked at Ryston (1867). Ewan Christian was responsible for the old Bishop's Palace and Woodbastwick Hall (demolished), also for work at Docking and Pynkney, while Teulon enlarged Shadwell. Garboldisham Manor, built by George Gilbert Scott jun. (1873), has gone, except for the stables.

Ken Hill at Snettisham is by J. J. Stevenson (1879–80) and in 1899 Sir Edwin Lutyens built the Hall and The Pleasaunce at Overstrand. The new 20th-century houses include Happisburgh Manor by Detmar Blow (1900) and Home Place at Holt (1903–5) by E. S. Prior, the work being superintended by Randall Wells; Templewood, Northrepps, by Seely & Paget (1930), and the neo-Georgian Hockering (1968) by Cecil B. Smith, whilst substantial additions were made to Lexham Hall about 1950 by J. Fletcher-Watson.

The break-up of many estates (about 110 in Norfolk since 1900) and the changed circumstances of those that remain have led to the conversion of many houses to institutional uses and to the separation of others from the land that formerly supported them. The future of older manor houses like Flordon, Kirstead and Wilby as viable farm-houses looks more doubtful than ever, and these are now joined in uncertainty by the Halls at Melton Constable and Letton. It is a melancholy necessity to record a long list of country-house demolitions: Ashwicken, Bagthorpe, Barmer (1956), Beaupre (1966), Boyland (1947), Brooke Hall, Buckenham Tofts (1946), Bylaugh (ruinated 1952), Clippesby, Congham (burnt), Costessey, Didlington (1956), Elmham (1947), Garboldisham (both the Old Hall, fire 1955, and the Manor), Gawdy Hall (1939), West Harling (1931), Haveringland (1947), Hemsby, Hillington (1946), Hingham (c. 1947), Honington (1966), Marham (1931), Great Melton, Mileham, Necton (1949), Petygards, Rollesby (1949), Spixworth (after 1946), Thursford, Toftrees (1958), West Tofts, Weeting (1952), Weston (1926), Witton Hall, Woodbastwick (1971), Worstead (1939), Wretham and Wroxham.

The great estates of Norfolk were sometimes responsible for the building of parsonage houses, as at Warham where the house north of the church (now Church Farm) is a typical Holkham building of about 1802; sometimes a college patron (as at Saham Toney where the arms of New College, Oxford, are on the fine Georgian former rectory), but more often it was the Church itself. One of the most attractive features of Norfolk villages was the closeness of church and parsonage house; sometimes in a grove of trees, cedar and copper beech predominating, with a short path and a wicket gate to the church and often a snowdrop-carpeted shrubbery as a 'sermon walk'. Two of the oldest parsonages are at Methwold (early 16th century) and Great Snoring (1525); some of the others have 16th- and 17th-century cores, though many were enlarged and refronted in the 18th and early 19th centuries when restoration of the church itself was not the first consideration. But it was the whole group that was so attractive and made such a significant point in the village, socially as well as aesthetically. Nearly all the parsonage houses have now been sold away from the church; but old memories of fêtes and parish teas still persist; it is not so easy to bowl for a pig on the handkerchief-size, toy-strewn lawn of the up-to-date, easily-run, cheap-to-heat box into which the clergy are now fitted. It is all part of social change which has hit Norfolk as hard as anywhere else.

The gardens

Norfolk is not particularly famous for its gardens. It has one famous gardener, Maurice Mason at Fincham, who has vast knowledge as well as tireless enthusiasm and has created acres of extremely interesting planting. There is the wonderful garden at Blickling, which has everything, from the bluebells and azaleas lining the vistas and rides in the woodland round the Temple, and the spring flowers under the huge Oriental plane, to the great *parterres* re-designed by Norah Lindsay in 1930, which are full of colour and interest until late in the autumn. Felbrigg, another National Trust house, has an interesting, recently made garden inside its very fine brick walls. Oxburgh has an interesting *parterre* of an old French design beside the moat. These are all National Trust houses, and few private owners can compete, though in the village of Heydon three or four owners of the pretty old houses there open their gardens on the same day. There is a river and lovely trees, and it is a charming place. Sheringham Hall is probably the best of the private gardens: there are acres of rhododendrons, magnolias, azaleas

and many extremely interesting rarities, and beyond them are a lake and beautifully planted pleasure grounds. Raveningham Hall is a garden full of interest. Opening times for all these, as well as the Sandringham gardens (where there are some fine old trees), must of course be checked, and there are other gardens which often have something special, like the old fashioned roses at Alby Hall or the snowdrops at Walsingham Abbey.

What are the dangers to Norfolk which threaten its individuality? The influx of newcomers, whether attracted by new industry or in retirement, certainly has its effect. Some villages are increasingly populated by the elderly or those who live there only at weekends or on holiday. By no means all new housing has been of as high a quality or as sympathetic to historic patterns as one would like, though there are definite signs that planning officers in the councils are increasingly aware of our heritage, whether in secular or ecclesiastical buildings. The holiday industry has proved a mixed blessing, with bungalows, chalets and cabin cruisers all culprits. The effects of hedgerow removal have already been touched upon. Public transport has deteriorated; Norfolk has the highest private car ownership per capita, and it is uncertain whether this is cause or effect.

However, there is still much to enjoy in Norfolk; it is less vulgarized than other coastal counties, and its natives value it for its oddness and unspectacular beauty. Norfolk women who marry outside the county are known for bringing their husbands back to work or to retire. It still just manages to be different, as it has always been proud to be; this difference cannot last much longer, so let us enjoy it while we can.

Castle Acre Priory

Gazetteer

The number in brackets following the place name refers to the square on the map at the back of the book where the place is to be found

Acle [12] There are interesting old houses in the centre of the village. In St Edmund's Church, whose round tower has battlements built in 1472, at a cost of £16, is a font of 1410 whose panels include, as well as the symbols of the evangelists, wild men or wodehouses, lions, angels and a pietà. Early 15th-century inscription in Latin, under chancel window. Chancel built by William de Culpho, rector, 1362. Money left for screen and north porch, 1496–7.

The Acres [8, 9] *Castle Acre* is a small town within the outer bailey of the castle, the motte with considerable remains of the curtain wall being on the south side. Extensive excavations have been carried out recently. There is a fine wide street leading from the church to the gateway, originally one of the entrances to the castle built by the de Warennes, standing at the opening of Bailey Street with its rows of cottages running down to the river, and the fine Tudor house up a narrow street on the right. To the west of the town on the banks of the Nar is the Cluniac priory, the finest monastic remains in East Anglia. There is a very noble west front flanked on the south by the prior's lodgings in which there is a small museum. The church of St James, an imposing 15th-century building, contains a most beautiful font cover, a fine screen, and 15th-century pulpit. *South Acre* in a pretty, wooded churchyard, has a finely restored church of St George, containing an early 16th-century font cover on top of a Norman font. There is also a magnificent brass to Sir John Harsicke (1454) and a carefully restored table tomb with effigies for Sir Edward Barkham 1621), Lord Mayor of London. The Revd Edmund Daubeney (d.

1914) carved the lectern and other fittings. At *Westacre* are remains of a house of Augustinian canons, once larger than Castle Acre priory. The gateway still exists, as do some of the conventual buildings. On the other side of the river are the ruins of the boys' school maintained by the canons and on the high ground on the road to South Acre, in the decayed village of Custhorpe, the ruins of St Bartholomew's Chapel. In the east window of All Saints' Church, Westacre, is a splendid gentleman in hunting pink dated 1907. Westacre High House was built in the 18th century. A castellated front and Doric pilasters and pillars were added in 1829. The principal rooms are on the first floor.

Alburgh [17] All Saints' Church tower has a cap with curiously buttressed crockets, unusual Great War monuments adorned with marble shako and helmet; remains of old gesso-work screen.

Alby-with-Thwaite [5] St Ethelbert's Church has 15th-century tower and woodwork, and makes a charming group with its former rectory beside it in the trees.

Aldborough [5] The small, much restored, church of St Mary contains very good 15th-century brasses; and an east window whose glass commemorates a Victorian rector who was a famous bulb grower. The spring flowers in the churchyard are thought to be due to him. He was the Revd J. G. Nelson and he gets a mention in Miss Gertrude Jekyll's *Wood and Garden*. Aldborough Hall is late Georgian and is prettily sited.

Aldeby [18] Fragmentary ruins of the Benedictine Abbey. St Mary's

Church has a Norman west door in a restored front, and a central Norman tower with very high narrow arches at the crossing, on one of which is carved THIS STEPEL WAS BELT 1633; double sedilia and piscina (13th century). A modern Virgin and Child looks well in the niche over the north porch.

Alderford [10] A pretty village with a stream running through it. The well-restored church of St John the Baptist has a very good Seven-Sacrament font. Piscina for the altar in the former north aisle remains in the outside wall.

Anmer [2] The 18th-century Hall, built round an earlier house, is in a well-landscaped park. The church of St Mary near it has the arms of George II and many hatchments. There is a baptistry in the south aisle with a pretty screen. Three interesting Victorian paintings by Sir Noel Paton in the chancel, and two fine chairs with the Order of the Garter in woolwork. An atmospheric, unusual church with interesting monuments to the Coldham family. The Hall was formerly the seat of this family but is now the residence of H. R. H. The Duke of Kent. It is part of the Sandringham estate.

Antingham [5] Two churches, St Mary's and St Margaret's, stand side by side but St Margaret's is in ruins. St Mary's contains a brass to Richard Calthorpe and family of nineteen. A window on the south side of the chancel shows Martha and the two Marys, in memory of Mrs Martha Dolphin, wife of a former incumbent. Martha carries a saucepan, ladle and jug.

Appleton [2] Consists of Appleton House where Queen Maud of Nor-

Aylsham

way lived, a farm, and the ruins of a church with a 12th-century round tower and a stone slab commemorating some 17th-century Pastons—a younger branch of the famous 'Letters' family. There is a holy well near the church. A sour little book, *Eighteen Years on Sandringham Estate*, was written by King Edward VII's first tenant here; it is scarce because the Royal Estate agent ordered all available copies to be burnt. The estate is part of Sandringham. The Hall was built in 1863. The Italianate water tower, a splendid landmark, was designed by Martin ffolkes in 1877, and has been beautifully converted into holiday accommodation by the Landmark Trust.

Arminghall [11] There was once a late Neolithic temple site, or woodhenge, here. St Mary's Church has old poppy-headed bench ends as well as Victorian benches designed by J. P. Seddon.

Ashby St Mary [11] Has a nice Hall with 1850ish additions in white brick to a 17th-century gabled house and a (probable) 18th-century tower—use unclear —nearby. St Mary's Church with continuous nave and chancel has a Norman door, heavy 17th-century altar rails, small font cover of same date and a plain poor box, probably earlier. There are some old benches restored, return stalls in the choir and good wrought-iron brackets in the nave.

Ashby with Oby and Thurne [12] (near Thurne) Here one is in the most remote corners of Broadland. The lane from the main road at Clippesby goes meandering on and on with numerous tracks leading off onto the marshes and among the scattered cottages of Ashby and Oby. At the very end is Thurne Mouth where the Thurne joins the Bure, and not far away is Thurne

Church (St Edmund) which has a 17th-century altar table and rails.

Ashill [9] St Nicholas' Church has a window to the memory of the Revd Bartholomew Edwards rector for 77 years, and some 15th-century glass.

Ashmanhaugh [11] A scattered village. There is a good 18th-century house with pedimented gables, east of the church. St Swithin's Church itself, up a path beside thatched cottages, has a small, rebuilt round tower. A table tomb in the sanctuary for Hono Bacon (1591), a few old bench ends and a well-preserved stair turret with plain indications in the wall of the extent of the rood loft.

Ashwellthorpe [16] The interesting 13th/14th-century church of All Saints, which has the unusual feature of a step down into the chancel contains a splendid alabaster tomb with effigies of Sir Edmund and Lady de Thorpe (c. 1417). There were originally two villages here and in Chantry House near Wreningham Church the arch braced roof of the former parish church of Ashwell is preserved Ashwellthorpe Hall is a Tudor revival building dating from 1831 and 1845, built by Lady Berners. The village is full of new development

Ashwicken [8] The approach to All Saints' Church by a chestnut avenue is charming. The interior is Victorian; the font is in 14th-century style.

Aslacton [16] The village has nice old houses, the remains of a wind mill, and St Michael's Church with a pre-Conquest tower. The pulpit carving of David and Goliath is probably 16th-century Flemish Porch, 1438.

Attleborough [16] Renowned for turkeys and cider which Norfolk people are sure is just as good as any that comes from Somerset or Devon. Though the town is one of the least interesting of the Norfolk market towns, there is a pleasant

Baconsthorpe Hall

row of 19th-century villas along the main road towards Thetford, and a most interesting church dedicated to St Mary. This has a Norman central tower, the bottom stage of which is now the chancel as the original east end is destroyed. There are transeptal chapels and a lofty 15th-century nave; but the glory of the church is the magnificent 15th-century screen right across the nave and aisles, and complete with rood loft, along the front of which are painted the arms of the twenty-four bishoprics then established in England. Along the top is an Elizabethan inscription, a

quotation from the 3rd chapter of Proverbs. Above are mediaeval frescoes. The pulpit is said to have been carved by Grinling Gibbons; the mediaeval font was originally in Booton Church, and came here in 1975 from St Mary Magdalene, Norwich. The Hall, basically a large Victorian farmhouse, is surrounded by a dry moat.

Attlebridge [10] A small village on the Wensum. St Andrew's Church contains a good example of the Norfolk type of chalice brass commemorating George Cunyngham, rector, 1525.

Aylmerton [5] The round-towered church of St John the Baptist stands above the village. John of Gaunt was patron for some time which may account for the castellated south door. Mid-14th-century chancel windows by architect of Acle chancel. There are remains of a chapel on the north side, reduced when the nave was rebuilt about 1400.

Aylsham [5] Has a splendid market place surrounded by graceful 18th-century houses and a plaque to the memory of Christopher Layer, one of Norfolk's few Jacobites, who suffered at Tyburn in 1723. There are many fine mansions set in pleasant grounds. The 14th/15th-century St Michael's Church with lofty west tower with galleries, transepts and remains of a rood screen, has many memorials including an imposing one to John Jegon, Bishop of Norwich (1618). In the churchyard to the south of the chancel is a neat Gothick memorial and a few rose trees marking the grave of Humphry Repton, the landscape architect. Woodgate House is a Queen Anne house of nine bays and three storeys, with attractive grounds and a lake.

Babingley [2] On the Sandringham estate. Here the tower of the ruined 14th-century church of St Felix can be seen in the fields west of the old road. The nave is roofless; the buttressed carrstone tower still looks fairly solid except for crumbling parapets. There is a nice decorated window in it, and an even better one re-set in the wall which shortened the nave at some unknown date. There is a two-bay south arcade and a blocked one to match on the north. The porch has the remains of brick and stone benches. There are two odd arched recesses west of the east wall. It is a lovely place. The old Hall was a fine Jacobean house refronted in 1820. The present church, which

Banham

doubles as a parish room, was built in 1894, as a gift from King Edward VII when Prince of Wales. It has atmosphere, in spite of being built of corrugated iron and pitch pine.

Baconsthorpe [4] In the fields towards Bodham are considerable remains of the Castle (well cared for by the Department of the Environment), a defended manor house built by Sir John Heydon. It was begun about 1450 and completed in 1486 by Sir John's grandson, Sir Henry. It is moated on three sides; on the fourth is a mere. There are two gatehouses; the inner one has fine vaulting and was quite a spacious dwelling. But it was the outer gatehouse, known as Baconsthorpe Hall, which was inhabited long after the main castle was dismantled in the 17th century. An engraving after Repton shows it (in 1781) with two pepper-pot turrets, one of which remains. The other fell in 1920 and the place ceased to be lived in. The grouping of the church and the 18th-century former rectory is charming. The

latter was completed in 1770 at the expense of Zurishaddai Girdlestone, rector and Lord of the Manor, and the parishioners. The tower of St Mary's was rebuilt in 1740 and much restoration was done on the rest of the church in 1768 when it was 'in a very ruinous and deplorable state', for it was the boast of a villager that 'he had been churchwarden off and on for forty years and had never put the parish to any expense.' There is a good monument to Sir William Heydon (1592) in the south aisle, and some brasses of importance. There is a fine Easter Sepulchre in the chancel and opposite is an attractive angle piscina c. 1260–80.

Bacton [5] Here is the vast North Sea Gas installation. Conservationists opposed this site on the grounds of spoiling an area of outstanding natural beauty and the operators have made a pathetic effort to 'landscape' the site. St Andrew's Church has a fine tower of 1471, and good 14th/15th-century font; and even better than the church are

the remains of Bromholm Priory —famous in the Middle Ages for possessing a relic of the true Cross. Bromholm is mentioned often in the Paston Letters. The village has somehow retained a nice seaside character.

Bagthorpe [2] A hamlet with a row of very pretty cottages and St Mary's Church built in 1853, by W. J. Donthorne—almost all that is left of this attractive place. The Georgian Hall in a well-planted park was demolished after the war. The church once contained a fine Norman font, now in a Norwich museum. There is a large Chad monument on the south wall. This church, which was falling into disrepair, has been rescued by the Norfolk Churches Trust.

Bale [4] There are pretty farmhouses and cottages here, and on the little green by All Saints' Church, where the famous giant oak was felled in 1860, there is now a grove of fine ilex trees. The church itself is mainly Perpendicu-

Barmer

lar with a 13th-century chancel, but its great interest is the glass in the south window, which includes two 14th-century representations of prophets with scrolls. The rest of the window is filled with 15th-century Norwich School glass; among the golden feathered angels, many with musical instruments, is an Annunciation of great beauty. There are painted consecration crosses on all four walls of the church; and interesting Stuart royal arms dated 1698, re-inscribed for one of the Georges.

Banham [16] The spired church of St Mary forms one side of a square

with interesting houses and lime trees all round it. In the church is a wooden effigy of a knight with a very hooked nose, early 14th century. Interesting Victorian glass; and in the south aisle a window of 1914 by Kempe.

Banningham [5] St Botolph's Church here has a splendid 15th-century tower, and makes a lovely group with the former rectory, a 17th-century gabled brick house standing among trees. The church has a good hammerbeam roof, some box pews, wall paintings and interesting stained glass. It has also preserved its rood beam.

Some new development in the village.

Barford [10] The village is gathered about a bridge over the Tiffey. St Botolph's Church has a wide nave with remains of a 14th-century screen. The stained glass in the east window came from the closed Snoring workhouse chapel.

Barmer [3] There are a few houses on the Fakenham–Docking road here, but the Hall, which belonged to the Kerslake family, was demolished in 1956 and the little church of All Saints stands alone on what must be a pre-Christian site in

Barningham Hall, **Barningham Winter**

the fields. It has a round tower and in the churchyard a touching inscription, 'After long suffering God gave the call, And sad was the parting for one and for all. Though longing to stay with those she loved best, She longed more for heaven, she needed the rest.' The church is vested in the Norfolk Churches Trust, who arrange for 'occasional' services here.

Barney [3, 4] Stretches along a street joining it with the next village of Fulmodestone. The church of St Mary has a tower to which money was left about 1520 and a transept chapel built about 1490. Both the chapel and the nave have original arch-braced roofs, the latter turned a lovely silvery-grey with age. The 15th-century font has some good carved emblems; there is a Jacobean pulpit bearing two mediaeval brass inscriptions, and some old benches.

Barnham Broom [10] Here, just off the road, is the fine red-brick Hall with a Tudor porch and Jacobean wings, in those days the seat of the Chamberlaynes. There are fine plaster ceilings inside, one dated 1614. In St Peter and St Paul's Church is a very good screen; on the panels there are two local saints, St Walstan with his oxen and St Withburga holding a church, as well as the better known St Clement, and St Ursula with her maidens. The church tower was built c. 1430–40.

Barningham Norwood [10] (near Sustead) Two farms and a few cottages are all that survive of the parish where the Palgraves had a splendid house whose ruins can be seen in a farmyard down a lane east of the church. The church, dedicated to St Peter, now vested in the Redundant Churches Fund who arrange for a splendid Patronal Festival annually, contains im-

portant Palgrave monuments of the 17th century—a fine tomb chest to John Palgrave, who died in 1611; to Mrs Pope, under a baldacchino whose curtains are held up by angels; and to Sir Austin Palgrave who died in 1639, with two white marble busts in grey oval surrounds. There is also part of a brass to Henry Palgrave, 1516, and his wife. There is a curious unexplained tiled pattern on the floor, probably mediaeval. The former rectory, about a mile west of the church, is a most attractive Victorian-Jacobean house with very tall chimneys.

Barningham Parva or **Little Barningham** [10] This beautifully placed church of St Mary contains good woodwork, notably a very strange pew made by Stephen Crosbie in 1640 with a carved skeleton in a shroud on the end, and the inscription, 'As you are now, ever so was I, Remember death for you

East Barsham Manor

must die.' The pew was reserved for 'couples joined in wedlock'.

Barningham Winter [10] (near Matlaske) In the fine park, an avenue of oaks leads to the west front of Barningham Hall, built in 1612, for a junior branch of the Pastons. In 1736, the Pastons here, like those at Oxnead, went bankrupt, and the house was acquired by the Mott family (whose descendants are still there). In 1805, John Thruston Mott asked Humphry Repton to remodel the house which did not contain one room that was comfortable'. Luckily Repton was very conscious of the picturesque character of old houses, and he left the west front of Barningham untouched though he added bow-windows to the south. The ruined church of St Mary in the park retains its chancel intact and this is now the parish church. It contains

a military brass to John Winter (1410) and some heraldic glass.

The **Barshams** [3] *East Barsham* Here the traveller has a wonderful surprise and treat when, on the Fakenham–Wells road, he suddenly comes upon the magnificent early-Tudor Hall, built by Sir Henry Fermor about 1520. The two-storeyed gatehouse, with much moulded brick, including the royal arms, leads to the embattled south front. Though the house has had several big restorations and additions, it is still a most interesting example of a Tudor mansion—and very impressive in its colour and site. The property descended to the Calthorpes, the L'Estranges of Hunstanton, and the Astleys. All Saints' Church to the south-west of the house lost its tower but is a real unspoilt country church, with a Norman south door, benches with

poppy-heads, a little very good stained glass including two female figures, almost certainly a Visitation, and angel musicians. There is also a fine monument, representing a shrouded Mrs Calthorpe, rising from her coffin. She died in 1640 and the monument is signed by John and Matthias Christmas. *North Barsham* is a hamlet beside the little River Stiffkey. All Saints' Church on a little hill has a 17th-century pulpit, a 13th-century Purbeck font and a nice monument to Philip Russell, died 1617. *West Barsham* The Church of the Assumption has recently been almost entirely rebuilt. The nave shows early 11th-century work with circular windows in the north wall with deep splays on the outside. The bench ends and south chancel windows were designed by M. W. Tarrant, a famous artist and illustrator of children's books.

Barton Bendish [8] Is one of the most attractive villages in the region of the Wissey and has two churches: St Andrew's with small box pews (1623) and a Norman south door, and St Mary's with 14th-century windows, and wall painting of St Catherine. St Mary's has been vested in the Redundant Churches Fund and given a new thatched roof.

Barton Turf [11] The village green is near the Broad. St Michael's Church has a superb rood screen surpassed only by Ranworth. It is embellished with magnificent painting and gesso work, the figures representing the Nine Orders of Angels with Saints Apollonia (with tooth), Sitha and Barbara (1440). The panels in the aisles, by a different hand, have pictures of St Edmund, Henry VI, Edward the Confessor and St Olaf. Monuments to Anthony Norris (inscription) and his widow Sarah, the latter by John Ivory. The Georgian Hall was built in 1742 by the Revd Stephen Norris who was followed by his son, the antiquary Anthony Norris, who died in 1786.

Barwick [3] The church of St Mary has long since been a ruin. Barwick House and Little Barwick are very attractive houses.

Bawburgh [10] Village on the Yare with a former mill. Bawburgh Hall has stepped gables and a three-storey porch with the date 1634. It was later landscaped by Repton. Nearby in a field are two mysterious but pretty little buildings, called variously The Slipper House (for pilgrims), the dovecote, the summerhouse, etc., but not really identified. The pilgrims would have gone to St Walstan's Well, remains of which can be seen in a farmyard near the church. He was a local saint whose shrine was formerly in the church, dedicated to St Mary and St Walstan. The church has a pre-Conquest round tower and some good glass; the two

small angels in the north window of the chancel probably belong to the rebuilding of the chancel in 1309; the rest of the glass is later, some of it of very high quality and resembling that at East Harling. Wall paintings have recently been uncovered here. Arms of Charles II.

Bawdeswell [10] Chaucer's Reeve came from this village. The Norman revival church of 1845 was destroyed a century later in an aeroplane accident. The present elegant classical building, All Saints', in the colonial style, designed by James Fletcher Watson in 1953–5, has a modern three-decker pulpit and western gallery in the true pre-Tractarian tradition. The Hall, with Dutch gables, bears the date 1683.

Bawsey [8] This ruined church of St James stands prominently on a hillock. It has a central tower with some Saxon long-and-short work though most features are Norman and later.

Bayfield [4] Bayfield Hall, originally Elizabethan, belonged to the Jermy family before being acquired by the Jodrells who refronted it in the 18th century. It stands in a timbered park beside a lake, in the most lovely part of the Glaven valley. The ruined church beside it with a 14th-century western bellcote, was in use in 1603, subsequently ruined, and now used annually for a service for the Girl Guides who camp in the park.

Beachamwell [8] Has 18th-century cottages and St Mary's Church whose Saxon tower has a later octagonal top. There are a Jacobean pulpit, quite good modern benches and a very nice hexagonal brick floor. There are ruins of two other churches, All Saints' and St Mary's, and there is said to have been a fourth. The Devil's Dyke, a linear earthwork of Saxon times, runs near here and is mentioned in a charter of 1053. The

Hall was rebuilt in 1906 by Wimperis & East after a fire.

Beckham [4] There are two villages, *West* and *East Beckham*, the latter really a hamlet a mile to the east of the church of St Helen and All Saints, West Beckham. In 1890 the church of St Helen, East Beckham, was a ruin, and All Saints, West Beckham, was in poor repair. Through the initiative of the Revd Edward Catmur Jarvis, both churches were dismantled and used to build the present church on a completely new site near the centre of population. The architects were Habershon and Faulkner and the cost £1,245. The plan adopted was that of East Beckham church; the chancel arch and south porch stonework came from East Beckham, and parts of some of the windows and doorways from West Beckham. The abandoned and ruined buildings on the way to Holt are what remain of the Gothic workhouse designed by Donthorne in 1851.

Bedingham [17] Here there are an old house called Priory Farm and a splendid unspoilt church, St Andrew's, with box pews in the aisles, old benches in the nave, old brick floors, pulpit with carved swags and altar rails, both 17th century. There is English glass of the 14th and 15th centuries and the two St Paul panels came from King's College, Cambridge, the patrons.

Beeston-next-Mileham [9] A most beautiful church, dedicated to St Mary, away in the fields. 14th-century tracery like that at Gt Walsingham. Hammerbeam roof with carved figures on wall posts. Three very fine screens, old benches, old floors, font cover. Very atmospheric, though particularly badly mutilated, probably by Cromwell's men; a church not to be missed.

Beeston Regis [4] All Saints Church on the cliffs amongst th caravans has a fine 15th-century screen. Good Kempe glass; brass, 1527. The church porch has a cobbled floor. There are considerable remains of the Augustinian Priory between the church and Beeston Hill. The north chapel remains and the site of the cloister can be seen in the farmhouse garden. The Hall, now a school, belonged to the Cremers from the 18th century.

Beeston St Lawrence [11] St Lawrence's Church has an early round tower and was 'new roof'd and repaired 1803' in 'gothick'. The Hall was built about 1785. It is faced with flint and has restrained Gothick windows, a very early example of Gothic Revival in Norfolk. It overlooks a lake.

Beetley [9] The Old Hall, of the 17th century, has a gabled porch. St Mary Magdalene's Church has the remains of canopied sedilia and piscina, and a Jacobean font cover. The north aisle was demolished in 1795.

Beighton [12] All Saints' Church, thatched, was once known for possessing an early 17th-century yew chest with representation of Susanna and the Elders on the lid, but this has been removed to Hunstate Museum in Norwich. Much of the chancel is of the Decorated period; note the ogee arches and crockets of the sedilia. The glass, however, is 1849.

Belaugh [11] (near Wroxham) A most attractive village where St Peter's Church stands on a high promontory overlooking a bend in the River Bure which enclosed the Old Hall and Belaugh Broad. There a good Norman font. Fine 15th-century apostles painted on the screen, whose faces were rubbed out in 1643 by 'a godly trooper from Hobbies'.

Bergh Apton [11/17] Good 17th-and 18th-century houses in this village and a County Council estate

built by Tayler & Green in 1950 and 1956. Any work by these architects (cf. Hales, Lowestoft) is worth looking at; they brought an unusual grace to post-war housing. St Peter and St Paul's Church was much rebuilt in 1837. It has one nice Kempe window (1910) and two by Ward & Hughes, described by Pevsner as 'horrible', and there is a memorial to Bishop Pelham, appointed to Norwich by Lord Palmerston. The Georgian manor house has six bays with a porch on two pairs of columns.

Bessingham [4] St Mary's Church is very prettily sited above the village. It has one of the earliest round towers (mid 11th century). Interesting glass by Powell and Kempe. Though the village almost died after the last war, a few devoted parishioners kept the church going and now, with a change of ownership, the whole place flourishes again.

Besthorpe [6] All Saints' Church, standing alone, is a perfect example of the 14th-century style throughout. In the chancel are a fine group of piscina and sedilia and a magnificent monument to Sir William Drury (1639) and his wife Mary, the daughter of Sir William Cockayne, Lord Mayor of London. After her husband's death she married the Viscount Kilmorey and their son, Robert Needham, Viscount Kilmorey, died on 29 May 1668, aged 13. But when the vault was opened in 1877 the boy's coffin, which did not appear to have been tampered with in any way, was found to contain a load of old books. Besthorpe Hall, north of the church, incorporates fragments of the former seat of the Drurys, with remains of an old tilting yard, and fine brick piers surmounted by pineapples at the entrance to the walled garden.

Bexwell [7] Has the remains of its 16th-century Hall built into a barn on the main road. There is an

octagonal belfry above the round Norman tower of St Mary's Church.

Bickerston [10] (near Barnham Broom) Some fragments of St Andrew's Church, about half a mile north of Barnham Broom, by the roadside.

Billingford [16] (near Diss) Has a few cottages on the Diss road, including one dated 1818 decorated with bottle ends. Up a rough track through a field are St Leonard's Church, the Hall and the rectory, and a view over the village. Monument to Charles le Grys 1601, restored 15th-century screen, plain Jacobean pulpit with tester and remains of wall painting.

Billingford [10] (near Elmham) St Peter's Church stands on high ground. It is unusual in having a tower that is octagonal from the base up. Apart from a 13th-century Purbeck font bowl and fragments of the screen worked up into benches, the most interesting feature inside is the splendid 15th-century eagle lectern of latten, the alloy of copper and brass from which the memorial 'brasses' of the period were made.

Billockby [12] In this tiny village only the chancel of All Saints' Church remains, but this makes a conveniently sized place for worship for the small population. The parish register runs: 'Memorandum: That on Thursday ye 15th day of July 1762 there happened a most violent storm of thunder, lightning, hail, and long continued rain, by ye violence part of ye roof of ye parish church of Billockby fell into ye said church and broke down ye seats and greatly damaged ye pulpit and desk....'

Bilney, East [9] This village is claimed as the birthplace of Thomas Bilney in 1495. He is shown in a stained glass window in the church, preaching from the Bible and then being burnt at the stake in Norwich, with the cathedral in the background. He preached justification by faith alone, denied the mediation of the saints and condemned the worship of relics. He was tried for heresy before Cardinal Wolsey, condemned to prison, released, re-arrested by order of Sir Thomas More, and finally burnt in 1531. His ashes were buried in this churchyard. St Mary's Church is mostly a Victorian rebuild, though there are unusual Jacobean choir stalls. There are very nice 1838 almshouses and a fine 1848 Tudor-style former rectory standing in its own meadow. The Hall was built about 1866. It is now an old people's home.

Binham Priory

Bilney, West [8] Small roadside church which has lost its chancel, unusually dedicated to St Cecilia, patron saint of musicians.

Binham [3] Very nearly the most interesting monastic remains in Norfolk. The priory was founded about 1091; the ruins are now in the care of the Department of the Environment and are well documented; they stand above the river and ford. You enter through a gatehouse into a farmyard. The church was a vast cruciform building, the nave of which is still standing, and is the parish church. Much of the ruined east end and choir is there, with most beautiful clustered stone columns. In the nave are

Norman arcades, triforium and clerestory, though the westernmost bays have the pointed Early English arch, and this is also the period of the great west front. The present church ends where the former choir began, and on the straight wall behind the altar hangs a modern dossall designed by Isobel Clover and worked by Susan Gurney. There are good benches, a Seven-Sacrament font and the base of an old screen, on which the Puritans painted texts over the saints. On the green there is the tall shaft of a cross, and there are stones from the priory built into many of the cottages. There are several very nice small farmhouses here too, though the most interesting

early 17th-century example was demolished in the 1960s.

Bintree or **Bintry** [10] A spreading village of 18th-century houses and a charming water mill, with St Swithin's Church containing 14th-century work. The statue of St Swithin over the porch commemorates a former vicar, the Revd R. W. Enraught who was imprisoned under the Public Worship Regulation Act, 1880.

The **Birchams** [2] *Great Bircham* has very pretty farms and cottages and there are the remains of a windmill between the village and the Peddars Way, a Roman (or pre-Roman?) road running from Holme-next-the-Sea to Bury St Edmund's, which here skirts fields of lavender as well as corn. St Mary's Church has Norman, 14th- and 15th-century work. It is always pleasant to find seats around the piers, and there are box pews and a 17th-century pulpit and altar. *St Andrew's, Bircham Tofts*, close by, was ruinated soon after the last war and is now almost completely overgrown with ivy, though the tower is still visible from the road and memorial tablets are still legible to those who brave the quicksand of pigeons' dung. *St Mary's, Bircham Newton*, is an unspoilt and very atmospheric country church with small box pews of 1858 (very late for these), royal arms for George III, and two other things well worth seeing—a priest carved on a stone slab in the chancel, a rarity in Norfolk; and on the south wall of the chancel a monument to Nelson's 2-year-old grandson, the child of Horatia, his daughter by Lady Hamilton, who married the Revd Philip Ward, once incumbent of Bircham. There is also a Norman font. A church not to be missed.

Bixley [11] A tiny village overlooking Norwich. The church is mainly 14th century but much rebuilt. At the south-east corner a stone records its foundation by William

of Dunwich; it is notable as being the only church in England dedicated in honour of St Wandregeselius, or Wando, a 7th-century monk from Normandy.

Blakeney [4] The last port left on the Glaven estuary but now open only for small boats at high tide. There is a most attractive high street with brick and flint houses leading down to the quay and the old Guildhall, only the undercroft of which, with 13th-century brick vaulting, remains. Once a flourishing port, the coasting trade was maintained until the early years of the present century. Blakeney Point (also approached from Morston) now owned by the National Trust, is a long stretch of sand dunes with the bird sanctuary at its western extremity. It can be reached from Blakeney at high tide or on foot along the beach from Cley. St Nicholas' Church has a magnificent west tower built in 1435, and a 13th-century chancel with groined roof. The whole building was sympathetically restored in the present century and the rood screen has been rebuilt across the chancel arch. An unusual feature is the small turret at the east end of the chancel containing the staircase rising to the chamber above the chancel vault. The turret extends higher than the chancel roof and may have been used as a lighthouse guiding ships into Blakeney haven. It still has a light in it from dusk. There are fragments of mediaeval glass in the north aisle and some carved misericords in the chancel. There are interesting 17th- and 18th-century gravestones in the churchyard.

Blickling [4] The Hall was built (1619–28) for Sir Henry Hobart, Chief Justice of the Common Pleas, by Robert Lyminge who was employed at Hatfield House. There is much elaborate plasterwork, especially in the Long Gallery. Building accounts survive for the years 1619–21 when over £5,400

was spent, and in the first two of these years 1,288,500 bricks were used. Robert Lyminge received £103 17s 6d over this period. Edward Stanyon, plasterer, was paid 5s 6d, a third square measure for 'frett ceeling' in the gallery, and those in the Great Chamber, drawing chamber and parlor, and he was to receive 18d a yard over the normal rate of 12s a yard for similar work in the hall. The contract is signed by himself and by Lyminge. The lead for the roof came from Derbyshire from the estates of Thomas Eyre of Hassop and Sir George Manners of Haddon. The house was extensively altered, enlarged and redecorated in the second half of the 18th century by the second Earl of Buckinghamshire to the designs of William Ivory of the Norwich architectural family, with plasterwork by William Wilkins, grandfather of William Wilkins, born in Norwich, the Norfolk architect who designed the National Gallery. The house is in the possession of the National Trust and is surrounded by the most beautiful gardens, redesigned about 1930 by Mrs Norah Lindsay. The fountain and basin came from Oxnead Hall. In the Park, the design of which is attributed to Humphry Repton, is the mausoleum for the second Earl of Buckinghamshire by Joseph Bonomi. In St Andrew's Church, restored by Butterfield and with a tower and porch by Street, is a 17th-century pulpit and many brasses including a fine military one for Sir Nicholas Dagworth (1401), the figure of Isabel Boleyn, wife of William Cheyne (1485), in a butterfly head-dress, and of Anne à Wode, second wife of Thomas Astley, holding twins with whom she died in childbirth in 1512. At the west end of the nave is a marble table tomb with supporting angels and recumbent effigy of the fourth Marquis of Lothian by G. F. Watts.

Blofield [11] The old village, containing a number of pleasant thatched cottages, gathers around the church of St Andrew and St Peter, which has a lofty 15th-century tower (1465) and the remains of a 15th-century rood screen. Unfortunately most of the chancel windows are blocked, but the seating is interesting and the font unique, in being carved with scenes from the Life of Christ—an exceptionally vivid one representing the Nativity.

Blo Norton [16] St Andrew's Church is of the Decorated style with nave, chancel and west tower. The collecting shoes are very good 20th-century copies of those at Bressingham. The Tudor timber-framed Hall bears the date 1581 and the initials of Elizabeth Brampton and Henry, her son. Since the reign of Edward I the property has never been sold. Prince Frederick Duleep Singh, a notable historian of Norfolk, son of the deposed ruler of the Punjab, Queen Victoria's maharajah, and supposed grandson of Rajah Ranjit Singh, was tenant until his death in 1926.

Bodham [4] At Lower Bodham, near the well-restored All Saints' Church, are a number of pleasant brick and flint cottages and farmhouses. Most of the church is 14th/15th century and is well cared for, in contrast to the observation of a 1602 writer, 'The Wholl churche there greatlie decaied, and redie to fall down'. There are holy water stoups, the arms of Queen Anne, a nicely carved Victorian pulpit (1890), and riddel-posted altars.

Bodney [15] Scarcely a village, only huts, military roads, and a farm. Among huge oaks stands the small flint church of St Mary, very neat and plain and holy, like a candle shining in the wastes of the Military Training Area. Mediaeval benches originally in Tottenhill church, an original consecration cross, and some Anglo-Saxon carving in the north-east buttress.

Booton [10] This small village, so near Reepham, has unexpected links with the worlds of art and literature through the 50-year incumbency of an intellectual—and eccentric—parson, the Revd Whitwell Elwin, who was appointed to this family living in 1849 and who died in the rectory on 1 January 1900. He was born in 1815 at nearby Thurning Hall and the delightful church there is full of memorials to his family. For many years he edited the *Quarterly Review* for John Murray from Booton, and he had many literary friends including Thackeray, Scott, Lockhart, and others, many of whom came to stay at Booton in the rectory which Elwin built for himself and his family—the pretty house in the trees beside the church, whose architect was Thomas Allom. In 1876 he started to rebuild the decaying church; he was his own architect and was totally untrained. He borrowed ideas from buildings he liked at home and abroad, and in spite of many vicissitudes the church was finished when he died in 1900. Sir Edwin Lutyens, who married the daughter of Elwin's great friend Lord Lytton, said of the church that it was 'very naughty but built in the right spirit'. Locally it is known as the Cathedral of the Fields; Elwin himself said, 'I have had but one end in view, which was to give the church the aspect of a House devoted to prayer.' In the north porch is a mutilated 14th-century statue of the Virgin and Child from the old church, but the figure of St Michael in the niche outside is probably by Elwin's son. There are some monuments from the old church inside, and there is a dramatic account in that superb book *A Blessed Girl* by Lady Emily Lutyens, of the removal to the churchyard of the remains of former Elwins (where they are marked by a cross near the eastern boundary). Elwin himself is buried near the southwestern boundary. Next to the idiosyncratic nature of the architecture, the main interest of the church, dedicated to St Michael and All Angels, is its complete set of stained glass. There were at least two separate designers; the easternmost windows were by someone called Buckley, but he did not satisfy Elwin and all the nave windows are by Booker and Purchase. They represent processions of angelic girls; the very pretty ones in the vestry look as though they may be portraits. The spacious baptistery was an important feature, dear to Elwin, and he was unusual for his time in having no pulpit and no pews. Elwin also built the village school and designed the house known as the Hollies. He left all his Booton property to the Lutyens family, and Robert Lutyens, Sir Edwin's son, designed the house on the north side of the road known as Booton Manor. The red brick Georgian Hall was sold in 1713 by Christopher Layer, the Jacobite, to his father-in-law, Peter Elwin, in which family it remained until this century.

Boughton [8] A very attractive place. There are scattered 18th-century houses round its green and rushy pond; the tower of All Saints' Church has a little steeple and weathercock which appear over the houses. Apart from the tower, the church was rebuilt in 1872 (architect R. J. Withers, who worked at Shouldham at the same time).

Bowthorpe [10] St Michael's Church is a ruin. A vast new suburban development is taking place there now.

Bracon Ash [16] St Nicholas' is an attractive little church ablaze with the hatchments of the Berney family who had a mausoleum on the north side of the chancel. Early 16th-century terracotta work. Bracon Ash was the birthplace of Lord Chancellor Thurlow, and its rector from 1661–2 was Thomas Tenison afterwards Archbishop of Canter

bury. Mergate Hall is an old gabled and crenellated house, altered at the end of the 18th century.

Bradenham [9] *East Bradenham* Church of St Mary, chiefly 14th/15th century, has one or two good monuments and a mediaeval altar stone in the south aisle. St Andrew's, *West Bradenham*, has 13th-century arcades and an Easter Sepulchre. West Bradenham Hall, red-brick Georgian, looks well across the park, and on the lavender bushes beside the garden gate Nelson's uniforms were spread out to air by his sister, Mrs Bolton, to whom they were sent after his death. She was the one member of the family who was kind to Lady Hamilton who, with Horatia, often stayed at Bradenham. Later it belonged to Sir Rider Haggard's family.

Bradeston or **Braydeston** [11] St Michael's is an isolated little church, dating perhaps from the 11th century onwards, pleasantly situated on high ground between Brundall and Blofield, revived by William Joseph Blake, father of Lord Blake, the historian, in the 1940s.

Bradfield [5] St Giles' Church has a well-proportioned chancel with 14th-century windows and elaborate buttresses rising to pinnacles at the top. Tower built 1450–1500.

Bramerton [11] A pleasant village among trees. The early west tower of St Peter's Church is narrow and supported on massive arches. 14th-century font.

Brampton [11] The little church of St Peter, standing by the Mermaid Stream, has brasses to the Brampton family, with a beautiful Virgin and Child.

◁   **Blickling** Hall and a term in the gardens

Booton ▷

Brandiston

Brancaster [2] The Roman Branodunom, but nothing left to see. The village, however, is charming and so is the golf course and the beach. Brancaster Staithe is the old harbour, now very popular for sailing. St Mary's Church has a 15th-century font cover, arms of William IV and interesting brass to Robert Smith (1596).

Brandiston [10] A tiny village. The Hall is an interesting 17th-century house with most interesting late 15th-century glass roundels in one of the windows which are said to have come originally from a Norwich house. The 14th- and 15th-century church of St Nicholas is interesting and has monuments to the Athill family who once owned the Hall. The church is now vested in the Redundant Churches Fund.

Brandon Parva [10] Called 'Brand' by Parson Woodforde who sometimes visited here. All Saints' Church stands above a farm; it has a battlemented tower and a wide nave with nice head-stops to the windows. Inside there are Victorian texts around the altar and a good monument (1702). The 18th-century farmhouse overlooks the meadows by the Yare, beyond which Barnham Broom church tower appears on the high ground.

Breckles [15] The 16th-century brick and timber Hall is in pleasant grounds. St Margaret's Church nearby with its round tower has a square Norman font with the Evangelists in high relief.

Bressingham [16] A Suffolk border village with many colour-washed high-pitched cottages and farms. The church of St John the Baptist, largely rebuilt and refurnished c. 1527 by Sir Roger Pilkington, has bench ends of that date, Jacobean pulpit, and three collecting shoes (1631). The tower is earlier, c. 1431. Bressingham Hall, a Georgian house of three bays with a pediment, is the home of Alan Bloom and is noted for his gardens as well as his collection of railway locomotives and traction engines.

Brettenham [15] On the River Thet, has very large 19th-century brick cottages with Tudor-style chimneys and a great air of prosperity. St Mary's Church was rebuilt in 1852 and has been much renewed, mostly with marble since. Over the river is Shadwell, a handful of cottages only, and inside the park of Shadwell Court, a fine 19th-century house enlarged by J J. Teulon, is St Chad's Well, a charming flint grotto with a bubbling spring, remains of niches for statues, and stone seats.

Bridgham [15] A red-brick villa intrudes into the nice plastered houses. St Mary's Church has a carved 15th-century font with the Assumption and the arms of Canterbury and Ely. A second font came from Roudham church. There are sedilia with tracery, some old stalls, one given by 'John Watsin and Alys hys wiff' (c. 1475) screen, glass fragments (14th century) and splendid 18th-century paintings of Moses and Aaron. Monument in chancel to George Robert Comyn (1816) who 'having

Shadwell Park, **Brettenham**

served his time in the navy with honor to himself and highest approbation of his commanders fell a Victim to the Climate of the West Indies'.

Briningham [4] The church has a beautiful 14th-century window with curvilinear tracery in the south wall of the nave; a screen has been erected right across the chancel arch to conserve heat in the winter. Briningham House is late Georgian. South of the village on the high ground overlooking Melton Park is a circular tower built by the Astleys of Melton Constable, used as a look-out post at the time of the Armada, the Napoleonic War and the two World Wars.

Brinton [4] There are several pretty houses and an old barn once used as a soap factory. The church has a very good roof with half-angels, and post-Reformation texts on the wall. A bequest of 1529 left 20 marks towards a new roof—possibly this one. Brinton Hall is a medium-sized Georgian house.

Brisley [9] The village, with its wide green, moated Tudor manor house and barns, gathers about the fine church of St Bartholomew, dating from 1350–1450. Building began with the chancel, which has a crypt at the east end, for it has both Decorated and Perpendicular tracery. All the remainder is Perpendicular; the porch was leaded in 1435 and the grand tower built around 1450. It has freestone panelled buttresses with niches for statues. Inside, the church is imposing and clerestoried with box pews, three-decker pulpit and lofty 15th-century screen.

Briston [4] Now a suburb of Melton Constable. This was a railway village, the former centre of the Midland & Great Northern Joint Railway. Now there is not even a station, but a bus shelter makes nostalgic use of spandrels from the station roof dating from the times of the Central Norfolk Railway, precursor of the M & GN. Marriott Way is named after the Chief Mechanical Engineer of the latter, whose reminiscences, *Forty Years of a Norfolk Railway*, have recently been reissued. Much restored Briston All Saints' Church has graceful 14th-century piscina and sedilia, and a cast-iron 'cello used in the church band in the 18th century. Burgh Parva Church is in ruins, and a serviceable and surprisingly atmospheric 'tin tabernacle' has been erected alongside.

Brockdish [17] A delightful village on the Waveney, with many good stream-side houses. Some glass and woodwork survive the restoration of St Peter and St Paul's Church (1864–5); note the monument in the chancel whose inscription begins 'If the virtues which ADORN life could PRESERVE it, this tablet had not recorded the death....' Francis Blomefield, the historian, was once rector here. The Hall has a three-storeyed porch dated 1634.

Brooke [17] Has a reedy mere down its middle, some typical south Norfolk cottages with steep gables, a strict Baptist chapel (Gothick 1851), a village sign and

51

much wrought iron and gilding on gates before villas. The round tower of St Peter's Church is Norman, and there is a particularly good though defaced Seven-Sacrament font.

Broome [17] St Michael's Church lies in splendid isolation nearly a mile from the village and has a particularly fine 15th-century tower.

Brumstead or Brunstead [6] A small village near Stalham. St Peter's Church has a tower towards which money was left in 1390 and a thatched nave. The chancel was cut off in 1827 and the whole church restored at the sole expense of the Revd H. N. W. Comyn in 1867; he was Nelson's godson and his father was Nelson's chaplain, the younger Comyn being buried here. Read the tablet on the chancel wall.

Brundall [11] Very much a dormitory village but, like the village, St Lawrence's Church is well kept and is unique in Norfolk in having a mediaeval leaden font bowl.

Buckenham [1] The Buckenhams are bounded by a large common with meres and marl-pits. There was a castle at *Old Buckenham* which was removed to *New Buckenham* (hence the name) about 1136. The 12th-century circular shell-keep of the second castle remains within a larger earth ringwork. In a nearby barn, which was once the church of St Mary, are Norman arches. *New Buckenham* has large old houses round a village green and a market house with a whipping post and some heraldic carving. Near the door of St Martin's Church is the tomb of John Hill, died 1765.

Of this world's goods he had his share/Both wine and punch as well as beer/His whole life thro' he did not spare.

There is a fine 15th-century tower with good flushwork, a 15th-century wooden church door, an unusual font with hairy animals

Buckenham St Nicholas

dated 1619, one good tomb and a Jacobean altar table. *Old Buckenham* has a large green with several ponds and less grand houses round it than at New Buckenham. All Saints' Church is thatched and has an octagonal tower; inside, some heraldic glass, fine carved stall ends in the chancel, a drop-handled bier, and a good modern memorial to Lionel Robinson, d. 1922.

Buckenham St Nicholas [11] (near Cantley) A station, a ferry over the Yare, an interesting old rectory and a few cottages. The main interest, though, is the church and its associations. It has a most unusual 13th-century octagonal tower with arcading at the top, and two probably Norman doorways. Inside there is a fine 13th-century north doorway and an unusual 15th-century font with figures around the stem and bowl. There is a good wall monument in the chan-

cel to Ann Newbury (1707) with a flaming urn. The church was considerably restored in the 1820s; it was given an east window full of interesting stained glass in 1823, most of which has been vandalized, as has much else in the church; the ancient bell and royal arms were stolen. Although long neglected, the church is now being repaired and is vested in the Redundant Churches Fund. From 1863 to 1871 William Haslam was rector here. He was a noted Evangelical preacher who drew overflowing congregations so that he was forced to preach, from a semi-circular pulpit (still visible) in the rectory wall, to vast masses of listeners, many of whom were converted as a result of his preaching. He left Buckenham in 1871 for an appointment at the Curzon Chapel in London and his book *Yet not I* relates many of his experiences at Buckenham.

Buckenham Tofts [15] The stately 19th-century mansion is now level with the ground (1946) and the park, one of the most beautiful in Breckland, is now in the Stanford Military Training Area. The fine stables alone remain.

Bunwell [16] There are attractive groups of thatched cottages in Bunwell Street and an old mill at Bunwell Bottom. The church of St Michael stands finely: it has an impressive tower (to which money was left 1499–1508) and big Perpendicular windows in the nave and chancel. There are royal arms of Queen Anne, an east window by Hardman and Powell (1914) and an impressive high altar.

Burgh-next-Aylsham [11] A pretty village along the north bank of the Bure. St Mary's Church has a chancel with lovely 13th-century arcading, shortened in about 1570 and then rebuilt to its original length in 1877 by R. M. Phipson. The north chapel dates from then. The nave is mainly 19th century but the tower is 15th century

New Buckenham

There is a slightly defaced Seven-Sacrament font.

Burgh Parva [4] The church has long since been a ruin. The 17th-century Hall, with later additions, was part of the Melton Constable estate and often used for younger members of the Astley family.

Burgh St Margaret [12] A little Broadland village overlooking the marshes of the Muck Fleet which joins Filby, Rollesby and Ormesby Broads to the Bure. St Margaret's Church has two Norman door-ways and inside a small figure brass for John Burton (1608) kneeling at a prayer desk in ruff and M. A. gown, 'Rector for about 8 Years'. Also an unusual

inscription for the Rt Revd George Carnac Fisher, Bishop of Ipswich and incumbent 1898–1921. Curious dormer window in the thatched roof.

Burgh St Peter [18] A long straggling village within a wide bend of the Waveney with the church standing on a ridge at the eastern extremity of the parish, and of Norfolk, looking across the river to the Isle of Lothingland with Lowestoft in the distance. Altogether a most beautiful spot with a staithe leading from the Waveney Hotel directly to the river. The church is a very long 13th/14th century building, thatched, and with a nice arch-braced roof; the nave is continuous with the chancel, so there is no

chancel arch. The tower, which is a landmark to all the country round, is a most odd erection of 1793 (on the original base of c. 1500), put up as a Boycott Mausoleum. It looks like the sort of edifice a child would construct with a box of bricks, consisting of a series of brick cubes piled one on top of the other in diminishing size, the penultimate one being of white brick. An unusual series of memorials is the family history of the Boycotts (or Boycatts) told on brass plates entirely covering the outside of the pulpit.

The **Burlinghams** [11, 12] St Andrew's and St Peter's stand close together beside the Norwich–Yarmouth road. St Peter's is a ruin but

Burnham Deepdale font

some of the best fittings have been transferred to St Andrew's which is a fine 15th-century church (tower 1466–79). The screen from St Peter's (showing angels holding St Peter's keys) is now the tower screen in St Andrew's, and St Andrew's itself has a fine roof screen with figure painting and gesso work (c. 1530). The saints represented include the local saints, Walstan and Withburga. Most remarkable of all, however, is St Edmund's, *South Burlingham*, which has a magnificent 15th-century pulpit with Jacobean tester. Round the pulpit itself, which retains its original colouring, is the inscription 'inter natos mulierum non surrexit major Johanne Baptista' (among those that are born of

women there hath not arisen a greater than John the Baptist). St Edmund's also contains some mediaeval pews and two wall paintings representing St Christopher and the martyrdom of St Thomas Becket.

The **Burnhams** [3] Are seven parishes. *Burnham Market* containing the parishes of Burnham Westgate, Burnham Sutton and Burnham Ulph. St Mary's, *Westgate*, church, whose tower has fine carved parapets, stands at the west end of the wide street which runs eastward between fine Georgian houses. Westgate Hall, 1783, now an old people's home, is from a design by Soane. The road divides round the green and then meets

again near *Ulph* church. The ruir of *Sutton* church are just beyond th former railway station, and *Norto* (St Margaret) stands to the nort and has the most interesting churc of them all. Parts of it may be Saxc and it has a well-restored interior, Norman font, and a superb 15th century pulpit with paintings of th four Latin Doctors. Fine views fro: the churchyard. Just to the east Norton church is the priory gat way, a building very similar to th 14-century Slipper Chapel *Houghton St Giles*. Beyond Norte village on the coast road is *Burnha Deepdale*. St Mary's Church has early round tower and an exce tionally fine Norman font wi high-relief figures representing th Labours of the Months. *Burnha*

Bylaugh Hall

Bylaugh church

Overy, St Clement's, on the bank of the Burn, is a 13th-century building with a Norman central tower and interesting interior. On the main coast road is a most attractive group with a watermill and cottages—now owned by the National Trust. On the rising ground above the watermill is a windmill overlooking Overy Staithe. Most famous of all is *Burnham Thorpe*, though the rectory in which Nelson was born no longer exists, but All Saints' Church in which he was baptized is full of Nelson relics of much interest. There are good sedilia and piscina in the chancel and a fine brass to Sir William Calthorpe (1420). At *Overy Staithe* the harbour, with remains of the quay, is one of the most attractive of the north Norfolk ports.

Burston [16] Has pretty farms and good trees, especially willows. The church has an unusual 14th-

century font. The school 'strike' which began in April 1914 led to the building of the 'Strike School' on the edge of the green, which was used as such until 1939; it is now a village meeting room. The rectory was designed by Vulliamy in 1840.

Buxton [11] The 15th-century tower of St Andrew's Church is at one end of the village street and the Flemish gables of the Crown at the other. Behind the Crown is the long terrace of 'Feoffees Cottages'. In the church is a monument to Mary Kent (1773), 'who died under "innoculation"'. Her fond parents, deluded by prevalent custom, suffered the rough officious hand of Art to aid the flourishing root of nature.'

Bylaugh [10] The great house, Bylaugh Hall, seat of the Lombes, is now a ruin; it was designed by Charles Barry jun., and finished in

1852. It was in the late 16th-century style. It was sold in 1917 and was ruinated in 1952. St Mary's Church is well worth seeing; it was rebuilt in 1810 by Sir John Lombe (note the self-effacing inscription on the tower arch) and contains two spacious box pews with fireplaces, a three-decker pulpit (access from both transept and chancel) and a military brass to Sir John Curson (1471). It owes its unrestored condition to the fact that the Revd Louis Norgate was rector here from 1836 to 1908; Parson Armstrong wrote of him, 'Norgate, though evangelical, dresses in the most popish style'. East of the church is the 17th-century Old Hall, with shaped gables.

Caister-by-Yarmouth or **Caister-on-Sea** [12] Almost a suburb of Great Yarmouth with holiday camps and caravan sites in abundance. Holy Trinity Church has a

◁ **Castle Rising** church; the west front

huge 14th-century font (bought from Eye, Suffolk, in 1901 for £5) and royal arms with Hanoverian quarterings but the motto of James I; large commandment boards with figures of Moses and Aaron. Caister Castle to the west was built by Sir John Fastolf and passed into the hands of the Pastons after years of contest, described vividly in the Paston Letters. In recent years important excavations have revealed much of the Roman town of Caister, which can be seen near the old rectory, now a hotel.

Caistor St Edmund [14] The site of Venta Icenorum, the most considerable Roman remains in Norfolk, on the bank of the River Tas. Holy Trinity Church incorporates fragments of the fortress and dates back, in part, to Saxon times. The font is c. 1410. The church stands on the south-east corner of the fort. Venta became a town, a fortress, and garrison centre, and during the Roman occupation of England it must have been one of the most important places in East Anglia. The Old Hall dates mainly from 1612 and 1647 and has mul-

lioned windows. The Georgian Hall, with late Georgian additions, has a handsome curved porch on Doric columns.

Calthorpe [5] St Margaret's Church has a wide nave with 15th-century bench ends which are in their original plinths. There is a 17th-century pulpit, altar rails, and communion table now serving as a side altar. The church has been well restored with good modern furnishings, and a little of the colourful splendour of the 15th-century has been given back to it in

57

15th-century angels, **Cawston**

a painted rood beam and font cover. In the nave is a ledger slab with two skulls and a curious emblem.

Cantley [11, 12] Has a large sugar beet refinery on the bank of the Yare, along which ply not only the barges connected with the factory itself but also a good deal of sea-going shipping on its way to Norwich. St Margaret's Church has some fine 15th-century nave windows.

Carbrooke [9] This little village with attractive houses once had the only house in Norfolk of the Knights Hospitallers of St John of Jerusalem. The monastery stood in the fields just to the south of the magnificent church of St Peter and St Paul which has a dominating 15th-century tower. A pair of early 13th-century slabs in the chancel are believed to mark the burials of the Countess of Clare, who founded the house, and one of her sons. Also in the chancel are fine carved 13th-century sedilia and 14th-century east window; two mediaeval altar stones have been restored to use, there is a well-carved 15th-century screen and a few leaves from a mediaeval antiphoner. A church not to be missed.

Carleton, East [10] An attractive little village among the trees with some Suffolk-type high-pitched thatched cottages. The Hall is now a Cheshire Home. St Mary's Church has been much restored, including the tower which was rebuilt and heightened by 12 feet in 1895.

Carleton Forehoe [10] Has large old houses round a green with a pond; one house (now two cottages) has a good early Dutch gable over the porch. St Mary's Church is a little way out of the village, standing in a meadow where there are three enormous very old oaks. The flint and brick tower with tall thin crockets was rebuilt 1713 and inscribed VIVAT A REGINA. At the other end of the village are the Regency lodges and fine gates of red brick, turreted Kimberley House (q.v.) which can be seen across the park. The good planting, the numerous farms and ancient cottages, are all part of the estate owned by the Wodehouse family for over 500 years until its sale in 1958.

Carleton St Peter [11] Here St Peter's Church, surrounded by Scotch firs, stands in the middle of a large field. The village is scattered about and below. The flint and brick tower is mentioned in wills of 1500–25. Some beautiful bits of 14th-century screen have been worked up into a new one. Splendid inscription to 'Mr Saletts five children'.

58

Carleton Rode [16] All Saints' Church has a squat tower rebuilt in 1717 and a fine late 13th-century chancel. There is a screen base with the Twelve Apostles, a most graceful double piscina and some very fine consecration crosses.

Castle Rising [2] On the old road between this village and Babingley is Onion Corner, so-called because of the strong smell of garlic from the roadside wood. The 12th-century church of St Lawrence has been restored by Salvin and Street but the Norman west front, font and chancel arch are fine. Across the road, the Hospital of the Holy and Undivided Trinity is almost exactly as it was when Henry Howard, Earl of Northampton (ancestor of the present squire) built it about 1614 as an almshouse for 20 spinsters. It is a low brick building with little towers round a quadrangle with a mown lawn and a few flowers round each old lady's door. The chapel, though rebuilt and restored, has the old pews and altar table, and there is more Jacobean furniture in the dining hall. The old ladies go to church in long red cloaks bearing the Howard badge and pointed black hats, as they have done since the foundation. Surrounded by huge earthworks is the romantic ruin of the Norman castle, to which Queen Isabella, Edward III's mother, was banished. Extensive excavations are proceeding.

Rising was a sea-port
When Lynn was but a marsh
Now Lynn is the sea-port
And Rising fares the worse.

It was also, until the Reform Bill, a rotten borough, and Pepys and Horace Walpole both sat for it.

Caston [15] An interesting village with a mysterious, recently restored mediaeval cross on the green and a pretty 16th-century farmhouse. Holy Cross Church is mainly 14th-century with a beautiful west window and door in the tower; it has recently been given a new thatched roof.

Catfield [12] Has a reed-grown staithe on Hickling Broad. The 14th-century All Saints' Church with arcaded chancel has faded wall paintings and there is a 15th-century screen with sixteen painted kings. Hourglass stand by the pulpit and Georgian royal arms inscribed V^{ist}R. The poet Cowper stayed in the former rectory as a child with his cousins, the Donnes.

Catton [11] Once a pleasant late Georgian village suburb, now almost part of Norwich. St Margaret's Church has an early round tower with 15th-century octagonal belfry stage. The pulpit is dated 1537. Christ Church, New Catton, was built by John Brown of Norwich in 1841–2 and is a riot of pinnacles and a good example of 'Commissioners' Gothic'. The Hall is a late Georgian house, the grounds being among the earliest laid out by Repton. It is now an old people's home.

Cawston [10] An attractive little country town with two wide parallel streets and, towering above the houses, St Agnes, one of the most splendid of all the great mediaeval churches of Norfolk, with a tower built by Michael de la Pole, Earl of Suffolk, early in the fifteenth century. The tower is faced with freestone and there is a hammerbeam roof with angels and a well-preserved rood screen having figure paintings (c. 1504) of the apostles and others; note St Matthew with spectacles. Much of the old seating remains and there is a wall painting of St Agnes in the south transept and nearby a piscina ornamented with a dragon and a Wild Man. There is a fine tower screen with an inscription showing that it was erected on the proceeds of a 'church ale'—the mediaeval equivalent of a fête. The old sign of the Plough Inn of Sygate, the street west of the church, stands beneath the tower gallery. Near the junction with the Norwich road is the 'Duel Stone', marking the spot where Sir Henry Hobart of Blickling was slain in a duel with Oliver Le Neve of Great Witchingham in August 1698. Cawston Manor, built in 1896, is now a Woodard School.

Chedgrave [17] Between here and Thurton are two groups of ornamental 18th-century gates with lodges designed by Soane, into the park of Langley Hall, a house by Matthew Brettingham and containing remarkable rococo plaster work by C. Stanley. All Saints' Church, a curious conglomeration of styles having two Norman doorways and a Norman north-east tower, stands on a hill above the village and opposite a red-brick, early 18th-century house, with curly Dutch gables. The east window has bright 17th-century glass, traditionally brought by a Lady Beauchamp Proctor, of Langley Hall, from Rouen Cathedral—the sort of extraordinary thing that went on in former centuries which enriched many Norfolk churches.

Claxton [11] A ruined castle of the Kerdistons by the Yare containing the remains of a 17th-century manor house. St Andrew's Church has a reed-thatched roof, some box pews and old benches. Royal arms of George I.

Clenchwarton [7] In the flat fen, amongst the potato clumps, some 17th- and 18th-century houses are grouped in the trees by St Margaret's Church. There are the remains of an old cross in the churchyard and headstones near the south porch. The church contains an Elizabethan table and a Jacobean pulpit with decorative carving. On the south wall of the chancel is a monument to the rector who behaved gallantly in the 'terrible inundation of Feb. 16th 1735'; this low-lying marshland is never wholly safe from the sea.

Cley-next-the-Sea [4] Once the largest of the Glaven estuary ports with a fine 18th-century Custom House on the coast road. The quay still remains near the picturesque Cley Mill, but the old harbour at the southern end of the village near Newgate Green has long since disappeared and, since the building of the bank on the 'New Road' towards Blakeney at the time of the Enclosure Award in 1823, has been green meadows. Cotman's picture shows what it was like before the making of this bank, with a high-arched wooden bridge over the tidal creek, with Blakeney Church in the distance. In the narrow main street are some large houses with rows of cottages in between. In particular the former Fishmongers' Arms and the shop, sometimes called 'Knucklebone House' for its curious cornice with panelling which seems to be made up from sheeps' vertebrae, are attractive. Many back alleys and courts known as Lokes lead up to the high ground to the east of the village near the Hall. St Margaret's Church, on Newgate Green, is one of the finest in Norfolk. Originally it was quite a small building, as can be seen from the weather mould against the inside wall of the present tower which belonged to the earlier church. But it was rebuilt in the 14th century on such a magnificent plan that not even the Middle Ages could realize it to the full. No doubt a soaring west tower was intended, but after the Black Death of 1348–9 there was not the means to go on with the scheme in its entirety. Hence the small chancel which contrasts a little oddly with the splendid nave, and the great 15th-century window at the west end instead of a tower. The transepts have been in ruins since the 16th century. To the 15th century belongs the beautiful south porch with chamber above, in which there is a huge cupboard which must have been made at the time the porch was built. There are many of the original 15th-century

bench ends. The return stalls with their miserere seats have been re-erected against the chancel walls behind the choir stalls, and there is a pulpit dated 1611 and a royal arms board for Charles II repainted for Queen Anne. There are many brasses including the figure of John Yslington D.D. (c. 1430) and the Symondes family in shrouds (1511) with the repeated *memento mori*—'Now Thus'. In the churchyard just outside the south transept a table tomb commemorates Mr James Greeve 'who was assistant of Sr. Cloudesly Shovel in ye burning ye Shipps in ye Port of Tripoly in Barbary Jan. 14th 1676 and for his good services perform'd was made Capt. of the Ship called Orange Tree of Algeir, in 1677 presented with A Medal of Gold by King Charles ye 2nd, he died April 1686 aged 45 years'. The Hall was built about 1800; the Old Hall on the coast road is a 16th-century house which was restored, and a round staircase tower added, by Seely & Paget, immediately after World War II.

Clippesby [12] St Peter's Church is mainly 13th century but the Norman round tower has a Victorian octagonal belfry and there is Norman work in the doorways, whilst the font bowl is supported by angels. Brasses, including one of John Clippesby in armour with his family (1594).

Cockley Cley [8] Had two churches, All Saints' on the main road from Swaffham to Stoke Ferry, which suffered a vigorous restoration in 1866; 13th-century south aisle and chancel. The other (on the road towards Hilborough) is St Mary's, which is apsidal, has been restored recently, having for many years been used as a cottage—a reversal of the current trend. The Hall was built in the Italianate style in 1870–1 by R. M. Phipson.

Cockthorpe [3] A small village which was the birthplace of Admiral Sir Cloudesley Shovel. In All Saints' Church is a fine monument to Sir James Calthorpe and his wife Barbara, who 'was much comforted by the sight of 193 of her children and their offspring at the age of 86 years'. There is a Jacobean tomb chest to Sir James Calthorpe (1615) and good 15th-century font and roof. Some of the descendants of these Calthorpes, together with the Redundant Churches Fund and the Norfolk Churches Trust, have recently restored this church which was fast becoming derelict. There are now 'occasional' services here.

Colby [5] A scattered village. St Giles' Church has a plain unbuttressed 14th-century tower and a 15th-century porch and font. The 15th-century glass in the east window has just been restored; the reredos is 17th century. Another charming grouping with its former rectory.

Colkirk [3] On high ground near Fakenham, this compact village has a church, St Mary's, with an interesting circular Norman font bowl.

Colney [10] From Earlham Park one sees the Saxon round tower of St Andrew's, Colney, in the distance. The church stands a little below the level of the road, and over the porch there is a memorial to a waggoner who lost his life when his horses bolted. 'Reader if thou drivest a team, be careful and endanger not the life of another or thine own.'

Coltishall [11] Although on the upper reaches of the Bure, it has a lot of river traffic, and in summer there are many launches moored by the riverside which is separated from the village street by meadows. In the centre of the village, just east of the bridge over which Sir Thomas Boleyn (father of Anne) is

said to ride on certain occasions, is a triangle of streets with pleasant red-brick houses. The thatched church of St John the Baptist has a 15th-century tower and porch. The Hall, a Georgian building to the east end of the village, is now an hotel.

Colton [10] St Andrew's Church has an early 15th-century rood screen, faint wall paintings, and a west gallery and organ, both of 1855. There are old bench ends.

Congham [5] Is a straggly village with a narrow path leading up to St Andrew's Church which is almost hidden in a little wood. There is a 13th-century font. Sir Henry Spelman, the antiquary, was born in the village in 1562.

Corpusty [4] St Peter's Church on the hill has interesting window tracery and a partly mediaeval screen. The Friends of Friendless Churches hope to save it from further vandalism and restore it for occasional use. The River Bure divides this village from adjoining Saxthorpe. On the river bank is a white-painted water-mill with a superb garden behind a 'tapestry' hedge.

Costessey [10] Now a suburb of Norwich. The old church of St Edmund has a 14th-century tower with modern spire, a 15th-century font and a very interesting 15th-century screen which has brackets at the end which supported the rood loft. Jacobean pulpit and other woodwork originally in Booton Church. The new church of St Helen in New Costessey was designed by Andrew Anderson in the 1970s. Costessey Hall, a neo-Gothic house of 1826, which incorporated an early brick E-shaped house, was destroyed by fire about 1925. It was the seat of the Jerninghams, Baronets (extinct in 1935), who did so much to ensure the legitimate succession to the crown of Queen Mary in 1553. The per-

manent showground of the Royal Norfolk Show is alongside the main road.

Coston [10] A small village with an important small church dedicated to St Michael, all of the 13th century. Jacobean pulpit. The church is vested in the Redundant Churches Fund.

Cranwich [14] A hamlet with farmhouse, St Mary's Church with interlacing stonework in the Saxon round tower (recently given a new thatched roof) and white brick Regency rectory, which form a pretty group amongst meadows and hazelnut trees. Circular churchyard.

Cranworth [9] The 14th-century St Mary's Church contains monuments to the Gurdons, whose home was Letton Hall, a fine mansion by Soane with splendid trees in the park and a very fine monkey-puzzle by the house. Bequests to build church porch c. 1520. Stocks by church gate.

The **Creakes** [3] *North Creake* is the larger of the two villages with a fine church, St Mary's, though rather drastically restored. The nave has a 15th-century hammerbeam roof and a good figure brass for Sir William Calthorpe (1500) holding a model of the church. Fine sedilia and piscina, and Easter Sepulchre in the chancel, mediaeval panels including St Veronica, and a Victorian opening font-cover with painted interior. Tower 1435–50. North of the village stands Creake Abbey, an Augustinian house which went into voluntary liquidation, and so escaped damage and destruction. The nave has disappeared but there are considerable remains of the choir and crossing, and the cloister and conventual buildings can easily be traced in the grounds and buildings of the adjoining house. At *South Creake* the church of the Assumption is a splendid mainly Perpen-

dicular church of the East Anglia type, excellently restored, so tha the graceful piers of the arcades ca be seen coming right down to the bases which have been widened form seats. There is a beautifi single hammerbeam roof, and well-preserved 15th-century roc screen and pulpit. This wonderf church is in many ways the finest i Norfolk; it has the atmosphere of very holy place, a sense of timeles ness. The little Burn river runs th whole length of the two villages an through the garden of the enchan ing South Creake rectory just belo the church, amazingly still lived i by the incumbent (1981).

Cressingham, Great [9] Grea Cressingham Priory is a very fir brick house dated 1545, but pos ibly earlier, with three turrets; a decorated with terracotta panel alternately a monogram and hand holding a hawk. St Michael Church has a fine tower (144! brooding over the council hous and a chancel of about 1300 wi very pointed arcades and nice wi dow tracery. In the nave, Norwi School glass, including feather angels in north aisle, and four go brasses. The porch is 1439.

Cressingham, Little [9] Pretty v lage with old windmill and miller house, on the River Wissey, wi Clermont House, 1812, by Willia Pilkington, seen across the fields. Andrew's Church is entered exc ingly through ruined west tow and arcade. It has a Decorat chancel.

Crimplesham [8] Despite hea Victorian restoration, St Mary Church retains Norman doorwa and windows. Mediaeval scre across tower arch originating North Weald Bassett, Essex. T Hall is a Victorian house with folly.

Cringleford [11] Now a suburb of Norwich, newly by-passed, with a mediaeval bridge and St Peter's Church with a Saxon nave and chancel.

Cromer [5] The fishing village and small port was developed into a seaside resort by the coming of railways at the end of the 19th century. St Peter and St Paul's Church is an imposing 15th-century building with magnificent west tower, but it has been rather tastelessly restored inside. Along the sea front were some splendid Edwardian hotels backing onto the narrow street which forms the core of the old town but these have almost all been demolished now, leaving only the magnificent Hotel de Paris, built in 1895 by the Norwich architect, Skipper. The Hall was built by Donthorne in 1829 for the Wyndham family. It is splendid Gothick, built in flint on a lavish scale.

Crostwick [11] A wide green bisected by a main road, a few cottages, and St Peter's Church with a 15th-century font having a Trinity and apostles on the bowl.

Crostwight [5] The ruined 16th-century Hall remains. The unspoilt oil-lit All Saints' Church has a 13th-century font and a tower that was lowered in 1910. Mediaeval screen and some good 14th-century wall paintings, including the Seven Deadly Sins.

Crownthorpe [10] This hamlet has an ivy-clad 13th-century church, St James', which will soon be a complete ruin. It has been much vandalized, but to balance this a family of local children is doing its best to preserve what is left, in the hopes of an eventual restoration.

Croxton [15] Is a pretty village built of dark flint, on a hill. The

◁ **South Creake**

Great Cressingham Priory

little church of All Saints in the middle has a round tower with a hexagonal top and a spire, brick-mullioned windows to the clerestory and a hammerbeam roof.

Denton [17] St Mary's Church has the remains of a Norman round tower, rebuilt in 1843, and a fine porch with a groined roof and bosses showing the Joys of the Virgin Mary. Interesting piscina and sedilia, and painted panels from a screen worked up into a chest. In the east window is a remarkable collection of stained glass assembled by John Postlethwayte in 1717. Denton House has a garden landscaped in the 18th century with Gothick ruins, good trees and a shell grotto dated 1770, erected by Stackhouse Thompson, using stones and coral from the Great Barrier Reef.

Denver [7] The key point of the drainage system of southern fen-land, where the Bedford River, coming straight across from Earith in Huntingdonshire, rejoins the Great Ouse, now increased by waters of the Cam. There is a vast sluice gate preventing the tides from sweeping up the river and opening at low tide to allow the fresh water to flow down towards the Wash. The sluice is more than a mile from the village which is on the main road from Downham Market to Littleport. St Mary's Church has been much restored, but there is some of the 15th-century wood-work in the nave roof and choir stalls. The Hall, although it has the front of a small Georgian house, incorporates at the back and side the Tudor manor house of the Willoughbys.

Deopham [10] The church has a magnificent west tower with stepped battlements on the parapet. Inside are the remains of a 15th-century rood screen.

Dereham, East [9] An important mid-Norfolk town with some industry; the wide market place has some 18th-century houses remaining despite recent 'improvements', including at the north-east end that of Sir John Fenn, first editor of the Paston Letters. The Congregational chapel stands on the site of the house where Cowper died in 1800, and the poet is also commemorated by a Victorian stained glass window and a monument by Flaxman in St Nicholas' Church. This is a cruciform building with a lantern tower at the crossing and a detached 15th-century bell tower in the churchyard. In the churchyard at the west end of the church is St Withburga's Well; Withburga, the daughter of Anna, King of the East Angles, and sister to St Etheldreda Abbess of Ely, founded a convent at Dereham, but in the 12th century when the cathedral at Ely was built, her body was stolen and reinterred there beside the remains of her sister. The church has been much restored; there is a Seven Sacrament font (which cost £12 13s 9d in 1468) and a mediaeval brass eagle lectern. The mediaeval screen in the north transept came from Oxborough Church when its tower fell in 1948. The Revd B. J. Armstrong, the Tractarian vicar (1850–88) kept a daily diary, of which two volumes of extracts have been published, and which shed considerable light on the times. In the street east of the church are Bonner's cottages with thatch and pargetry work, rather uncommon in Norfolk. To the north of the town, on the Fakenham road, is Quebec Hall built by Samuel Rash in 1759, but considerably altered since, now an old people's home. Dereham includes outlying hamlets, Toftwood (although modern buildings have really joined it on to Dereham) and Dillington, and separate groups of houses at Etling Green, Dumpling Green wher

◁   **Cromer**

George Borrow was born in 1803 in a neat and many-sashed farmhouse, and Neatherd Green, which still have the appearance of separate villages. The woods around Quebec House were laid out in accordance with the military dispositions at the battle of Quebec (1759). Dillington Hall is a Georgian house of c. 1800, a mile to the north-west. As well as George Borrow, Dereham also gave to the world William Hyde Wollaston, F.R.S. (1766–1828), whose family produced rectors from 1761 to 1872. Among his discoveries in the field of natural sciences was the isolation of the chemical elements palladium and rhodium.

Dereham, West [8] St Andrew's Church has a very wide Norman tower made of large chunks of carrstone topped by a brick Tudor belfry. Inside, it has a pillar poorbox (with a text from Tobit IV), drop-handled bier (1683), 15th-century angels in a nave window and Jacobean pulpit. Other Jacobean woodwork is found in the lectern and stalls. Three-sided altar rails given by Mrs Green, sister of Col. Edmund Soame, who is commemorated by a splendid monument by Robert Singleton of Bury (1706), showing the colonel as a life-sized armoured figure. Another is in Florentine mosaic to Sir Thomas Dereham (1722), envoy of James II to the Grand Duke Cosimo III of Tuscany. There are remains of the Premonstratensian Abbey founded in 1198 by Hubert Walter, a native of West Dereham, who became Archbishop of Canterbury.

Dersingham [2] Has nice cottages built of the local brown carrstone, and interesting new development. There is a large sandy heath with silver birches and views of marsh and sea. St Nicholas' is a big church surrounded by yews and contains good tombs, an unusual incised black marble one of 1607, and a very rare 14th-century chest carved

Deopham

with emblems of the evangelists. The Hall apparently incorporates part of the 17th-century manor house of the Pells. Fine barn north-west of the church (1671).

Dickleburgh with Langmere [16] The painter, Cattermole, was born in this large village in 1803. It is grouped round All Saints' Church in a well-treed churchyard. There is a school, built in 1820, in restrained Gothick. Inside the church are arms for Charles II hanging on the west gallery and a wonderful monument to Dame Francis Playters who died in 1659 and whose family were great sup-

porters of King Charles I. The long inscription is worth reading. Also a Crimean monument. The village suffers a pounding from the heavy traffic using the A140.

Didlington [14] A tower and colonnade are all that remains of the vast Italianate Hall (demolished in 1950). St Michael's Church in the park has an arch brace and cambered tie-beam roof and some 15th-century benches. The nave has been cleared of most of its fittings and is now used for social events; the chancel, with noteworthy continental marble altar rails, affords adequate seating for

◁ **West Dereham**

Downham Market: cast iron clock tower △

he small population. The Hon. Alicia Amherst, daughter of the first Lord Amherst of Hackney who lived here, was a famous botanist and gardener and author of *A History of Gardening in England*, a superb book published in 1895.

Dilham [11] Was once joined to North Walsham by the only navigable canal in Norfolk. St Nicholas' Church was rebuilt in 1931 but it has an interesting 15th-century font; the base of the round tower is an early 19th-century version of a Norfolk speciality.

Diss [16] John Skelton, poet and tutor to Henry VIII, was rector of Diss, the most attractive country town in south Norfolk, largely because the Mere is in the middle of it. The tortuous narrows of Mere Street widen a little at the top to form a small market place dominated by St Mary's Church. This is a spacious building, somewhat over-restored within, with an early 14th-century tower and 15th-century west doors. The Manning family supplied four successive rectors (1778–1916) including a noted local historian; another of the family, Thomas Manning, was the first Englishman to reach Lhasa. This is John Betjeman's favourite Norfolk town, and Mary Wilson, wife of Sir Harold, lived here as a child. The Corn Hall is a fine classical building, and along the street on the other side of the Mere are some very pleasant Georgian houses. North of the church is the Georgian Manor House, five bays with an elegant semi-circular porch on Corinthian columns.

Ditchingham [17] The Hall (variously dated at 1702, 1715 and 1727), stands by a lake in a park landscaped by Capability Brown. St Mary's Church has a noble flint tower, with original statues each side of the west door, and a basecourse carved with the Sacred Heart bearing the Crown of Thorns; inside is a restored screen, a black marble 1914–18 Memorial (by Derwent Wood, R.A.) with a life-size bronze effigy of a dead

69

soldier and an interesting window to the author of *She* (Rider Haggard), who lived at Ditchingham House. The Anglican Community of All Hallows was established here in 1859 and the sisters run a girls' training centre, a hospital, two schools and a retreat house, and St Anne's House, a home for the elderly. Ditchingham House was built about 1780 by the Revd William Buckle.

Docking [2] In the highlands of west Norfolk, known as 'Dry Docking'. There are attractive old houses in the village. St Mary's Church is a spacious 14th-century building with a font of the period and a north aisle added in 1875. The tower, however, is 1415. St Henry Walpole, the Roman Catholic martyr, was baptized here in 1558. The Hall, partly Elizabethan, has belonged to the Hares since the 17th century. The estate was inherited by the Christian family who took the names and arms of Hare in 1798, and the Victorian work in the Hall is by Ewan Christian.

Downham Market [7] All yellow and brown (brick and carrstone), standing on high ground at the very edge of The Fens. St Edmund's Church, in a big churchyard well planted with yews and weeping ash, stands higher still and is reached by steps or a steep lane. It is built of carrstone and has a Romanesque crucifix outside and a Queen Anne gallery with her arms above it. 'That gallery is getting old now,' a church cleaner remarked threateningly. The church has a rather unusual glass chandelier, c. 1730. Though the church stands well, the approach road to the town has been badly mauled and an unattractive retaining wall erected below the churchyard. There are four Nonconformist chapels, of which Mount Tabor in Bridge Street has a most unusual and imposing façade (1809). The old workhouse, now Howdale House,

is in good workhouse style of about 1835, and some 17th-century gables on a shop in High Street show the Dutch influence so strong in these parts. The Gothic clock tower (1878 by William Cunliffe) in the market place is a great source of local pride. The Castle Hotel has a very attractive 18th-century façade.

Drayton [10] The growing community on the outskirts of Norwich still has some village character; the rebuilt St Margaret's Church by the green has a thatched roof. Punning village sign.

Dunham, Great [9] This good church dedicated to St Andrew has a Saxon central tower with interesting mouldings. Good flint buildings in former railway station on road to Little Dunham.

Dunham, Little [9] Village full of pretty houses, mostly Georgian, including former rectory beautifully grouped in trees by St Margaret's Church; note curious head over church door and bases of arcade piers widened to form seats, in the days before pews. Dunham Lodge is a Georgian house.

Dunston [11] This church dedicated to St Remigius, has a simple 15th-century screen and some mediaeval glass. The neo-Elizabethan Hall is probably by the Norwich architect, Boardman; there is also a small Queen Anne manor house.

Dunton-with-Doughton [3] Dunton is a tiny hamlet, Doughton has vanished. St Peter's Church has a well-proportioned tower built in the 1440s, a modern rood screen (1910), good glass (1863) probably by Powell, and an interesting window with fine peacocks, an unusual symbol, and a memorial slab to Sir Matthew Lancaster (1658). This church is now vested in the Norfolk Churches Trust and a small community of Anglican monks lived there for a while.

Earlham [11] The University o East Anglia, a distinguished mod ern building by Denys Lasdu (though with additions by Bernar Fielden), stands above the Rive Yare, in the former park of Earl ham Hall where John Crom taught the Gurney girls to dra and Joseph John Gurney caugh George Borrow fishing. The Ha itself, now an administrative part c the university, dates from 1642; i is very lovingly described in *Ear ham*, a book published in 1922 b Percy Lubbock, himself descende from the Gurney family who gav the house its fame through th philanthropist Joseph John Gurne and his better-known siste Elizabeth Fry. Although the Gu neys lived there from 1786 to 189. it never belonged to them; it wa built by Robert Houghton, an passed through various owner until the university acquired it. . recent addition to the university the striking Sainsbury Centre, prize-winning building by Fost Associates. St Mary's Church much restored but has a 167 Bacon monument.

Earsham [17] The Hall stands in fine park. It is now a school but wa built early in the 18th century b John Buxton, 'an amateur archite of some ability', who sold it in 172 to William Windham of Felbrig great-uncle of the statesman. It ha later additions, including some b Sir John Soane. The much-restore All Saints' Church has a Seve Sacrament font and some famou Flemish glass.

East Bilney *see* Bilney, East

East Carleton *see* Carleton, Eas

East Dereham *see* Dereham, Eas

East Harling, *see* Harling, East

Easton [10] An expanding villag stretching along the A47, b towards Ringland the scenery is times reminiscent of Devon ar you would never guess how near Norwich was. The church has a good Norman doorway; the pulpit with hourglass stand came from the closed Norwich church of St Mary Coslany.

East Ruston [5] The great Cambridge professor, Porson, was the son of a farm worker here, and a curate, the Revd Mr Hewitt, taught him Latin. He became Regius Professor of Greek at the age of 33. The isolated church of St Mary in this little Broadland village has a 15th-century font and the lower part of the screen, with good paintings of the Latin Doctors and evangelists, as well as unique treatment of the mullions. The church has been closed but is being restored, and is vested in the Redundant Churches Fund.

East Tuddenham *See* Tuddenham, East

East Walton *see* Walton, East

East Winch *see* Winch, East

East Wretham *see* Wretham, East

Eaton [11] The old village with its splendid Red Lion Inn and Dutch gables is on the main road and the mediaeval thatched church of St Andrew is prettily situated near Cringleford Bridge. Christ Church, Victorian Gothic of 1873 by J. H. Brown and Pearce, with a porch and aisle added in 1913, has some interesting 20th-century glass, as well as some fragments of mediaeval glass in the porch.

Eccles [16] (near Attleborough) A small village with new housing development between St Mary's Church and the railway station. A delightful little church up a drive lined with young trees; it has a Norman round tower. The chancel arch has interesting carvings and is flanked by niches over former nave altars; there is a Jacobean pulpit and a fine modern rood group. In the chancel are a good 13th-century double piscina and huge mediaeval stone altar. The late 17th-century Hall has unusually shaped gables.

Eccles-next-the-Sea [6] The church is a ruin on the beach, near Hempstead.

Edgefield [4] A scattered village, chiefly remarkable for St Peter and St Paul's Church which was moved from the original site and rebuilt in the geographic centre in the eighties of the last century by Canon W. H. Marcon, rector for 63 years, with the assistance of J. D. Sedding. Canon Marcon's little book, *The Reminiscences of a Norfolk Parson*, is very revealing about Norfolk village life. With the exception of the tower and chancel the old church was faithfully reproduced. There is a fine parclose screen with figure painting of the donor, William Harstong. The old tower, octagonal in shape and built of flint with large blocks of carrstone, stands in a farmyard a mile away. The Old Hall has a three-storey porch with angle shafts, and pedimented windows and is early 17th century.

Edingthorpe [5] All Saints' Church, isolated in the fields with only footpaths leading to it, has a round tower and a 14th-century painted screen with wheel tracery above the ogival arch in the centre. There are remains of wall paintings and a reading desk dated 1587.

Ellingham [17] (near Bungay) Scattered village on the Suffolk border; mainly 14th-century church of St Mary, with box pews. The charming water-mill is now a flourishing art centre.

Ellingham, Great [16] (near Attleborough) Has a spacious 14th/15th-century church, St James, with a beautiful east window and base of rood screen with figure paintings, set in a commanding position at the north end of the village. There are wall paintings in the south aisle including an angel in a niche, and there is a splendid two-tier west gallery to accommodate both choir and ringers. The Old Hall is a timber-framed Tudor house with a four-bay front.

Ellingham, Little [15, 16] An attractive group of cottages round St Peter's Church, restored after a fire in 1867; porphyry font and glass by Kempe; the village also has a curious clock tower with living accommodation in the bottom, dated 1855, the same year as the Hall.

Elsing [10, 13] St Mary's Church, of the Decorated period, has an extraordinarily wide nave, a most beautiful 14th-century font cover and one of the finest military brasses in England for Sir Hugh Hastings (1347) who built the church. There is 14th-century glass in the chancel. Elsing Hall is a perfect example of a 15th-century moated manor house still retaining its great hall with oriel windows. It was restored in 1852. The property belonged to Wimer, Steward to the Warrenne family, at the time of the Domesday Book, and passed through his descendants until it was finally sold, for the first time, in 1958.

Emneth [7] Straggles, and has a nice house with brick pilasters between here and Outwell, and handsome stone piers outside a large 17th-century brick house near St Edmund's Church. This is one of the famous Marshland churches with a beautiful hammerbeam roof and very lovely carved angels. There is an old screen with some colour left, and in the south aisle is an altar tomb of Sir Thomas Hewar by Nicholas Stone, 1631, and an 18th-century one to another member of the same family.

Erpingham [5] St Mary's Church has a lofty west tower (c. 1484) finely embellished with panelled buttresses in stone and flint; the name ERPINGHAM is spelt out round the parapet. Inside is a good military brass for Sir Thomas Erpingham dating from c. 1415; *not* the Sir Thomas who was the companion of Henry V at Agincourt. The east window has some panels of 16th-century German glass from Steinfeld imported about 1800 by J. C. Hampp. An atmospheric church looked after with loving care. There is a 14th-century font from the bombed St Benedict's, Norwich.

Fakenham [3] A pretty market town which once had two railway stations; it has none now, of course, and though mainly an agricultural centre, it has a few light industries. St Peter and St Paul's Church, with a splendid west tower (c. 1450), received a thorough restoration in the 19th century. There are 15th-century brasses, and some interesting glass roundels in the windows. The view of Fakenham as you approach from the south across Hempton Green is very attractive; once in the town, there are fine brick buildings in the market place, and many very pretty small lanes and courts, with charming old houses and 18th- and 19th-century buildings, like the Fire Station, west of the market place down towards the river. Close to the Great Snoring boundary of the parish is Thorpland Hall; a fine 16th-century red-brick house with brick mouldings.

Felbrigg [5] Has a beautiful park possibly landscaped by Repton and overlooked by the south front of Felbrigg Hall, dated 1620, to which a western wing was added in 1686, the work of William Samwell, an architect from Watton in Norfolk who, according to Evelyn, built a house for Charles II at Newmarket. The Gothick library on the first floor of the south wing and the staircase were designed in 1750 by James Paine. The stables to the east of the house with the colonnade were built in 1825 to the designs of

W. J. Donthorne, another local architect, this time from Swaffham, who was a pupil of Sir Jeffry Wyatville. The house was built by the Wyndham (later Windham) family, of whom Rt. Hon. William Windham was Secretary at War in the younger Pitt's Cabinet. It was sold with its contents in 1862 to the Kettons and passed by marriage to the Cremers. It was left to the National Trust by R. W. Ketton-Cremer in 1969. St Margaret's Church, standing in the park, contains many brasses including one to Sir Simon de Felbrigg and his wife (1416) and two post-Reformation ones as well as splendid Windham monuments, including William Windham (1686) by Grinling Gibbons, and another William Windham (1813) by Nollekens.

Felmingham [5] St Andrew's Church has a strong squat tower (c. 1530) without a parapet, which dominates the village. The rest of the church was rebuilt in brick in 1742 after a fire but does not have a Georgian character, perhaps because the Perpendicular south doorway and some of the Decorated windows were kept. There are two interesting brasses and some scraps of old glass.

Felthorpe [10] Much-restored church and a 19th-century Hall.

Feltwell [14] Is a large straggly village with two churches and nice old houses. The church of St Mary has grey 15th-century benches with carved ends; ladies in sentry boxes, three people weeping over a corpse, and a camel. Also 16th-century monuments in chancel and a triple sedilia and piscina with cinquefoiled heads. St Nicholas' Church has flint panels on its outside walls and a Norman arch inside, survivor of a round tower which fell in 1898 while men repairing it were having breakfast at a nearby pub. It is now vested in the Redundant Churches Fund and cared for by the local archaeological society.

Fersfield [16] In the chancel of St Andrew's Church is a monument on the floor to Francis Blomefield, rector of this parish and the great historian of Norfolk. The old rectory where the history of Norfolk was written and printed can still be seen in the trees to the west of the church. The church itself has an exceptionally narrow west tower, a 15th-century arcade, and a most interesting wooden effigy of Sir Robert du Bois (1311) restored by Blomefield himself. The sanctuary has 17th-century panelling and altar table.

Field Dalling [4] Is a straggling village with an interesting church St Andrew's. The chancel was restored in the Tractarian manner. In the north aisle are box pews and in the south windows of the nave is some good 15th-century glass. There are interesting tombstones outside. Opposite the church is a pretty cottage with a Jacobean front, and there are several other nice old houses in the village.

Filby [12] A Broadland village on the old main road which runs down to the bridge between Filby and Rollesby Broads. Down the side road to Thrigby are pleasant cottages and orchards. All Saints Church has a 15th-century tower with flint flushwork and statues of the Latin Doctors acting as pinnacles. The door to the belfry stair has seven locks and probably enclosed a strongroom; there is 14th-century ironwork on the north door, a very fine screen base with some vivid figure paintings and mediaeval pulpit. In the churchyard extension to the south, a tombstone to a couple whose combined ages totalled 200 years. People called Filby from all over the world turn up here for occasional celebrations.

Fincham [8] Is strung out along the main road from which the Hall, a Tudor house with Victorian additions, is visible. It belonged to the

Felbrigg Hall

Finchams, extinct in the 17th century. St Martin's Church has a fine tower (bequests 1458–76), a Norman font with crude carvings of Adam and Eve and the Serpent; a strange naked-figure brass in the middle of the nave, painted texts (1717) and some good monuments. Robert Forby, author of *The Vocabulary of East Anglia*, was rector here until he died in his bath in 1825. The Moat House, just out of the village to the south-west, has a square moated island, possibly a mediaeval cattle enclosure.

Fishley [12] The church, St Mary, of this hamlet has a pre-Conquest round tower, a Norman doorway, a poorbox cut out of a log, and an organ case of 1781.

Flitcham [2] Stands on the River Babingley. There was once an abbey here of which there are a few remains near the house known as Flitcham Abbey. St Mary's Church has Norman arcading in the central tower.

Flordon [16] The village stands amongst water meadows and willows. St Michael and All Angels' Church has two Saxon windows, a 17th-century pulpit, complete rood stairs and fragments of mediaeval glass. The good Tudor Hall has for centuries been used as a farmhouse.

Fordham [7] The little church of St Mary is of carrstone with a 19th-century bellcote and no tower. Snore Hall, of the 16th century but much restored, was the seat of the Skipwiths, and Charles I stayed here on 30 April 1646 on his journey from Oxford to Newark.

Forncett St Mary [16] Has pretty south Norfolk cottages, colour-washed cream or pink with very steep roofs, sometimes thatched. The church has a Jacobean pulpit. J. W. Colenso, later a controversial colonial bishop in South Africa, was once rector here.

Forncett St Peter [16] There are some gabled houses including the Queen Anne rectory which stands in trees and makes a fine group with the church. The latter is a most interesting building with a splendid Saxon round tower with a fine arch inside. There is a good 15th-century porch, and pews with magnificent carving including a woman shut up in a sort of sentry-box; also fine roofs, a table tomb, and interesting Victorian glass.

Foulden [8] The delightful Hall, of many different dates and with some Elizabethan chimneys, looks like a 17th-century sampler with its rectangular pond in front, edged with a double row of pleached limes. All Saints' Church has a 14th-century nave full of 15th-century benches with carved ends; in the aisles are 18th-century box pews. There are remains of a 15th-century painted screen, and a huge monument of 1656 in the chancel; also a fine floor of old flint and yellow brick, some laid in herring-bone patterns. The wrought-iron lampholders on pews in aisles were well placed to give an agreeable light. A recent painting in the south aisle depicts a 17th-century communion service.

Foulsham [4] The well-proportioned 15th-century tower of Holy Innocents' Church rises high above the pleasant market place, rebuilt

73

after a great fire in 1771 with graceful Georgian houses. The long range of the Ship Inn, with its elaborate sign, is described by Parson Woodforde who came here for a 'Visitation Dinner'. The 16th-century Old Hall was built by the Themelthorpes and was later acquired by the Skippons, who produced the famous Parliamentary General Philip Skippon.

Foxley [10] The well-restored church of St Thomas has a shapely western tower and 15th-century screen with figures painted on the doors. It also has plastered ceilings, a two-decker pulpit, box pews at the front of the nave and poppy-headed benches at the back. A west gallery completes the ensemble; one almost expects to hear the violins being tuned up to accompany the singing. The early-Victorian former rectory was built in 1842.

Framingham Earl [11] An early Norfolk church, St Andrew's, whose round tower and nave and chancel with circular windows are mainly Saxon; there are two Norman doorways and a Norman chancel arch. The 17th-century pulpit came from Sotterly in Suffolk. Monuments to Edward Rigby (1822) and two pieces of 15th-century glass showing St Catherine and St Margaret (the latter with a very red dragon). Note curious tree-gravestone in churchyard for Samuel Bligh 1834–1913.

Framingham Pigot [11] Pleasant small village whose tiny Saxon church was pulled down in 1859 and replaced by the present building, St Andrew's, by Kerr, which retains a Norman piscina. The Victorian fittings repay examination. The manor house was built in 1862.

Fransham [9] *Great Fransham* All Saints' Church has a brass to Geoffrey Frensham (1414) and the 15th-century font from St

Etheldreda's, Norwich, and at *Little Fransham* St Mary's there is a square Norman font, simple 15th-century hammerbeam roof, some old benches, and many Dickens memorials. The Old Hall dates back to the 16th century.

Freethorpe [12] A rather bleak village which seems to be at the end of everything, but there is a lane which leads to the even more remote Wickhampton. The village consists of one street with the usual flint and brick cottages and there are a few more scattered about Freethorpe Common on the road to Southwood. All Saints' Church has a round tower. It was restored in 1849.

Frenze [16] St Andrew's is a tiny church in a farmyard, containing the famous Blennerhassett brasses, 1475–1527, and others, including Thomas Hobson in his shroud, Joan Braham and one Richard Nixon. There is also a splendid Jacobean box pew opposite a pulpit with tester; note the nice monkeys on priest's stall. Mediaeval altar stone. The church is now vested in the Norfolk Churches Trust.

Frettenham [11] St Swithin's Church has a good 14th-century tower and arcade, and Purbeck marble font.

Fring [2] This pretty hamlet is at the source of the River Heacham. The Hall was built in 1807 and was rebuilt in this century after a fire. All Saints' Church, on high ground above the river, is 14th century with typical Y-tracery and ogee moulding. Wall painting of St Christopher and traces of others.

Fritton [17] Is scattered round a large green. It has a delightful round-towered church dedicated to St Catharine, some way up a grassy track. There is part of an early 16th-century screen, with painted figures including those of John Bacon and his wife, who gave it; a

beautiful modern rood, and good wall paintings including a particularly fine St George and the Dragon.

Fulmodestone [3] The old St Mary's Church stands in ruins. Near it is an attractive late 18th-century farmhouse, the pediment of the west front being filled by a large bas-relief representing a shepherd with his sheep. Christ Church, the Victorian church in the village centre, is by W. Bassett Smith, 1882.

Fundenhall [16] St Nicholas Church with Norman central tower stands isolated in a beautiful grove of pines. It has a Norman south door and the remains of a screen.

Garboldisham [15] Has one or two pretty cottages, an inn and two churches, one now in ruins. The other, St John the Baptist, is very fine outside, with a Latin prayer on the flint porch and a tower of the 1460s. In the porch is a 13th century bell; in the church is a ringer's jug or gotch with a hearty inscription, 1703. There is a modern rood-beam with figures; and some pre-Raphaelite glass. The Hall, which was by G. G. Scott, was burnt down in 1955. The stables of Garboldisham House, by the younger G. G. Scott, survive. The Devil's Ditch is a Saxon earthwork designed to block the Roman road (now the A1066).

Garvestone [10] St Margaret Church has a 14th-century west tower which is a landmark.

Gateley [3] The Hall (1726) belonged to the Sharrocks from the 17th century until about 1835. It is well restored, as is St Helen Church, approached through farmyard. The latter has Saxon work in the nave, a 15th-century screen with paintings (c. 1485) which include the uncanonized Henry VI and John Schorne, chancel of 1866, good Caroline

Fulmodestone church

royal arms, nice carved bench ends, and a monument, now needing repair, by Robert Page of Norwich to Mrs Segrave (1727) who 'in her conjugal life was not so happy as deserving'. She built the Hall and was the daughter of Archdeacon Sharrock of Winchester, a very learned man and an authority on legal matters, also 'very knowing in vegetables', who is said to have introduced the artichoke into this country.

Gayton [8] The village has tall lime trees and two tall buildings, one the 14th-century church tower of St Nicholas' Church with a pointed black roof and four large statues at the corners in place of pinnacles, and the other the old black body of a windmill whose sails have now gone. Outside the village is Eastgate House, a former workhouse, by Donthorne, 1835.

Gayton Thorpe [8] A hamlet whose church, St Mary, by a little green has a round 11th-century tower with Saxon splayed windows. Inside it has a hammerbeam roof and a good Seven-Sacrament font.

Gaywood [8] In the brick church, St Faith, rebuilt by W. D. Caroe in 1906–9 are two pictures, one of Queen Elizabeth I reviewing her troops and ships at the time of the threatened Spanish invasion, and the other of the Gunpowder Plot; they were given by Thomas Hares, the rector who died in 1632, so they are probably contemporary records. Also a font with interesting 17th-century inscriptions, and a fine Elizabethan altar.

Geldeston [18] St Michael's Church is much restored and has a modern east window by Leonard Walker, but the village is pretty, and the Hall is a nice late Georgian house with an even better one standing below it beyond the road and River Waveney.

Gillingham [18] Has three churches close together by the realigned road; one is a ruined tower, All Saints, in the park. Next is a Norman one, St Mary (substantially rebuilt in 1858–9 under the supervision of Penrice of Lowestoft), whose interior would please those Victorians who loved a dim 'religious' light; a former rector, the Revd John Lewis, was a keen horseman, and it is said that, in his old age, he had his saddle fixed in the pulpit so that he could preach sitting down. Finally Our Lady of Perpetual Succour, a Roman Catholic church built by John George Kenyon, a convert, in brick with two towers designed by F. E. Banham, 1898; with an unspoilt interior. Good Tayler & Green terraces 1955–8 on main road. The Hall is an E-plan Jacobean house acquired by Sir Nicholas Bacon, the premier Baronet, of Redgrave, from the Everard family in the reign of James I. The fenestration is now Georgian, and a south wing with a drawing-room was added in this style.

Gimingham [5] All Saints' Church has a south porch with a parvise having a watching window looking into the church. Stuart royal arms, and a nice tower built about 1500.

Gissing [16] Has good oaks and chestnuts. From the 14th century until very lately, it was the home of the Kemp family, many of whom are buried in St Mary's Church and in the small Kemp chapel. There is

△ Ivy Farm, **Grimston**

Mermaid in **Grimston** church ▷

a fine double-hammerbeam roof to the nave, a Saxon round tower, two Norman doorways, and a nice 15th-century porch. The Hall was built in the 19th century in Elizabethan style.

Glandford [4] St Martin's Church, which was built on the site of an earlier church by Hicks & Charlewood for Sir Alfred Jodrell in 1900, is a galaxy of all the splendours of an East Anglian church building. Rood and parclose screens, hammerbeam roof, marble Seven-Sacrament font copied from the one at Walsoken, carved pew ends (one derived from Landseer's celebrated picture *The Shepherd's Chief Mourner*, representing a dog resting his sorrowful head on his master's coffin), a side altar with figure painting on the front with gesso work. There are some fine candelabra and very beautiful windows—in the nave and aisles by Heasman, with the east window by Kempe. All this was placed here by the pious Sir Alfred Jodrell of Bayfield Hall in memory of his mother. The church stands in a beautifully kept churchyard with a charming prospect down the Glaven valley towards Cley. The model village, built by the Jodrells, consists of very well-designed cottages with Flemish gables; and a

little building of a similar design just north of the church contains a collection of shells brought from every part of the world, and other objects of interest including an embroidered panel by the Sheringham fisherman-artist John Craske 1881–1943. This unsophisticated little museum is absolutely not to be missed. The water-mill in the village has been converted into a charming house.

Godwick [9] The church is a ruin, as is the Hall (built by the Drurys in 1586), which was the principal seat of the Cokes before they moved to Holkham. (*See also* Tittleshall.)

Gooderstone [8] St George's Church contains a square-headed rood screen with prickets for candles and paintings of the apostles, a two-decker Jacobean pulpit, benches with pierced backs, and a memorial on the west wall to Mrs Mary Thornton (d. 1799). The font was given to the church by a vicar who died in 1446.

Gorleston [12] A suburb of Great Yarmouth but still a seaside resort with a distinct character of its own; it was, after all, there before Yarmouth. The parish church, St Andrew, contains one of the earliest and most interesting military bras-

ses in England representing a knight in chain mail (c. 1320) a member of the Bacon family; also a Seven-Sacrament font, mediaeval altar stone restored to use, and a fine set of Caroline royal arms. The Roman Catholic church (1938) by Eric Gill is a cruciform brick building with a central altar, an early example of the Liturgical Movement.

Great Cressingham *see* Cressingham, Great

Great Dunham *see* Dunham, Great

Great Ellingham *see* Ellingham, Great

Great Melton *see* Melton, Great

Great Ryburgh *see* Ryburgh Great

Great Yarmouth *see* Yarmouth Great

Gresham [4] John Gresham of Gresham was the great-great-grandfather of Sir Thomas Gresham who founded the Royal Exchange. John Gresham, uncle of Thomas, was born in his father's manor house at Holt which he afterwards converted into

Gresham's School. Gresham village also had a connection with the Paston family and the remains of their fortified mansion—Gresham Castle—can be seen in the meadows surrounded by a moat just opposite The Chequers at the south side of the village. All Saints' Church has a very fine Seven-Sacrament font.

Gressenhall [9] At one end of the village stands splendid Beech House, 'the House of Industry' mentioned by Parson Woodforde, built in 1777 and now a very fine Rural Life Museum. At the other end of the village is the 12th-century church of St Mary with central tower and battlements formerly dated 1491. The Hastings chapel in the south transept has a coloured roof and incised slab with large figure, 1360. The Revd Dennis Hill was rector here from 1807 to 1873; a parson of the old school who drank a bottle of port a day and was a keen shot and bowls player, he would have delighted John Keble as he played cricket with the village youth on Sunday evenings. On the Longham road notice Sparrow Green Farm, an attractive Elizabethan house.

Grimston [8] Is dominated by the tall 15th-century flint tower of St

Botolph's Church. Good 15th-century carved bench ends, in the choir a chrism child in swaddling clothes, a woodpecker, and a mermaid with very long hair and a short curly tail. More at the west end of the nave, including Apocalyptic beasts and a man in the stocks. There is an old pulley for the new font cover, large canopied niches at the east end of the chancel and a restored screen and crucifix. Faint wall paintings and a nice 13th-century south door. The Revd Mr Unwin, husband of Cowper's friend, was incumbent here, although in later years he spent most of his time at Huntingdon.

Griston [9, 15] St Peter and St Paul. '1568 was this steple tope newe set up to the great cost of landed men' is the inscription on the bowl of the font, referring to the parapet of the tower ('new' in a will of 1477). There is a 15th-century screen, stained glass figures, and bench ends, and a fine Stuart pulpit with backboard and canopy.

Guestwick [4] The Saxon tower of St Peter's Church, now in the angle of the nave and chancel, was originally central. There are some beautiful incised slabs with figures for members of the Bulwer family and also a good 18th-century

monument for William Bulwer and 18th-century communion rails. Very interesting 15th-century font with the emblems of apostles, the symbol of the Trinity, and the Instruments of the Passion. There is some 15th-century glass and a most unusual flight of stairs to the rood loft. By the church is the former Independent manse, c 1700, which served the chapel in a field north of the church. This date from 1652 (although altered in the early 19th century), one of the earliest in the country, and still contains many of its original furnishings, though sadly dilapidated.

Guist [4] A model village laid out in the present century by the family of Thomas Cook & Son, with a neat clock tower on the village green. Much restored church of S Andrew. The gates on the Fakenham road are the entrance to a fine park surrounding Sennowe Hall, the splendiferous mansion built by Skipper in 1908 around an 18th-century core.

Gunthorpe [4] St Mary's Church has interesting Crimean War memorials, a 15th-century heraldic font, and a High Victorian chancel. Tower built c. 1417–21. Sir John Soane extensively altered Gunthorpe Hall (1788–9) for the Revd Charles Collyer, who died in 1830. It was re-fronted by Butterfield about 1880. The park is attractive, wooded with a lake. There is an interesting village school by Preece (1869).

Gunton [5] The beautiful little church of St Andrew, now vested in the Redundant Churches Fund, was built by Robert Adam in 1769. With its Doric portico, stalls and return stalls, it is like a college chapel. Each of the return stalls is equipped with a beautifully bound prayer book for the use of the Suffield family. Gunton Hall was

Haddiscoe (*above*)
Hales (*below*) ▷

built by Matthew Brettingham who was associated with William Kent at Holkham, and was subsequently enlarged by James Wyatt and partially burnt in 1882. The remains, still inhabited, stand in a charming formal garden. There are fine classical entrances to the park on the north and west and a strange, attractive look-out tower-cum-lodge, now being restored.

Hackford [10] (near Reepham) A little rubble remains of the church, burned down in 1543, in the same churchyard as Reepham and Whitwell churches. The Hall estate, having been acquired by George Coke, first cousin of Sir Edward, the Chief Justice, was left by him to his half-brother Augustine Messenger. It passed eventually by descent to Messenger Monsey, the eccentric physician to Chelsea Hospital, the only man who could and would beat Sir Robert Walpole at chess. It is an attractive late-Georgian house with a porch on two pairs of columns, in a small park a mile west of Reepham.

Hackford [10] (near Wymondham) 'John Daynes, churchwarding' put his name to a 16th-century chest in St Mary's Church, which has a Norman doorway and piscina and sedilia of the early 14th century.

Haddiscoe [18] St Mary's Church is on a little hill overlooking the Waveney marshes—made famous as the subject of paintings by Arnesby Brown, who caught the feeling of the east Norfolk landscape beneath the wide arch of the East Anglian sky. The magnificent church tower with triangular-headed belfry windows dates from the late 11th century; over the Norman south door is a contemporary figure, possibly Christ in

79

Sculpture above the south door, **Haddiscoe**

The thatched roof has recently been renewed. *Hales Green* is huge (66 acres) with a farm at either end. One is late Georgian, the other is part of a house built by Sir James Hobart, Attorney General to Henry VII. It includes, through its Tudor gatehouse, the moated remains of a mediaeval house and one of the largest barns in the county, with triple rows of light slits and a splendid timber roof.

Halvergate [12] St Peter and St Paul's Church contains a 'palimpsest' brass showing on the one side the head and shoulders of a Franciscan friar of Great Yarmouth 'Frater Wilms Jernmy', and on the other Alice, wife of Robert Swane of 1540. There are two good early 19th-century white brick houses and an old windmill.

Hanworth [5] St Bartholomew's Church, set amid a group of firs, has a memorial to William Doughty who 'after eleven years travell into ye Barbados and other Trancemarine Countries safely arrived at his native towne, and when he had with great oy seen his Friends and Neighbours, took his leave and return'd to ye universall place ye Earth, where all must rest till ye sound of ye Trump'. The Hall is a fine house of the early 18th century, built by the Doughty family. The park has recently been improved by planting and the restoration of the lake; in the garden is a gigantic Spanish chestnut tree 20 feet around and probably 700 years old.

Majesty. A 15th-century font and remains of a St Christopher and other wall paintings. Mrs Arnesby Brown is commemorated by a window, and in the nave is a monument to the Dutchman, Jan Piers Piers, 'the master of the dykes' at the time when the land in this part of the county was reclaimed. Memorial to William Salter in the south wall of the churchyard.

Hainford [11] Dormitory village north of Norwich with one straight street. The old church, part of which still stands outside the village, was replaced in the 1830s by All Saints, nearer the village centre, designed by the architect, John Brown, in his favourite 13th-century style.

Hales [17, 18] Has many new houses by Tayler & Green in a well-designed layout, and cheerfully coloured. St Margaret's Church is Norman, with a round tower (with some evidence of Saxon work), arcaded apse and splendid doorways. Inside it is colour-washed cream, has 15th-century wall paintings and fragments of a painted screen; it is now vested in the Redundant Churches Fund.

Happisburgh [6] A lighthouse warns passing ships of the dangerous Happisburgh Sands. Not far away is St Mary's Church with its lofty west tower and fine 15th-century font and rood screen. The 16th-century 'Monastery Cottage' stands in the village street; in the churchyard are many memorials to the victims of shipwreck. When Jonathan Balls was buried in 1846 at his own request a plum cake,

Bible, a poker and a pair of tongs were also interred with him; it appears that 'he poisoned people's drinks with arsenic but one day drank from the wrong glass'. Happisburgh Manor (1900) is one of Detmar Blow's most important houses.

Hapton [16] St Margaret's Church is mainly 14th and 15th century, but the tower was built in 1847–8. There is a 13th-century iron knocker on the door and 15th-century ironbound chest; notice lively 14th-century carving on the chancel arch and fragments of the old screen made up into the back of the sedilia. The interesting former Nonconformist chapel (1741) has been converted into a house.

Hardingham [10] St George's Church is a fine 13th/14th-century building with south tower and a notable piscina; it stands midway between Low Street and High Common, which are more than a mile apart. The Old Hall, with two-storeyed porch, stands south of the church. The present Hall is of the early 18th century with additions of c. 1830.

Hardley [18] Hardley Staithe consists of a small landing stage and boathouse amongst the willows, reeds and burdocks of the River Chet which winds through marshes, past the relics of windmills, to join the Yare at Reedham. St Margaret's Church has wall paintings, remains of screen and fine piscina, all 15th century, and the mediaeval bench ends have been encased in 18th-century panelled pews of a lovely faded colour, on some of which are graffiti of sailing ships. The 16th-century Hall, nearly a mile south of the church, is a longish house with two-storey porch and the initials W and M joined in a knot for William Drake and his wife.

Hardwick [17] St Margaret's Church has a 12th-century door and a wall painting of St Chris-

Happisburgh font

topher. The rood screen is badly mutilated and rather clumsily restored by John Ebbs and Joseph Cock, church wardens in 1661. A large box pew, with tester, now serves the purpose of a vestry.

Hargham [16] The tower and most of the nave of All Saints' Church are ruinous, but the remainder and the chancel have been repaired by local enthusiasts pending leasing to the Norfolk Churches Trust.

Harleston [17] A very pretty place with Georgian houses (note particularly 'Candlers') and elaborate

wrought-iron inn signs in its long straight street. The church is at Redenhall but there is a daughter church dedicated to St John the Baptist designed 1872 by R. M. Phipson, F.S.A., of Norwich, in the Decorated style, with an apse of much stained glass. The Corn Exchange (1849) has an immensely heavy Doric façade.

Harling, East [15] This little town has the most splendid church in the district, dedicated to St Peter and St Paul. The 14th-century tower is surmounted by a lead-covered flèche which was copied at St Peter

Mancroft, Norwich. The 15th-century nave has an unusually high-pitched hammerbeam roof, with a beam extending across the nave from the penultimate hammerbeams at the eastern end. This carries a pulley and was probably intended for raising and lowering the lamp in front of the rood. The screen base (c. 1510), now at the west end of the nave, has a series of carved panels; note especially the one representing the Cross as the Tree of Life. In the south aisle, where there is a fine tomb to Sir Robert and Lady Harding (1435), is a splendid screen with vaulted loft, one of the most magnificent in Norfolk. In the chancel is the canopied tomb of Sir William Chamberlain (1462) and the tomb of Sir Richard Lovell (1524). In the east window is some magnificent 15th-century Norwich-School glass. The various panels represent scenes from the Life of Our Lord, the most interesting being that of the Ascension showing Christ's feet disappearing into the clouds, with His footprints on the rock beneath. Below are the kneeling figures of the donors, Sir William Chamberlain and Sir Robert Wingfield.

Harling, West [15] All Saints' Church stands closed and isolated in what was the park of the Hall, demolished in 1931, a familiar story of the death of a community. It is now vested in the Redundant Churches Fund. It has some good carvings and monuments, including several brasses, one to Ralph Fuloflove, a rector (1479).

Harpley [2] St Lawrence's is a spacious 14th/15th-century church with a tower at the south-west corner, which permits a large west window. The chancel was built early in the 14th century by the rector, John de Gurney, and has a fine priest's door; much of the rest of the church was built by the Knowles, or Knollys, family. The south aisle has a fine parapet outside and sedilia inside, and there

are many mediaeval benches; the original south door is a lovely piece of carpentry.

Hassingham [11] St Mary's Church has an early round tower with 15th-century octagonal top; it was thatched until gutted by fire in 1970. It has since been imaginatively restored, and a crucifix made of two of the old thatch pegs now hangs in the nave. There is some mediaeval glass.

Hautbois [11] There is said to be golden treasure in the pond by the track leading to the old church at *Great Hautbois*, which has a round tower but is in ruins except for the chancel. The old churchyard contains some very interesting stones and some wooden crosses and is exquisitely pretty in the spring with snowdrops followed by daffodils. The new church, Holy Trinity, was built in 1864 in a rather feeble 13th-century style by Thomas Jekyll. At *Little Hautbois* the church stands in ruins in a picturesque place near the very fine Old Hall, a splendid example of the 16th- or 17th-century East Anglian type of house, probably built by the Baspole family.

Haveringland [10] Was ruined by the aerodrome which is now itself in ruins. St Peter's Church, with its Norman round tower (the rest was rebuilt in 1845), stands close to one of the runways and to what was once the park of the demolished Haveringland Hall, built by Blore for the Fellowes family, whose monuments, with those of the Hernes, previous owners of the estate, are in the church.

Heacham [2] Is a large and growing seaside village. A few pretty cottages, and St Mary's Church with solid square tower. Many interesting monuments, including a modern one to Princess Pocahontas, daughter of a Red Indian chief who in 1614 married John Rolfe (a member of the ancient family to whom this village belonged), but

who died sadly three years later in a ship off Greenwich on the way back to America with Sir Walter Raleigh's last expedition. Just outside the village is a romantic carrstone water-mill in the Tudor style. A mill on this site is mentioned in Domesday Book; the present one is used for making Norfolk lavender water.

Heckingham [18] A large House of Industry built in the shape of an H in 1764. The church, St Gregory, of this scattered village overlooks the Chet; the round tower has an octagonal top, the nave and chancel are thatched and there is an apse at the east end. There is a square Norman font and a magnificent Norman south door. Simple 18th-century urn in the churchyard.

Hedenham [17] Opposite the Mermaid Inn is a Tudor house with stepped gables and later additions, now a school run by the Community of All Hallows, Ditchingham. The 14th-century church of St Peter had a thorough restoration in the 19th century; note monuments, particularly that to Philip Bedingfield (1621), and altar rails. Stained glass in nave shows the arms of the Garneys; the mermaid on the arms explains the name of the inn. The Hall was remodelled about 1730.

Heigham [11] A suburb of Norwich, the old village is round the Gibraltar Inn, with gardens going down to the River Wensum, and at the Dolphin, a late 16th-century house, lived Bishop Hall when driven from his palace during the Civil War. He was buried in the old church, which in 1942 was destroyed by bombs (apart from the square, possibly Saxon, tower). Thus a calm and dignified old scholar and divine, the friend of Sir Thomas Browne, was driven from his home by one dictator, and blown out of his grave by another. The rest of Heigham is a suburb of

East coast at **Happisburgh**

Norwich, with two Victorian churches, St Barnabas (east-window glass) and St Thomas; at present much of the area between Dereham Road and the river is being rebuilt and redeveloped. A third Victorian church, St Philip's, by Edward Power, 1871, was demolished in 1978, in spite of local efforts to save it.

Helhoughton [3] The much reduced and rebuilt All Saints' Church in the centre of this small village is mainly 14th-century and has a curious font of the period. The organ, once a barrel organ, came

from East Raynham; there is a 15th-century heart brass at the east end of the nave.

Hellesdon [11] A suburb of Norwich. St Mary's Church has a lead-covered bell-turret and spire, and an attractive two-storey porch with vault. It has some good figure brasses. In Upper Hellesdon is the well-planned Mile Cross estate where the roads and avenues are designed in the form of a bishop's mitre. St Catherine's, Mile Cross, is an imposing brick church on the Aylsham Road by A. D. R. Caroe & A. P. Robinson (1935).

Hellington [11] From St John the Baptist's churchyard are lovely views of old farms and woods. The church porch is interesting, with three canopied niches; inscription to Sir Anthony Gawdy (1642): 'he is gon to Christ his Rocke To sing HAILVIAHS with his celestial flocke.'

Hemblington [11] Round-towered church of All Saints with a beautifully re-coloured font with the Trinity and saints on the bowl and stem. There is a most exceptional wall painting showing not only the usual figure of St

Christopher, but also the story of his martyrdom. Across the fields, Hemblington Hall, c. 1700.

Hempnall [17] A compact village with a much-restored St Margaret's Church, having Saxon fragments. On the tower is an elaborate wrought-iron weathervane dated 1727. The Royalist vicar, William Barwick, who was ejected from the living in 1644, was an uncompromising character who kept a gun at the vicarage and called Parliament 'a company of factious fellows'.

Hempstead [6] (near Happisburgh) In this coastal village is St Andrew's Church, whose nave has absorbed former aisles. It has a nice 15th-century porch and font, an attractive 17th-century pulpit, and a screen with some unusual saints including Saints Erasmus, Blaise, Leonard and Eligius.

Hempstead [4] (near Holt) A pretty village. All Saints' Church has a red-brick west tower dated 1744 and an apsidal east end (with thatched roof added in 1926 through the generosity of Sir Alfred Jodrell). There is a Norman door, one old bench end, and an unusual lectern (1886) with an angel standing on a globe.

Hempton [3] A wide expanse of common from which there is a fine prospect of the town of Fakenham with the church tower rising over the red roofs. Holy Trinity Church consists of a 19th-century chancel to which a nave was added in the 1950s. Parts of the nave are made of material from the bombed church of St Michael-at-Thorn, Norwich, and the ruined churches of Pudding Norton and Hempton. An interesting modern painted reredos in the nave.

Hemsby [12] A compact Broadland village with a good deal of modern holiday development. St Mary's Church has a tower and porch, both of the 15th century; the latter has a vaulted roof with the bosses representing the Nativity, Resurrection, Ascension, Annunciation, and Assumption of Our Lady.

Hethel [10] The church stands apart down the end of a lane and near the gnarled remains of a thorn tree said to be nearly 1,000 years old. In the church are many memorials to the Micklethwait, Branthwaite and Beevor families, and the altar with its marble mensa and reredos is a good example of late Tractarian restoration. In this parish is Potash Farm, famous as the residence of James Bloomfield Rush, who was publicly executed at Norwich Castle for the double murder of Squire Jermy and his son at Stanfield Hall in 1848. To commemorate this, one of the most famous murder trials of the 19th century, Staffordshire pottery models of Potash Farm were made.

Hethersett [10] A large village, now a residential suburb of Norwich. Along the main road towards Cringleford are large iron pumps for the purpose of watering the flocks that were driven to Norwich market. The church of St Remigius is a fine 14th/15th-century building, but poorly restored. In the south aisle is a good monument to Isaac Motham, 1703–4, by Stanton of London.

Hevingham [11] St Botolph's Church was originally cruciform, but the north transept has disappeared. It has a very wide nave and a simple modern hammerbeam roof. There is 16th-century German glass from Steinfeld, and a fine candelabra (1741) originally in St George's, Yarmouth. The chamber over the porch was used by local Parliamentarians as a store for gunpowder, bullets and guns during the early months of the Civil War; the feelings of the Royalist rector, Edmund Porter, can be imagined. The village is quite half a mile away to the south of the church; opposite the Fox Inn are the remains of a 17th-century house with gables.

Heydon [4] One of the most attractive villages in Norfolk. The houses and cottages surround a village green with a pleasant Gothic-revival brick pump-house in the centre. The church of St Peter and St Paul is 14th/15th-century with a west tower, a most unusual tub-shaped font, 15th-century pulpit with Jacobean tester and many memorials to the Earle and Bulwer families. The Bulwers have a mortuary chapel on the north side of the chancel, where there are many memorials and hatchments; and there is a good modern monument to General Earle Gascoigne Lytton Bulwer above the wainscotted family pew erected against the rood screen. Very interesting wall paintings have recently been uncovered. Heydon Hall is an Elizabethan house built in 1581–4 by Henry Dynne, and it belonged to the Colfer and Kemp families before being acquired by the Parliamentary lawyer, Erasmus Earle, about 1640. In 1762 it passed by marriage from the Earles to the Bulwers; the writer Bulwer Lytton was of this family.

Hickling [12] A typical Broadland village where the red tiles of the cottages are interspersed with thatch. There is a very attractive group of buildings round the Pleasure Boat Inn on the edge of the Broad at Hickling Staithe. St Mary's Church has an imposing, lofty west tower with a beautiful west door; the interior is restored. Opposite is Hickling Hall, early 18th century, once the possession of the Calthorpe family, which gave their name to the small Broad hidden in a wood about a mile to the north. On the road to Sea Palling is Priory Farm, where the remains of the cloister to the Augustinian house can be seen among the farm buildings.

Hilborough [8, 9] Was the home of Nelson's ancestors throughout the 18th century and his grandfather, father and brother were rectors here. All Saints' Church stands some way from the village, on the edge of the park of the fine Georgian Hall, built in 1779 by Ralph Caldwell. The west tower of the church has beautiful niches and a pierced parapet. Inside there are very large royal arms for James I, stone heads on the sedilia and a 17th-century brazier.

Hilgay [7] A narrow street of yellow brick houses opening into a little square at the southern end of the village. The somewhat over-restored All Saints' Church is approached through a thick avenue of limes and a holly hedge, and there is an old bridge over the Wissey. The brick church tower is dated 1794, and in the churchyard is a tombstone to the memory of Captain Manby, the inventor of the rocket life-saving apparatus, who was church warden when the tower was rebuilt. The old wooden eagle-lectern was originally in St Peter's, Manchester, and the board under the tower listing fees for installing monuments and the like (1819) repays attention. Wood Hall is an Elizabethan brick house built by Henry Hawe in 1579. Phineas Fletcher, the 17th-century poet and writer of hymns (including 'Drop, drop Slow Tears') was rector here.

Hillington [2] Is a carrstone village with cottages set back and raised above the road with extremely good gardens. Beyond the high wall and Gothick lodges is the park of Hillington Hall, through which an arm of the Babingley River winds past large beeches and oaks. The house was originally Elizabethan, then Gothicked in the 1820s by Donthorne and now largely rebuilt, but still keeping one gable, the old stables and various summerhouses

◁   Memorial and Easter Sepulcre
Hingham

Heydon Hall

and follies of great Gothick charm. St Mary's Church has several good monuments, one of 1611 to Richard Hovell and his wife, an early 19th-century one to Lady West and her husband and child, and two large 18th-century tablets, one of which describes Lady Browne who died in 1763 as pleasing, placid, personable, prudent, pious, and adds: 'She hath left a dear and onely daughter Mary/Married to William Folkes Esquire/And a dear and onely grandson Martin, a youth of fairest expectation/An Eton Scholar, now in the Third Form.' The memorial is signed Sir W. B., Archit., who was the boy's doting grandfather—which explains the proud reference to Eton's lowest division. There is a Snetzler organ (1763) in a good case.

Hindolveston [4] Just south of Melton Constable and consisting of one long village street. The old church is in ruins, but parts of it have been incorporated in the new

building, St George's, by H. J. Green (1935), nearer the centre of the village. Inside there is a quadrangular brass with figures of Edmund Hunt (1558) and his wife Margaret and family of fourteen, with rhyming inscription. Sir Jacob Astley, the Royalist, retired here, close to his Parliamentarian nephew and son-in-law, Sir Edward. Hope House is an attractive early Georgian house of seven bays.

Hindringham [3] Around the 14th-century St Martin's Church, with its graceful west tower, is an attractive group of cottages. The church contains a very early chest. The 16th-century Hall at the west end of the village is moated. West of the village is the site of the 16th-century manor house of the Godfrey family, and nearby is the present Godfreys Hall, a rather severe Regency house of three bays and two storeys, with a good porch on two pairs of Ionic columns.

Hingham [10] A most beautiful 18th-century town, with many stately Georgian houses. A perfect example of the winter assembly town for the surrounding gentry, who built houses there for times when the country roads would be impassable. St Andrew's Church is an example of the 14th-century style in all its splendour, built by Remigius of Hethersett, rector 1316–59, with a particularly fine tower; it received a rather too thorough 19th-century restoration. The east window is filled with splendid early 16th-century German glass and there is a fine 15th-century memorial in the chancel to Lord Morley, which also served as an Easter Sepulchre. A bronze bust of Abraham Lincoln in the north aisle bears witness to the fact that the Lincoln family came from here.

Hockering [10] Has a wide village street with some pleasant houses, especially the early 18th-century

Cock Inn. St Michael's Church has a well-proportioned 15th-century west tower. Hockering House is a nine-bay neo-Georgian house with three-bay pediment built in 1969 by Cecil Beadsmore Smith.

Hockham [15] The 'Heathly' of Mr Michael Home's Breckland novels, which describes so vividly what this district was like not so very long ago, when these light lands were farmed and not given over to advancing ranks of fir trees. The village gathers about the green. The church, a 13th/14th-century building, with 16th-century benches is in the park of the early Georgian Hall.

◁   **Holkham** (*left and above*)

Hockwold-cum-Wilton [14] Is a pretty village with some development, an old stone cross, taller than most, and two churches. St James' Church, Wilton, has a stone spire, one of the very few in Norfolk, a 15th-century chest, a splendid set of mediaeval benches, and a good 1683 monument. St Peter's Church, Hockwold, now vested in the Redundant Churches Fund, has a fine roof with alternate tie-beams and hammerbeams, and a splendid monument by John Ivory of Norwich and J. de Carle to Cyril Wyche (1780). Hockwold Hall, a gabled red-brick house, is on an E-plan, and was built by the Heveninghams who inherited it from the Pastons. William Heveningham, the regicide, lost his property at the Restoration.

Hoe [9, 10] St Andrew's is a mediaeval church much rebuilt in 1735; Gorgate Hall, centre of a large farm, is in part 18th century, whilst the grey Hoe Hall is a century later.

Holkham [3] Where once two rabbits fought for one blade of grass, is the most successful piece of landscaping combined with farming in Norfolk. In the early 18th century on the bleakest bit of the coast, amongst flat, windy marshes and grey sea, Thomas Coke (a descendant of the Lord Chief Justice) planted a noble park with great avenues of oak, ilex and beech, and built his beautiful Palladian house on the edge of an artificial lake. (Perhaps because the house was built of locally made yellow brick, perhaps because of something heavy in its classicism, the outside of Holkham has never been much admired by the neighbours.) Later in the 19th century terraces and fountains were added. William Kent was the architect of the house and much of the park, and Matthew Brettingham was also involved. Lords Burlington and Coke together planned the Hall with its pink marble pillars. In the chain of State rooms is much original furniture by Kent, and on the velvet and damask-hung walls are pictures by Van Dyck and Gainsborough, amongst others. There is a gold and white library full of beautifully bound books, and a famous collection of illuminated manuscripts, folios, psalters, as well as records of all kinds, and a long sculpture gallery with antique statues brought from Italy by Thomas Coke; these are supposed to have been packed in ilex seeds, accounting for the unexpected number of these dark evergreen trees which are such a characteristic and beautiful feature of the estate, both along the roads and grouped in the park. Next to Thomas Coke who conceived and built it, Holkham owes much to his great-nephew and heir, Thomas William Coke M.P. (Coke of Norfolk, created Earl of Leicester 1837), a most admirable and independent character and the greatest innovator in Norfolk farming. The Coke family still owns Holkham and lives there. The village was rebuilt outside the park during the construction of the house (1730–44) but St Withburga's Church is within the park walls. It was almost completely rebuilt in 1870 by James K. Colling and contains some interesting monuments from the earlier church, and a fine monument by Boehm of Juliana, Lady Leicester, who was responsible for the restoration.

Holme Hale [9] Has council houses pink-washed in the local tradition, and chestnut trees and old cottages. The beautiful church has a 14th-century screen, and bench ends with an elephant, a pelican and the devil; a roof with angels, window over chancel arch and lots of light from large 15th-century windows in south aisle. The Georgian Hall is of medium size, with a five-bay central section and wings added in 1820 and subsequently.

Holme-next-the-Sea [2] Has chalk cottages with gay gardens and old apple trees, and one or two very rich-looking stockbroker-converted houses with patios and *stoeps* occasioned by the nearness to Hunstanton Golf Links. There is also a very large caravan camp on the edge of the links. The church is well placed between village and marsh, with a good tower; it was partly rebuilt in 1771 and then restored again in 1887. The Peddars Way, a Roman or prehistoric road from near Ixworth in Suffolk, reaches the shores of the Wash between Holme and Hunstanton, and can be traced for most of its way, a lot of it being a very attractive green lane.

Holt [4] Is an attractive market town with fine Georgian houses dating from the time Holt was rebuilt after a fire in 1708; its new developments are tactfully sited, and it is a Conservation Area. At the top of Letheringsett Hill stands an unusual milestone, topped by a pineapple. From the Methodist church (Thomas Jekyll 1862), the pretty main street runs towards the parish church, St Andrew's, which was gutted by the fire of 1708 (traces of which can be seen in the discolouring of many pillars) and then further restored by William Butterfield in 1863. Among its interesting features are a consecration cross in the south aisle and very good glass by Kempe in the aisle windows and by Heasman in the east window. During the Civil War there was a small Royalist revolt in Holt, and William Hobart and the Revd Thomas Cooper (usher of Gresham's School) were executed in Norwich on Christmas Day 1650. Sir John Gresham founded the grammar school here in 1555. The Old School House in the market place was rebuilt in 1858. From its foundation, the school has been administered by the Fishmongers' Company and was enlarged in 1900 into a new and up-to-date public school with new buildings and spacious playing fields surrounded by woods along the Cromer Road. Most interesting of the new school buildings are the Memorial Library erected in 1931 (by A. E. Munby) and the chapel (1912–16) by Maxwell Ayrton. Holt Hall, to the north of the town stands on the site of an earlier house. Home Place, towards Cromer, is an amazing house built by E. S. Prior in the Arts and Crafts style (the work was superintended by Randall Wells) in 1903–5; it is now a convalescent home.

Honing [5] The Hall, built in 1748, was reconstructed in 1792 by Humphry Repton, who also landscaped the park and woods. The North Walsham & Dilham Canal runs through the village parallel to the railway, and there are the crumbling remains of locks on the edge of Honing Common. St Peter and St Paul's Church has a fine 15th-century tower; the rest was rebuilt in 1795.

Honingham [10] Is on the Tud, tributary of the Yare. St Andrew's Church has a well-proportioned 15th-century west tower. Honingham Hall was a Jacobean E-plan house. William Kent prepared plans for its Gothicization but this was not carried out. In fact, this interesting house, well known to Parson Woodforde, was demolished in 1966.

Horning [11] A popular Broadland yachting resort with boat-houses, trim lawns and a regatta; the street has reed-thatched cottages. The

14th-century tower of St Benedict's has the Four Evangelists on its pinnacles; the church has some consecration crosses and good mediaeval bench ends. About two miles away are the picturesque and much-painted remains of St Benet's Abbey and the windmill beside it, described more fully under Ludham (q.v.). The barn of Horning Hall, on the way to the abbey, was the chapel of St James's Hospital.

Horningtoft [9] A small, somewhat scattered village; the 13th-century St Edmund's Church has a very good 14th-century font with coats of arms (Castell) on the bowl. The screen is 15th-century and the pulpit 1620; more Jacobean woodwork is used in a prie-dieu. There was a tower which fell in 1796, and a high south porch which probably went in the 1871 restoration. Four pedestals around the altar came from the derelict church at Oxwick.

Horsey [12] The village beside the mere consists of a few houses near the church and the small hamlet of Horsey Corner, whence a lane runs down to the sand dunes at Horsey Gap—always a danger spot when the sea 'blows a rage'. Dead trees standing gaunt against the skyline show how very recently the sea has broken in and ruined the land for miles around. All Saints' Church itself is simple, but in the chancel is a 19th-century stained glass window showing a lady in the costume of the '80s and looking for all the world like Mrs Caroline Pooter. The Hall belonged to the Risings throughout the century and now is the home of Mr John Buxton, the naturalist. The windmill and the surrounding nature reserve belong to the National Trust.

Horsford [11] Now a Norwich suburb with a pleasant group of buildings round the Dog Inn with its stepped gables. All Saints' Church has a graceful 15th-century tower but has been much restored

within. At the northern end of the village is a row of cottages with the dates 1839 and 1845 boldly inscribed by means of bottles projecting from the pebbled walls. The site of the motte-and-bailey castle of the Cheyneys lies north-east of the village.

Horsham St Faith [11] Here was the Priory of St Faith, which was a Benedictine house founded about 1105. At Abbey Farm can be seen the remains of the cloister and chapter house, and the Norman door to the refectory. Recent restoration work in the refectory (now part of a private house) has revealed some remarkable late 13th-century wall paintings, including a series of scenes showing the legend of how Robert Fitzwalter and his wife, returning from a pilgrimage to Rome, were released from prison through the intercession of St Faith, and set up the monastery on their return. There are some pretty 17th-century and 18th-century houses near the spacious 15th-century church of St Mary and St Andrew, which has a rood screen of the lofty East Anglian type, figure paintings dated 1528 and a pulpit (1480), also with painted panels. There is a nice 17th-century font cover and a groined porch with a boss showing the martyrdom of St Andrew. A brass to Geoffrey Langley, prior of Horsham (1437) has recently been returned from St Lawrence's, Norwich. Housing development extends into the neighbouring village of Newton St Faith; part of the old military aerodrome is now used as residences by the University of East Anglia; the rest is Norwich Airport. St Robert Southwell, the Elizabethan martyr, was born at Horsham. The tall brick tower is part of the 1936 crematorium designed by J. P. Chaplin.

Horstead [11] Has a street with solid 19th-century villas and pleasant gardens. The Volunteer is an 18th-century house. All Saints'

Church has been extensively restored. Heggatt Hall, south of the village, in an attractive small park, was probably built about 1590, though now much altered.

Houghton [2] The village was rebuilt in the 18th century, and now a straight avenue of limes and discreet whitewashed cottages in pairs lead the eye to the white-painted wrought-iron gates in the long park fence. Inside the beautifully landscaped park is the great house built in the 1730s by the first Prime Minister of England, Sir Robert Walpole. His architects were Colen Campbell and Thomas Ripley, but Sir Robert himself left his own mark on the outside with its four little turrets, and still more inside where he gave William Kent his first big architectural job. The ceilings, mouldings, doors, state beds, tables and chairs are almost all by Kent himself. It is one of the first houses where mahogany was much used. The house has never been sold, though it was offered to King Edward VII who chose Sandringham instead—and the present owners are directly descended from Sir Robert through his daughter, Mary. The original collection of pictures was sold to Catherine of Russia to pay debts of Sir Robert's grandson, the eccentric Earl of Orford, which deeply upset his famous Uncle Horace, but since this time other pictures have found their way to Houghton, and there is a good collection again. There are rare Mortlake tapestries by Francis Poyntz, fine 18th-century book bindings and many other treasures. The carrstone stables, with a courtyard and fountain, are extremely attractive. St Martin's Church in the park was partly rebuilt by Sir Robert Walpole in 1729 but has no monument to the Prime Minister nor to Horace who, however, was buried there. It contains a coffin lid with a carved effigy of a prior of Coxford (1307), box pews in the aisles and a west gallery. There are hatch-

Houghton Hall

ments, and in the chancel some Jacobean woodwork. The house is open to the public in the summer.

Houghton-on-the-Hill [9]
(between Swaffham and Watton) The isolated and ruined St Mary's Church on high ground overlooking the Wissey and Peddars Way has a Saxon nave.

Houghton St Giles [3] Adjoining
Walsingham, this village is remarkable for the 'Slipper Chapel', so called as it was the place where the pilgrims left their shoes behind on the last stage of the Walsingham pilgrimage. It is a most attractive little 14th-century building with modern extensions and a very fine east window by Geoffrey Webb. It is now a Roman Catholic shrine with priest's house adjoining; the most recent development includes an outdoor altar and does not blend very well. The parish church of St Giles has a 15th-century rood screen with figure paintings, beautifully exe-

cuted on a gesso background, of apostles, doctors, and a Virgin and Child. It was almost completely rebuilt by W. Eden Nesfield in 1879.

Hoveton [11] A yachting centre
with shops and boat-houses, effectively part of Wroxham. Hoveton St John's Church has a nice brick tower of 1765. Hoveton House, about a mile east, is a very attractive 17th-century house with Dutch gables. Hoveton St Peter's Church dates from 1625. Hoveton Hall is perhaps by Soane, in a park with a lake to the north.

Howe [17] Is a handful of cottages
and old houses round a wide green with trees and ponds. The church has a Saxon round tower and in the chancel a brass plaque on which the Lady Elizabeth Hastings, patroness of the living in the 1730s, sets out some strict rules for the conduct of the incumbent and his successor. It is very long, but worth reading.

Hunstanton, Old [2] Has chalk

cottages, a sandy beach, and a golf course. The late 15th-century Hall, the mansion of the le Strange family, has one wing still intact, is moated, and has a Renaissance garden with high yew hedges. The head of the family is Hereditary Lord High Admiral of the Wash and can claim possession of anything on the beach or in the sea as far as a man can ride a horse and throw a spear. The estate was inherited by the le Stranges from the Domesday owners in the 12th century. On the extinction of the Norfolk line in the 18th century, it was inherited by the Styleman who subsequently took the name of le Strange and still continue in possession. The le Strange monuments in St Mary's Church include a magnificent portrait brass of Sir Roger le Strange (1506) and a tomb chest to Henry le Strange (1485). Another Henry le Strange (1862) is commemorated in the east window; he designed the glass in the east window of the south aisles here and painted part of the nave roof of El

Cathedral. There is also a painted Perpendicular rood screen and a Norman font.

Hunstanton St Edmund [2] Has a notable church, St Edmund, built by F. Preedy in 1865 and containing some stained glass by Comper, William and John Lawson, and Vera Flint. It is a most delightful seaside resort, partly designed by Butterfield for the le Strange family. Round the large green are carrstone hotels and shops. The old town has large Victorian houses in the French château style with turrets; the beach is the nicest in Norfolk, as the tide goes out for miles, leaving firm sand. To the north the cliffs are striped, red and white chalk and brown carrstone, and all along the beach there are little pools and low brown rocks. Years ago, children used to jump, with long poles, from rock to rock—quite a skilled game, which might return. L. P. Hartley in *The Shrimp and the Anemone* has written a sensitive description of the place. On the chalk cliffs to the north are the remains of a lighthouse and a few bits of St Edmund's Chapel, whilst to the south the place takes on the character of a modern seaside resort. The old G.E.R. station and the Sandringham Hotel beside it have gone, and so has the pier, but the place still has character.

Hunworth [4] A beautiful village in the Glaven valley (two fords cross the river). Some delightful houses surround the green, overlooked by Castle Hill (though the date of the earthworks on this hill is unknown). Up the road to Stody is the old (1699) Hall, now a farmhouse, with contemporary barn. A pretty water-mill stands in trees opposite the late 17th-century Hall, and there is a splendid barn here too, dated 1700. St Lawrence's Church has a Saxon window in the nave and a chancel built in 1850. The 15th-century south porch has a grid-iron in flushwork symbolizing St Lawrence, the patron saint.

Ickburgh [14] Is on the edge of the Stanford Battle Area. By the bridge over the river was once a leper hospital maintained by a community who raised the necessary funds by working a ferry over the Wissey. The foundations of their chapel are still to be seen by the river. The present church of St Peter, all except its 15th-century tower with nice flintwork in its top, was rebuilt by Lord Ashburton in 1865. On the eastern gable end of the church, just under the cross, is a 'signature'—the bottom of a beer bottle and a pint mug. There is an earlier 'signature' in the village, a large red brick heart in a flint wall just by the letterbox.

Illington [15] A small village very much off the beaten track. St Andrew's Church dates mainly from the 12th and 14th centuries and has a very nice carved Jacobean drop-handled bier.

Ingham [6] The chancel of Holy Trinity Church here, at the northern extremity of Broadland, was the conventual church of the Trinitarian Canons. There were only four houses of this order in England (Thelesford in Warwicks, Mottinden in Kent, Knaresborough in Yorks, and Ingham) which was almost indistinguishable from the Augustinian Canons Regular. The house at Ingham was founded in 1197 and made a collegiate church by Sir Miles Stapleton (one of the first Knights of the Garter) in 1360, at which time rebuilding of the church began, giving it the present magnificent nave and chancel; the nave is divided from the chancel by a stone pulpitum, of which there are considerable remains. The tower, over 100 feet high, was not built until a century later (bequests for its building are dated 1456–92). There is an unusual three-storeyed south porch and on the north side remains of the conventual buildings, including the cloister. There are a number of most interesting memorials. At the

Home Place, **Holt**

east end of the nave is the table tomb with effigies of Sir Roger de Bois and his wife Margaret (1300), and on the north side of the sanctuary is the effigy of Sir Oliver de Ingham (1343) lying on a bed of pebbles like Sir Roger de Kerdiston at Reepham. Sir Oliver's daughter, Joan, married Sir Miles Stapleton; they were buried in the centre of the chancel together with other members of the Stapleton family, but their magnificent military brasses, which were in existence in Cotman's time, have since disappeared. The church was restored in 1873 by Ewan Christian to the designs of J. P. Seddon, but plans to replace the pulpitum (for which Seddon prepared designs) never materialized. The Old Hall is mostly of 1904 but incorporates part of an earlier structure.

Ingoldisthorpe [2] Beyond the main road on the edge of the marsh is a small romantic Tudor farmhouse with an enclosed garden. St Michael's Church is up the hill in

Islington

the main part of the village. The chancel is mainly a Victorian rebuild (1857) with most interesting domestic scenes in the stained glass by O'Connor (1860). The Norman font has interlacing on its bowl, and there is an old screen. The Hall, built in 1745, has a small park and looks over sloping gardens to marsh and sea. In the 1770s the house was called Mount Amelia and was inhabited by a scurrilous, bad-tempered pamphleteer called Richard Gardiner or 'Dick Merry-fellow' who is, however, commemorated by a very affectionate inscription in the church. At the manor, now a hotel, Mrs Tylden lived to be nearly 105. 'Only at home to Royalty,' she said to the parlour-maid on her 100th birthday, when Queen Alexandra, Queen Mary and Queen Maud of Norway went to visit her.

Ingworth [5] St Laurence's Church has lost its tower (1822) but the rest of the thatched building has been well restored, and contains exceptionally fine carved royal arms of William III, box pews, and an hourglass for timing sermons. Brother Richard of

Ingworth was one of the first small group of Franciscan missionaries to arrive in England, in 1224.

Intwood [11] Although on the outskirts of Norwich, still an unspoilt little village, for the present at least. The round tower of All Saints' Church may be Saxon; there is certainly Norman work in the nave. The Hall was built in 1807 in the Tudor style by Arthur Browne.

Irmingland [4] The Hall was built in 1609 by Sir Nathaniel Bacon but only the much-altered east wing remains. Sir Nathaniel settled it on his stepson, Roberds Smith, and the heiress of this family married the Parliamentary General Charles Fleetwood (who secondly married Ireton's widow, Cromwell's daughter). There is no church in the parish.

Irstead [11] The thatched church attractively placed by the Ant serves a small village and is very little restored; it has an unusually-shaped screen base with figure paintings of the apostles, a 14th-century font with one panel showing the vernicle of St Veronica,

15th-century bench ends, and a Elizabethan pulpit with a hand-ra made out of a mediaeval mis ericorde. There is fine mediaeva ironwork on the south door. delightful atmosphere. The Ol Hall, of four bays and two-and-a half storeys, is originally of c. 160 but has Victorian fenestration.

Islington or **Tilney cum Islingto** [7] Here, in a wood where heron nested, was the 13th-centur church, the Hall (an old hous altered in the 19th century), an some cottages. Now the trees a cut down, the church is partly roo less but vested in the Redundan Churches Fund, the cottagers hav moved to new houses nearer Ti ney, and the park and woods hav become a muddy expanse of pota fields. The herons, unperturbe have moved to a wood a little wa to the south and continue to ne there. The bailiff's daughter cam from here and not from Nor London.

Itteringham [4] A pretty village o the Bure. The church has an ear. square unbuttressed tower an north of the bridge is a 17t

The Royal Arms, **Kenninghall**

century farmhouse with an elegant portico, now the property of the National Trust.

elling [4] An extensive parish with several hospitals set amid pine woods. There is a 15th-century Easter Sepulchre in the pretty church. The Hall is owned by the Peterding family, who built it, having bought the estate about 910. There are several pretty 8th-century houses in the street running down to the coast road, and a very charming Old Rectory. In the 18th century the owner of the estate was called Zurishaddai Girdlestone.

empstone [9] (near Great Dunham) In the ruinous church of St Paul is a good 15th-century chancel arch. The lodge is an attractive late-Georgian farmhouse built by the Holkham estate.

Kenninghall [16] A pleasant little town of two streets which join in a little square. The street leading up by the church, with many timber and plasterwork houses, gives the impression that it has been the principal thoroughfare, as no doubt it was in the days when Mary Tudor stayed at Kenninghall Place as the guest of the Duke of Norfolk at the time of her brother's death (1553) when she rode post-haste to Framlingham Castle to be proclaimed Queen. But what starts as a street by the church in Kenninghall soon changes into a country lane passing near Kenninghall Place, one of the last of the Norfolk

properties still owned by the Duke. The farmhouse is one wing of the old palace. But, for all its connections with Mary Tudor, Kenninghall was left in no manner of doubt who was the rightful queen a few years later, for in St Mary's Church there is a most splendid and exceptional royal arms board for Elizabeth I. The fine tower (bequests 1485–93) has a parapet dated 1637; there is a Norman door with lively carvings of animals on the jambs, also a 14th-century font with 15th-century telescopic cover, and a Suffolk-type cambered tie-beam roof.

Keswick [11] The Old Hall is a very attractive building of many dates but with 16th- and 17th-century gables. Keswick Hall

95

started as a Regency house part of which was designed by Wilkins, but was enlarged in 1951 by Seely & Paget and had many subsequent additions to transform it into a unit of the University of East Anglia. The round-towered All Saints' Church was partly ruinated by Sir Henry Hobart about 1600; the nave was restored in 1898 and a small apsidal chancel added in 1965; it has a lovely situation on a hill which was probably the site of pre-Christian worship.

Ketteringham [10] St Peter's Church stands near some pretty cottages almost in the Hall gardens. The tower was rebuilt in 1609 but the church has Norman and Early English work. There are box pews, a three-decker pulpit, and a west gallery, erected by Sir John Boileau in 1841. The main interest of the church is the large number of monuments; there are Victorian ones to the Boileaus themselves and to the family of Mr Andrew, the rector, whose quarrels with Sir John are recorded in Owen Chadwick's book, *Victorian Miniature*. The Atkins family is commemorated by a handsome monument by Sir Richard Westmacott, R.A., in the chancel, where there is also an attractive memorial by Flaxman to Harriot Peach (1825). In the sanctuary are monuments to the Heveningham family, a good heraldic brass (1490) above a table tomb on the south side; and on the north a monument to Sir William Heveningham. There is also an interesting brass to a child, John, son of Richard Colvyle, c. 1530, in swaddling clothes, and the remains of the brass to Sir Henry Grey (1470), 'Son of Sir Thomas Grey of Heton by Joan sister to the Duke of Norfolk that dyed at Venys'. Ketteringham Hall is a fine house rich in the same Gothick ornament as in the church; the house was designed c. 1840–52, first by Thomas Alla-son, then by Thomas Jekyll, for th Boileau family. It now belongs t Colin Chapman, owner of Lotu cars.

Kettlestone [3] All Saints' Churc has an octagonal 14th-centur tower and a 15th-century octagona font, and monuments to the Schulc ham family, formerly of Shoulc ham. There are very fine wooc lands round here; to the north of th A147 road, in a property of th Norfolk Naturalists' Trust, are th graves of the former owners wh planted many interesting trees.

Kilverstone [15] The villag stands among the Breckland wooc near the River Thet. The Norma church of St Andrew was muc restored in 1906. The Hall wa

King's Lynn: the Great Ouse, grair silo and the Customs House

originally built about 1620 but was very largely rebuilt in 1913. There is now a very interesting wildlife park there.

Kimberley [10] Round a green with huge oaks, limes and beeches are some very pretty cottages, one with a china plaque 1866. St Peter's Church with tower restored 1631 is full of memorials to the Wodehouse family, the two most interesting being a brass to John Wodehouse 1465 and a charming and life-like effigy of Dame Elizabeth Strutt, daughter of Sir Thomas Wodehouse, who died 1651. There are fine carved and painted royal arms, probably of James I. The Regency lodges in Carleton Forehoe lead to Kimberley House, formerly the home of the Wodehouses, built and rebuilt many times, possibly in the early 18th century by Talman and 100 years later altered by Salvin. The alterations in the 1950s were by James Fletcher-Watson.

King's Lynn [7, 8] Since the appearance of the first edition of this *Shell Guide* in 1958, one-third of the town within the lines of the mediaeval defences has been redeveloped. Individual buildings of note, many of them saved by the exertions of the King's Lynn Preservation Trust or by a handful of private owners, survive to be enjoyed, but the sense of a mediaeval town has been lost. Lynn has been, and still is, bedevilled by the notion of an 'historic core'—an idea that was suggested by conservationists in the 1940s. This core, which consisted of Nelson Street, Queen Street, King Street and the two market places, was held to contain the town's architectural gems and was to be safeguarded. However well intentioned, it proved an unfortunate concept because it was misread as envisaging and accepting the destruction of what lay outside the core. Furthermore, it has never been difficult for the determined to convince the planning authorities

of the 'necessity' for demolition within the core itself. Look, for instance, at what has happened in Queen Street where as recently as 1977 the Department of the Environment allowed the demolition of a 12th-century stone house. The pedestrianization of the shopping area has thrown an increased volume of traffic into the riverside streets that make up the core and, even more disastrously perhaps, pedestrianization was used to justify the construction of service roads which has given us vistas composed of little else but the torn and broken backs of buildings. Lynn is not a pretty town; on all but the sunniest of days much of its brickwork is sombre, and too many of its streets are disfigured by shabby and neglected buildings and patches of derelict land.

Early man seems to have avoided the marshy site on which Lynn was eventually to grow, favouring the higher land to the east of the town. To the visitor entering Lynn by the A148 and the northern bypass, the descent into the fen is particularly noticeable. Deep dykes and salt hills and reclaimed marshes stretching away to the Wash are evocative of the landscape the British knew and described with the Celtic word *lindo*—meaning 'lake', from which 'Lynn' derives. This swamp, always the haunt of fishermen and saltmakers, had dried out sufficiently by the 11th century to allow permanent settlement. The Domesday Survey suggests a number of scattered hamlets, only one of which had acquired a church, probably in Saxon times but certainly by 1100. This lay in the area later known as South Lynn, where All Saints' Church can justly claim the distinction of being the original church of Lynn. The focus for the rapid post-Conquest development of the town was St Margaret's Church and the priory founded about 1100 by Herbert de Losinga, Bishop of Norwich, at the request of the

inhabitants of his manor of Gaywood which ran down through the marsh to the banks of the Ouse and was separated from All Saints' parish by the Millfleet. Losinga gave the new township of Lynn to the Priory of Norwich Cathedral, but a century later Bishop John de Grey took it back. It remained in the possession of the bishopric until 1536 when it was seized by the Crown, and Bishop's Lynn became King's Lynn. The new town prospered and within half a century of its foundation it had outgrown the original limits—bounded by the Millfleet to the south and the Purfleet to the north—imposed upon it by Losinga, and it was allowed to expand into what a 13th-century survey calls the New Land, that is, the tract of land between Purfleet and Fisherfleet. Here the Chapel of St Nicholas was built and the Tuesday Market Place laid out. So, almost as improbably as Venice, Lynn grew on its marshy site between the creeks that drained into the Ouse. Recent archaeological discoveries have suggested that wooden stakes may have been driven into the mud along the creeks to encourage the accretion of silt and to consolidate the ground for building. The extent of the land gained in this way and also by the dumping of rubbish onto the river banks is dramatically illustrated in the courtyard of Thoresby College where a stone marks the line of the 13th-century quay. Today short stretches of the Millfleet, the Purfleet and the Fisherfleet are all that remains of a network of creeks that shaped the town's growth and survived into the 19th century. Timber from the Baltic, wine from France and coals from the Tyne flowed into mediaeval Lynn and were distributed inland by waterway. Petitioning the Crown in 1373, the merchants of Lynn claimed that they could supply the needs of seven counties—a claim that they maintained well into the 18th century. Out by the same waterway came the produce of the rich farm lands of East Anglia—in the early Middle Ages wool and salt, and always grain. With the coming of the railways in the 19th century, the colliers gradually disappeared from the river, but timber and grain (massive grain silos dominate the skyline) are still very much in evidence, with petrol from the Thames, motor cars from Czechoslovakia and steel from mainland Europe bound for the Midlands. Most of this trade is now conducted on the northern edge of the town from the two dock basins opened in 1869 and 1883. Until then trade was carried on from the premises along Nelson Street, Queen Street, King Street and the Tuesday Market Place. Each property in these streets represented a separate merchant business, with dwelling houses fronting the street and warehouses and yards running down to private wharves on the waterfront. A few of these businesses continued to operate in the traditional way until this century. It is the survival of so many of these groups of buildings that is the remarkable and characteristic feature of Lynn. The town's prosperity was built partly upon shipping, but it also derived in part from Lynn's role as market town and shopping centre for west Norfolk. At the end of the last century over seventy carriers' routes converged on Lynn from the surrounding countryside.

The Churches. All Saints' Church possesses an attractive interior, recently reordered to meet current liturgical requirements, but done with respect for the building and for tradition. The present building dating from about 1400 has a good nave arcade, mediaeval roofs and, at the west end, a Jacobean screen recently acquired from St Peter's, West Lynn. The tower collapsed in 1763. South of the chancel is the oratory of the anchoresses who lived here in the Middle Ages, and alongside may be seen traces of the 12th-century church. When the surrounding narrow streets of

post-mediaeval houses were demolished in the 1960s it was an imaginative step on the part of the church authorities to remove their churchyard wall and integrate with the new development. The nave, transepts and central lantern of the mediaeval St Margaret's Church were destroyed when the spire was brought down by a gale in 1741. The bases of the 13th-century nave arcade serve as foundations for Matthew Brettingham's new work. The 13th-century chancel has 14th-century screens and a 15th-century clerestory. Prints and photographs in the church suggest the quality of the 18th-century woodwork that Sir George Gilbert Scott removed in 1874. The pulpit with its carved foliage and sounding board survived, and the Elizabethan screen was shifted to its present position under the organ. The Corporation of Lynn bought this fine instrument by Snetzler at the bidding of Dr Charles Burney, the father of Fanny and town organist from 1751 to 1760. The sumptuous reredos is by Bodley (1899). In the south aisle of the chancel are two of the most important brasses in England, that to Adam de Walsoken and his wife (1349) and the even more splendid one to Robert Braunche and his two wives (1364). They are life-size effigies, and below the latter is a frieze showing the Peacock Feast offered, according to local tradition, to Edward II on his visit to Lynn in 1349 during Robert Braunche's mayoralty. They are of Flemish workmanship. Recent additions to the church include glass appliqué swing doors and an aluminium nave altar. The south-west tower displays a progression of styles through its various stages, which culminate in a belfry by the Ely Choir Mason of c. 1340 and a moon dial of 1681. On either side of the west door is 15th-century blind arcading which uses mid-14th-century tracery motifs from Ely Lady Chapel. In 1419 the mason of St Nicholas, Lynn, was called in to

King's Lynn: ▷
p. 100 St Margaret's, the south-west tower; *p. 101* Streetscapes near St Margaret's

avert the imminent collapse of the north-west tower. He inserted the east and north arches that bear his characteristic mouldings. Thirty years later the job of rebuilding the tower was completed by a different hand. St Nicholas', more striking than beautiful is a chapel of ease to St Margaret's, and also much in demand as a concert hall, particularly at the time of the King's Lynn Festival of the Arts at the end of July. The 13th-century tower carries a spire by Sir George Gilbert Scott, 1869. 'You will see,' he wrote, 'that I have adopted as a means of compensating for the want of height in the tower an octagon storey to the spire which ... will help to supply what is so much needed by the former without giving undue elongation to the latter.' The rest of the building, finished by 1419, has a richly ornamented south porch, angel roof and splendid east and west windows. Two striking hallmarks of this mason's work are the angularity of his tracery and his fondness for forms popular elsewhere nearly a century earlier, as, for example, the heads to the small north and south doors. Noteworthy among a number of good monuments is that designed by Robert Adam for Sir Benjamin Keene, British Ambassador to Spain, who died in 1757. Keene, although the son of a failed Lynn merchant, was the grandson of Sir Robert Walpole's election agent in Lynn, and the young Keene benefited from the patronage of that powerful figure who sat for Lynn in seventeen successive parliaments from 1701 to 1742. St John's is in Lancet Style by Salvin, 1846. It was built to provide for those who were excluded from St Margaret's and St Nicholas' by the pew system.

The Streets. Only the west side of Bridge Street survives. Tucked away at the southern end of the streets, a gateway of about 1400 is all that remains of the Carmelite priory. Arriving relatively late on the urban scene, in the 13th century, the friars in Lynn, as elsewhere, had to make shift with sites on the periphery of the built-up area. To the north a charming group, recently restored, includes the timber-framed and jettied Greenland Fishery House. As an inn, c. 1800, it was popular with seamen engaged in the Greenland whale fishery out of Lynn. Bombed during the last war, early 17th-century frescoes came to light during rebuilding. Nelson Street is Lynn's best surviving street. 19th-century maltings along the Mill-fleet were converted into flats by the West Norfolk District Council in 1978. In January of the same year flood water reached the door knocker of Oxley House next door

King's Lynn:
Greyfriars (*left*)
Red Mount chapel (*below*)

No. 15, built in the 1740s, has an imposing staircase. Notice the counting houses attached to this and to Oxley House. From Devil's Alley which runs between Nos. 13 and 15 it is easy to study the layout and development of these riverside properties. The front range of Hampton Court (it is named after a 17th-century occupant) was built about 1500 by Robert Amfles whose merchant's mark is carved in the spandrel of the entrance. The cannon ball in the entry is supposed to be the very one that crashed through St Margaret's when Lynn, almost alone in Norfolk, held out for the King against the Parliamentary forces, and was besieged in 1643. The south range is the oldest and represents the original house to which the other wings were added at various times. The west range was originally a warehouse with open ground floor and an arcade which is clearly visible from the garden. Priory Lane contains most of what remains of the Benedictine Priory of Lynn founded by Losinga in 1100. A plaque in the gateway records its restoration. To the west of St Margaret's Church is St Margaret's Place. The complex of buildings now called St Margaret's House was the Lynn Steelyard or depot of the German Hanse. Built around a courtyard for security—the German merchants were deadly rivals of the English for the profitable Norway trade and in the Icelandic fisheries—the timber-framed and jettied south wing is 15th century. From the 16th century onwards the property was regularly leased to Lynn merchants, but the Germans did not finally relinquish it until the mid 18th century when it was bought by the Everards, a Lynn merchant family, who rebuilt the street front. The whole has been well restored by the Norfolk County Council. In Saturday Market Place is the town hall (Guildhall), originally the Hall of the Trinity Guild, rebuilt after the previous Hall burnt down in

1421. A fire so near to St Margaret's might well have been fatal to the church, too, but for the intervention of Margery Kempe, a Lynn woman who, after a vision of Our Lord had become a mystic and a pilgrim; she persuaded her confessor to take the Blessed Sacrament out of the church and bear it to the fire. Margery meanwhile returned to the church where sparks were falling through the lantern and flying about the choir, and prayed earnestly for a miracle. She knew that her prayers had been answered when shortly afterwards men came rushing in with snow on their clothes and the news that the sudden storm had quenched the flames. The Town Hall is still much used and it is encouraging at night to see light streaming through the huge 15th-century window from some civic frolic within. The stone 15th-century Hall leads to the Georgian Assembly Rooms and Card Room. In the mediaeval undercroft the display of regalia and plate includes the exquisite so-called King John Cup (mid 14th century), silver gilt with enamelled panels. Next to the Guildhall is the former gaol with festooned chains over the door, built by William Tuck of Lynn in 1784. On the corner of Queen Street Thoresby College, which now houses the Lynn Youth Hostel and old people's flats, was built by Thomas Thoresby shortly after 1500 to house his own chantry priests and those of the Trinity Guild. The mutilated inscription on the entrance gate once sought prayers for the founder's soul. The former refectory with its fine hammerbeam roof is in the west wing overlooking the river. This building, like Hampton Court and the Priory, was restored by the King's Lynn Preservation Trust whose office is to be found here. Clifton House, with its baroque entrance and Elizabethan tower, is available for inspection. The present house of 1708 stands on the vaulted undercroft of its 14th-century predeces-

sor. Areas of 14th-century tiled floor are preserved and on display in two ground-floor rooms overlooking the pleasant courtyard, and in the same rooms are to be seen some of the mediaeval bench ends thrown out of St Nicholas' Chapel in 1852. In King's Staithe Square stands Bank House with its statue of King Charles I in a niche on the brick façade. Here, in the 1850s, Francis Cresswell, a banker, and his wife Rachel, daughter of the prison reformer, Elizabeth Fry, lived for five agonizing years without news of their son, Samuel Gurney Cresswell, who had gone on a naval expedition to the Arctic to search for the lost ships of Sir John Franklin. The expedition did not find these, but when Lieutenant Cresswell returned to Lynn in October 1855 he was the first man to bring confirmation of the long-sought North-west Passage, and he was suitably fêted in the Town Hall. King Street is one of the streets of the New Land extension. On the banks of the Purfleet stands the delightful Customs House, built in 1683 as an Exchange by the Lynn merchant Henry Bell (1647–1711), twice mayor and an architect of some note. He seems to have played a major part in the rebuilding of Northampton after the fire of 1675, and in Lynn he was responsible for the Duke's Head Hotel and the now vanished market cross of which prints survive in the town's museum. The range 28 to 32 King Street contains the two gable ends of a 12th-century stone house which was split into two properties in the 14th century when the stone street front was demolished and the present timber-framing inserted. The ground floor may have accommodated open-fronted mediaeval shops. Almost opposite is the 15th-century St George's Guildhall, once a theatre where Shakespeare is said to have acted, then for many years a warehouse and now, thanks to the vision and generosity of the late Alec Penrose, a theatre again and the centre of the

King's Lynn Festival. Warehouses behind have been skilfully converted into galleries and a restaurant overlooking the river. Next door a fine stone-fronted 18th-century house is now a museum of social history. In the large Tuesday Market Place the most notable house is the Duke's Head, 1689, originally of brick. Barclays Bank, opposite, had its attractive Victorian *porte-cochère* removed in 1960. A late 18th-century print of the building was used as a guide for the refronting. Lloyds Bank is by the Ipswich architect, Munro Cautley, known to lovers of East Anglia for his books on the churches of Norfolk and Suffolk. An increasing number of these houses is being gutted, and in some instances the front wall is all that remains of the original. St Anne's Street, leading to the docks, has some good timber-framed houses falling into decay. Pilot Street, to the east of St Nicholas' Chapel, has a pleasant row of mediaeval and later cottages restored by the Lynn Preservation Trust, and some new houses (1978) by Colin Shewring for the District Council. The latter, of red brick and pantile, are effectively and attractively grouped and the only new buildings of merit in the town so far. Chapel Street has suffered greatly, but the late-mediaeval Lattice House, 18th-century Westgate House opposite and, just round the corner in Austin Street, the sole surviving arch of the Austin Friars' once 'large, respectable, and stately edifice' merit a look. Eastgate House at the end of Littleport Street, once the family home of the Keenes, has been plucked from destruction and is currently being restored. The East Gate of the town stood here until 1800, and on either side of the road are a few remains of the mediaeval walls. In Gaywood Road gently curving terraces of late-Victorian villas lead to Basil Champneys' Grammar School of 1906—all red brick, white paint, green cupolas and high Dutch gables set in fields and trees. In its

shadow lies the miniature Hospital of St Mary Magdalene, founded 1174, for a prior and twelve brothers and sisters, of whom three were to be lepers; burnt down at the siege of Lynn in 1643 and rebuilt in 1649, it is a charming one-storey brick building around a little courtyard. In a park at the north end of London Road stands the Greyfriars Tower, the central lantern and sole remnant of the Franciscan church and friary. Its usefulness as a landmark to vessels sailing up the river ensured its survival at the Dissolution. The early 19th-century houses along London Road deserve better treatment than they are getting, and so does the South Gate, built about 1440 of brick and faced with stone in 1520 and an imposing piece of civic display. The Goodwins Road area nearby (just outside the mediaeval defence bank) was Lynn's first suburban development. Victorian and Edwardian villas in a pleasant variety of styles and materials repose in tree-lined roads and leafy gardens. High Street, distractingly paved in chequered concrete, has been cleared of motor cars only to be cluttered with concrete bric-à-brac. Numbers of quite distinguished 18th- and 19th-century buildings struggle to assert themselves above the usual inappropriate shopfronts.

In the Walks, a public park laid out in the 18th century, stands the Red Mount Chapel dedicated to Our Lady. Built about 1485 by the Prior of St Margaret's to attract pilgrims and restore the flagging finances of the Priory, it shows all the signs of hasty and cheap construction by a local builder. The venture proved a great success and by 1505 they could afford the services of a topflight mason to remodel the upper chapel. The man they engaged was John Wastell, master of the New Work at Peterborough Cathedral and creator of the high vault of King's College, Cambridge, who provided the very fine fan-vaulting

which adds distinction to this interesting little building. On Baxter's Plain, near the Post Office, is the very good museum housed in a Victorian Gothic chapel conversion, recently much enlarged and improved. The arrival in Lynn of the Campbells Soup factory in 1959 marked the beginning of a new phase in the industrial life of the town. Since then the usual plantations of sheds, assorted in size but uniform in dreariness, have appeared on the edges of the town to accommodate newly arrived light industries. However, Maxwell Fry's administration block for Dow Chemicals, by the estuary of the Ouse, has been praised; and the Bespak building (Furness & Thurlow 1980) on the northern bypass cheers the spirit and is one more reason for entering the town by that route. (*See also* West Lynn.)

Kirby Bedon [11] The church of St Andrew has a Norman south door with contemporary ironwork and 17th-century altar rails. Several interesting monuments including that to Gerald Fitzgerald 1872 ('Dein Wille geschehe'). The mausoleum (1868) was erected by Sir Robert John Harvey, who shot himself two years later after the collapse of the Crown Bank in Norwich. R. M. Phipson was responsible for a very thorough restoration of the church between 1876 and 1885. The ruined tower of St Mary's Church is visible across the road.

Kirby Cane [17] There are big cedars in All Saints' Churchyard with seats beneath them. The church tower is probably pre-Conquest, and there is a Norman south doorway. There are angels on the 14th-century font and a particularly nice Stuart pulpit. On the sanctuary floor are some black marble slabs of the Catelyn family and on the north wall two Renaissance memorials. A Lord Berners was squire and rector here for 66 years, dying in 1851, and there is a

Kirstead Hall

Berners hatchment in the church. The late-Georgian Hall has had several owners including the Lords Berners.

Kirstead [17] St Margaret's Church was rebuilt in very dark grey flint in 1864, but still had some old memorials and hatchments. Kirstead Hall is dated 1614—a splendid brick house with step gables, and wide stone mullioned windows. It is completely unspoilt and has all the atmosphere of an early manor house with its small enclosed garden in front, the dove house in the orchard, and good farm buildings.

Knapton [5] In this church, dedicated to St Peter and St Paul, is one of the finest double hammerbeam roofs in East Anglia. It was given by the rector, John Smith, in 1503 and has 138 angels arranged in three tiers. The font cover, 1705, has an inscription in the form of a Greek palindrome: NIΘON ANOMHMA MH MONAN OΘIN (Wash my sins and not my face only).

Lakenham [11] Once a pretty village but now engulfed in an enormous building estate and part of Norwich. There is a little group of old houses near the bridge across the Yare and the old parish church of St John and All Saints has a 15th-century font with representations of the Crucifixion and the Instruments of the Passion. St Mark's was built by John Brown of Norwich in 1844, in a scrupulous but rather insipid Gothic; attractive screenwork inside. St Alban's is a pleasant 1930s church (the 14th-century font came from Knettishall in Suffolk) in the middle of the late 19th/early 20th-century residential suburb. Norfolk play Minor Counties cricket on the ground here.

Lamas [11] Close to the Bure is an inn, the Anchor of Hope, and then a long village street with pleasant houses of brick and flint and here and there a thatched roof. The 17th-century Hall and the interesting manor house, probably of the same date, face the meadows, in which stands St Andrew's Church.

It has an 18th-century organ case, a very well-designed royal arms for Elizabeth II, and a heraldic window in the nave to the memory of the Norfolk antiquary, Walter Rye. In the graveyard of the former chapel beside the village street, Anna Sewell, author of *Black Beauty*, is buried among the yews. She was born in Yarmouth but her family had property in this neighbourhood.

Langford [15] The church of St Andrew is in the Stanford Military Training Area. The Norman church has a fine doorway and chancel arch, and there is a magnificent monument to Sir Nicholas Garrard (1727) by Christopher Horsnaile sen.

Langham [4] Captain Marryat lived at a farmhouse here. His grave, surmounted by a large urn, is in St Andrew and St Mary's churchyard, south of the tower. The tower itself is 15th century, as is the church. The north-east window of the nave contains Burne-Jones glass. The Hall was built about 1820.

Langley [17] Langley Park, now a school, is a fine house begun in about 1720 by John Buxton of Channonz. Matthew Brettingham added the towers and the wings. It has exciting stucco work inside by Carl Stanley, court sculptor to Frederick V of Denmark. The 13th- and 14th-century St Michael's Church has a plastered ceiling with arms of the Proctor-Beauchamp family and Hanoverian arms in the tympanum of the chancel arch. The 16th-century continental glass was supplied by Lady Beauchamp-Proctor about 1787. Until 1977 there were box pews (the family pew opposite the pulpit has its own door into the church), which were replaced by nice early Victorian pews from Snetterton Church. In a farmyard are the remains of a Chapter House, guest-house and other buildings (1195) of one of the larger Premonstratensian abbeys. Lady Beauchamp-Proctor, who died in 1798, left amusing accounts of her tours of Norfolk in 1764 and 1772.

Larling [15] The enchanting little church of St Ethelbert is down a very muddy field road but is well worth the effort. It has a good west tower (1473) and very interesting 14th-century window tracery in nave and chancel. But its glory lies in a superb Norman arch to the south door; unusually rich, and with two orders of shafts, elaborately patterned. A very exciting thing, and the pleasure of this church does not end there, because in the '90s of the last century the incumbent, the Revd J. B. Atkinson, who loved this church, did much to beautify it; he built the south porch to protect the Norman doorway and installed fine iron outer gates; he put in several stained glass windows, all inscribed, and he built a commodious vestry on the north-west side, with a charming tiled fireplace and a fine wash-basin in a wooden frame and a matching W.C. with a pull-up plug, serviced ingeniously by the rain water from the gutters. This remote, isolated church is loved and cared for; still a parish church, it is used for regular worship. Do not miss the memorial to an earlier rector, the Revd Peter Lynch, who died in 1817, on the outside of the east end. Middleton Murry, Katharine Mansfield's widower, lived for a time at the Old Rectory, the fine house now known as The Beeches.

Lessingham [6] The chancel of the thatched church of All Saints collapsed in 1961 and the painted screen is now in St Peter Hungate Museum in Norwich. There is a 17th-century pulpit with back-board and canopy and an altar table commemorating the burial of Anne, the wife of Edward Cooke, on 17 June 1634.

Letheringsett [4] A very pretty village. The Glaven is spanned by an iron bridge (1818) designed by William Hardy, whose work in laying out the estate here is mentioned by Cobbett. Hardy also added the Doric colonnade to the Hall, which is now an old people's home. Behind the Hall is St Andrew's Church which has an 11th-century round tower, and well proportioned 13th-century arcade in the nave. It was well restored in the 1870s by William Butterfield. In the churchyard there is a curious epitaph to Johnson Jex, the village blacksmith, who was also a self-taught horologist. His death mask is in the church. The church contains very good glass by Kemp and his pupil Heasman (about 1895–1900), and in the sanctuary some scraps of mediaeval glass found in the Hall summerhouse and a recent window by Webb.

Letton [9] The Hall was built by Sir John Soane (1785–8) for the Gurdons, later Lords Cranworth, and has a good central hall and staircase. There is a magnificent monkey puzzle tree beside the house. There has been no church here since the Reformation.

The **Lexhams** [9] Two attractive estate villages, both exceptionally well cared for. *East Lexham* is set amid woods with a beautiful avenue of oaks on the road to Litcham. A vineyard has been successfully established here. Both churches have very early round towers, probably pre-Conquest. That at *East Lexham*, St Andrew, is very fat, that at *West Lexham*, St Nicholas, very short. Lexham Hall at East Lexham, was altered to designs by J. Fletcher-Watson after World War II. As well as a pretty farmyard, there is what may be the last model estate village in Norfolk. The barns and farmyards at West Lexham are of a very high standard, too, and the farmhouse above the river, has great charm.

Leziate [8] (near East Winch on road to Gayton) The ruins of the church have virtually disappeared. Holt House is late Georgian. An earlier house on the site belonged to a branch of the Drury family.

Limpenhoe [12] Much of St Botolph's Church was restored in 1881 by A. S. Hewitt, but the base of the tower (to which money was left in 1460) and a good Norman doorway remain. Inside there is an interesting framed Flemish tapestry of the Sacrifice of Isaac, which was brought here from Southwood Church when it was abandoned late in the 19th century.

Lingwood [11] A compact village whose church, St Peter, has some nice woodwork including some poppy-headed benches, an arch-braced roof, and 17th-century communion rails.

Litcham [9] A compact and attractive little town. An 18th-century farmhouse at its southern end includes remains of the priory and in the attics is a 15th-century king-post roof. All Saints' Church has a red-brick tower (1669), a rood screen with figure paintings said to date from 1436, a 15th-century pulpit and a Flemish oak chest. On the middle pillar of the south arcade is a cryptic mediaeval inscription. Nice west gallery 1853. Fragments of 17th-century Flemish glass. The Hall is an attractive Georgian house at the west end of the village.

Little Barningham *see* Barningham Parva

Little Bittering [9] A hamlet church dedicated to St Peter, with a round Norman font, otherwise of the 13th century, standing remote in meadows. It was saved from dereliction a few years ago.

Little Cressingham *see* Cressingham, Little

Little Dunham *see* Dunham, Little

Little Ellingham *see* Ellingham, Little

Little Melton *see* Melton, Little

Loddon [17] Now that there is a bypass, something of its former atmosphere has returned to this small market town, built along a street of 17th- and 18th-century houses leading to the 15th-century Holy Trinity Church with its great embattled tower (1500). On the remains of the painted screen the boy-saint, William of Norwich, is being crucified; several other panels are interesting. The monuments include one to Lady Williamson (1684) who gave £200 to the rebuilding of St Paul's. There is a picture (1496) of Sir James Hobart, who built the church, and of his wife who built St Olave's Bridge. The Seven-Sacrament font (given in 1487) was conscientiously defaced for 6s in 1642 by one Rochester (a Beccles glazier, according to the church accounts) but still has some colour. In the churchyard, look for the memorial stone to a blacksmith who died in 1876. The council estate, like others in the area, is by the well-known architects, Tayler & Green.

Longham [9] The restored church of St Andrew stands in fields, has a 15th-century screen which has had its tracery and some colour restored, and a 17th-century altar table. Memorial to J. S. Hastings, who gave back to the tower in 1876 an upper storey in place of the one it lost in 1788. Unusual porch. The Hall is a good late-Georgian Holkham farmhouse.

Long Stratton *see* Stratton, Long

The Lophams [16] *North Lopham* is a long village of the Norfolk–Suffolk type with many colour-washed and timber houses with high-pitched roofs. St Nicholas' Church is mainly 14th century; there is a well-proportioned tower of about 1500, with inscriptions commemorating benefactors. The lordship of the manor belongs to the Duke of Norfolk and has descended in an unbroken line from the time of the Domesday survey. *South Lopham* St Andrew's Church has a magnificent central tower—quite the best Norman tower in Norfolk. Apart from the 15th-century parapet, it is a complete Norman structure with arcading on each of its four successive stages (c. 1110). But the north wall of the nave is even earlier, with a Saxon window high up; thus William Bigod, the Earl of Norfolk who was drowned in the White Ship in 1120, must have added his tower to an already existing church. The other 13th- and 14th-century parts of the church, and the nave heightened in the 15th-century with a lofty clerestory and hammerbeam roof, although well-proportioned, are eclipsed by the magnificence of the tower, which is worth going a very long way to see. There are some 15th-century benches with animals carved on the ends, and a very ancient hollowed-out chest.

Ludham [12] A most attractive Broadland village with a pleasant market place with fine 18th-century houses and a spacious 14th/15th-century church dedicated to St Catherine. It has a fine painted screen, given by John and Cicely Salmon and others in 1493, with saints including St Walstan and St Appolonia and (the uncanonized) Henry VI. The wheel emblem of St Catherine is worked into the tracery spandrels of the roof. There is a painted rood group on a tympanum (probably of 1553–8) above the screen and the arms of Elizabeth I are on the reverse. Ludham Hall was once one of the Bishop of Norwich's country houses and has 17th- and 18th-century work. The painter Edward Seago lived in the village. Towards the south-east, a narrow lane runs between the thatched cottages and boat-houses down to Womack Broad and Staithe, and towards the

south-west, Johnson Street runs down to Ludham Bridge over the Ant. Down on the marshes near the confluence of the Ant and the Bure is St Benet's Abbey where the remains of a mill rise up through the ruins of the gatehouse. St Benet's fell into decay after the Dissolution of the Monasteries because the last abbot became Bishop of Norwich and surrendered the episcopal estates to the Crown, retaining those of the abbey. Consequently, the revenues of the see of Norwich are those that once belonged to the abbey and the Bishop of Norwich is still the abbot. He makes a visitation of his abbey by water on the first Sunday of August each year—an event which usually draws a large congregation of holiday makers.

ynford [14] The Roman Catholic church of Our Lady of Consolation is by Henry Clutton, 1879, and the Hall by William Burn, 1856–61.

The iron gates, and the grounds, are very sumptuous. The house, burnt out and restored, is now used as auction rooms.

Lyng [10] A pretty village on the River Wensum. The view of the Mill House from the bridge is particularly attractive. St Margaret's Church, in the middle of the village, has a 13th-century west tower and a 15th-century nave. There is a nice Purbeck marble 13th-century font, but the real treasure is the very large and most beautiful late 15th-century Pall, made from fragments of three vestments, with embroidered representations of, among others, St Olave with an axe and sceptre, St Paul with a sword, St Philip with three loaves and St James wearing a pilgrim's hat. Some of the pews in the church are still marked 'Free'.

Mannington [4] The Hall is a 15th-century moated manor house, with flint flush work in the walls. Parts of the house were extensively restored by Horatio Walpole, Earl

of Orford, who died in 1898 and lies buried under an elaborate tomb in the ruins of the church on the other side of the road, hidden in the trees. The church fell into decay in the 17th century. Some of the original woodwork is in one of the rooms at the Hall, and in the archway over the 'drawbridge' is a church bell. Lord Orford's antiquarian eccentricities are commemorated in and around the ruins of the church by a number of pieces of Gothic ornament from various places, and Gothic archways form the entrances to the gardens, which were laid out south of the church, but there is much that is original in the house and it is of great interest. It still belongs to the Walpole family.

Marham [8] Holy Trinity Church has good Perpendicular tower (bequest 1450) and rare tympanum (lozenge motif) to Norman north door. Two interesting monuments: John and Anne Steward 1604 surmounted by a six-poster, and Henry Villebois (1847) by

R. Westmacott, jun., huge royal arms for James I, 15th-century benches, and lovely hexagonal tiled floor. In the farm opposite the church are the pretty ruins of a 13th-century Cistercian nunnery.

Marlingford [10] The fine trees in this village have been painted by John Crome in his *Marlingford Grove*, now in the Norwich Castle Museum. The Hall was rebuilt in 1868. The 17th-century Old Hall built by the Jermy family is in the village. St Mary's Church has a Norman doorway, a fine Commandment board, and an hourglass for timing sermons.

Marsham [11] The Hall stands on one side of the Mermaid Stream, and Bolwick Hall, landscaped by Repton, on the other, Titus Oates' father was rector here. All Saints', a very pretty church, has a 15th-century hammerbeam roof, painted screen panels and a fine Seven-Sacrament font.

Martham [12] Is a large village on high ground overlooking miles of Broadland. There are attractive greens and 18th-century houses. St Mary's Church has a massive west tower, a spacious nave, Seven-Sacrament font (c. 1470), 15th-century south door, and a very luxurious High Victorian chancel with elaborately traceried east window, rebuilt in memory of the Revd Jonathan Dawson in 1856—it includes an Easter Sepulchre. The south aisle altar is dedicated in honour of St Blide, mother of St Walstan, who is said to have been buried at Martham; in the window over this altar in the restored glass, is a 15th-century St Michael weighing souls against three very evil-looking devils. Under the tower is a slab with a surprising inscription by Christopher Burraway (1730) who commemorated his wife Alice, by saying that she was 'in this life my sister, my mistress, my mother and my wife'. The illegitimate child of an incestuous union, he returned

unwittingly to work as steward for his mother-sister, who discovered his identity after their marriage, by the presence of a mole.

The **Massinghams** [2 and 8] *Great Massingham* is most picturesque with a large pond and green, and cottages surrounding the graceful 15th-century tower of St Mary's Church. Notice also the south porch and 15th-century woodwork. The hamlet of *Little Massingham*, also in beautiful open country, has St Andrew's Church with 15th-century hammerbeam roof, and some quite interesting monuments. These are two charmingly rural villages.

Matlaske [4] Pretty flint and brick cottages and houses along the edge of the park of Barningham Hall. The round-towered church of St Peter has a nave only, in which are hatchments. The chancel collapsed in 1726—luckily outwards—as a service of Holy Communion was in progress; no one was hurt.

Mattishall [10] In this very pretty small market town All Saints' Church stands in the centre of a group of Georgian houses. The church has a west tower (1386), hammerbeam roof, remains of 15th-century rood screen with figure paintings of the apostles, and a Jacobean pulpit. William Cowper often visited his cousin, Mrs Bodham, who lived in the Georgian house at South Green. She often appears in Woodforde's diary. She sent Cowper the picture of his mother which inspired one of his most moving poems. The Georgian Hall was the home of the Donne family, Cowper's cousins. In the little 14th-century church of St Peter at *Mattishall Burgh*, the 18th-century barrel-organ with thirty tunes is still in use, and a sanctus-bell turret (but no bell) and mediaeval screen remain. There is much new development in this neighbourhood.

Mautby [12] A tiny hamlet in the fields, famous for Margaret Mautby, who became Margaret Paston. Mautby Hall is barely a mile from the Pastons' home at Caister Castle, across the marshes on a long lane leading down from the village to the Bure at Four Mile House. The thatched church of St Peter and St Paul with a round tower has a 15th-century font and cover, screen, graceful 14th-century carving on the piscina and sedilia, and the very large figure of a knight in a recess in the south wall. Unfortunately, the south aisle, where Margaret Paston was buried, has disappeared. Remarkable 20th-century glass showing St Thomas Aquinas saying Mass and St Clare with a monstrance.

Melton, Great [10] Here there are two churches in the same churchyard, St Mary's and All Saints' both in use until 1713, when All Saints' was allowed to decay. But in 1883 St Mary's was pulled down except for the tower, and All Saints' was restored. Some of All Saints' may be Saxon, and there is a good Victorian font.

Melton, Little [10] The well restored church of St Mary and All Saints, slightly apart from the village, has a 13th-century font remains of 15th-century woodwork, several Skottowe monuments, and faded 14th-century wall paintings, including an Annunciation. The manor farmhouse is an early 17th-century L-shaped house with stepped end-gables, and a three-bay front.

Melton Constable [4] The interesting church of St Peter in the park of the Hall has a Rubens-like triptych above the altar. There is an early Norman central tower with curious arcading above the chancel arch—two arches with a very large round pillar between them. In the chancel is an unusual low-side window with the sill hollowed out to form a seat. The south transept contains the Astley family pew and was built by Sir Jacob Astley in 1681. It is sumptuously furnished with fine chairs, folio prayer books, and the panelled dado is painted white and decorated with shields of arms. Round the walls are many Astley memorials, in particular that to Sir Philip Astley (1739) by Robert Page of Norwich, and that to Sir Jacob Henry Astley (1818) by J. Bacon and S. Manning. The Hall (c. 1670) stands some distance away, overlooking a most beautiful park and lake. It has been used in several recent films, notably *The Go-Between*. Inside, some rooms retain their 17th-century decoration, notably the Red Drawing-Room with a ceiling (1687) by a craftsman who also worked at Felbrigg. It was sold by the Astleys some twenty years ago. It is Sir Jacob Astley, the redoubtable Royalist commander (d. 1652) who is ever memorable for his prayer on the battlefield at Edgehill: 'O Lord, Thou knowest how busy I must be this day; if I forget Thee, do not Thou forget me.'

Merton [15] St Peter's Church has a round tower that was added to an existing church, for the west wall of the nave is Saxon. The fabric, however, is mainly 14th-century; there are two good windows of this period in the angle of the chancel and south aisle. There is a simple 14th-century screen and a good restored font cover above the interesting 15th-century font, with the crane for raising and lowering it. Also a 17th-century pulpit and reading desk—the hourglass stand is fixed to the screen. There is a brass to William de Grey (1495) kneeling in his tabard with his two wives and five sons. From the south side of the church is a fine view of the park and Hall; the latter, having been burned in 1956, suffered another fire in 1970. What one still sees is the gatehouse of 1620 and part of the Blore addition to the old house in the 1830s. It is the seat of the de

Greys, Lords Walsingham, who inherited by marriage from the Baynards in the 14th century, the estate not having been sold since the Domesday survey.

Methwold [14] A small town with some old houses, the best one, near the church, being the old parsonage with an elaborately moulded brick chimney, and Tudor gable end. It dates from the early 16th century, most of the windows having been replaced by 18th-century ones. St George's Church stands in a large churchyard with pollarded limes and wide views; it has a splendid crocketed spire rising out of the octagonal top stage of the tower. Inside are a nave roof with angels, a life-size brass to Sir Adam de Clifton (1367) against the north wall, and an 18th-century monument to Henry Partridge, Recorder of Lynn, with a portrait of him that must be more life-like than flattering.

Metton [5] St Andrew's Church has a little 14th-century piscina in the chancel and at the west end of the nave some good figure brasses for Robert Doughty (1493) and his wife, Matilda. Nice former rectory adjoining the churchyard, and interesting small Jacobean manor farmhouse across the road.

Middleton [8] Middleton Tower, a moated brick house, was reconstructed in 1860 but the gate tower is part of the house built in the middle of the 15th century by Lord Scales, author of the first book printed in England by Caxton, and writer of several of the Paston Letters. The 14th- and 15th-century church of St Mary is built of carrstone and much restored. Opposite is a low carrstone building, now several cottages, according to local tradition built in the early 18th century as an animals' hospital. Near a square carrstone farmhouse, in the valley of the Nar about a mile south, are a few remains of Blackborough Priory.

They are not much to look at but the valley and stream are charming.

Mileham [9] In this long straggling village are the remains of Mileham Castle, a motte-and-bailey type of mediaeval fortification. The 14th-century church of St John the Baptist has a later south aisle which has sunk, so that the arcade leans alarmingly; in the church are a three-lock poorbox (1639), mediaeval pulpit and a monument to Fermor Pepys, cousin of the diarist. The great interest of this church, however, is the glass, the magnificent west window with its large figures epitomizing a complete 14th-century glazing scheme. There is more glass in the chancel—in particular, note in the 15th-century south window two pack horses followed by a man and woman. There are some interesting old houses, notably Burwood Hall, almost opposite the church.

Morley [16] St Botolph's has thatched and colour-washed houses. St Peter's is the more interesting of the two churches, St Botolph's lately having been rebuilt following a fire. A mile westward is the Old Hall, a fine moated Elizabethan building, well restored.

Morningthorpe [17] Is a 'Norwich School' village with Crome-like trees and lanes. The Manor House is an old house restored, with fine stables. The church of St John the Baptist has a round tower (possibly Saxon) and is beautifully kept. In the chancel is a 14th-century piscina with crocketed ogival arch, and a 16th-century tomb chest, probably to Richard Garneys (1571).

Morston [4] A coastal village whose little quay is much used by small-boat sailors. All Saints' Church has a brick-patched tower (the result of being struck by lightning in 1743), often a subject for

artists. It has well-proportione[d] nave arcades, 15th-century scree[n] with the evangelists and Latin Doc[tors, and under the altar table a[n] unusual figure brass to Richar[d] Makynges (1596), rector, in hi[s] Geneva gown. In the south aisl[e] there is a tablet to Susanna Kinge[r] (1615) and a notable inscription t[o] the Revd Thomas Shorting (1718[)] who died after preaching his firs[t] sermon. The royal arms and th[e] Decalogue (1823) fill the space ove[r] the chancel arch. The marshes her[e] belong to the National Trust.

Morton-on-the-Hill [10] St Ma[r]garet's Church was severely dam[-]aged by the fall of the tower in 1959 but restored most generously i[n] 1980. The nave is Saxon and som[e] old screenwork remains in th[e] chancel. It is the church of the va[n]ished village of Helmingham, no[w] part of Morton. There is a lovel[y] view over the Wensum Valley. Th[e] Hall was built by Thomas South[-]well who died in 1609; a wing wa[s] added in 1830. The church is veste[d] in the Norfolk Churches Trus[t] with Lady Prince-Smith as gua[r]dian.

Moulton St Mary [12] (near Ya[r]mouth) The church near the Ha[ll] in the meadows has a round tow[er] and Tudor porch, a Jacobean pu[l]pit and reader's desk (17th ce[n]tury), and important 14th-centur[y] wall paintings. In the chancel is [a] very pleasing little memorial f[or] Edmond Anguish (1628). Th[e] church is vested in the Redunda[nt] Churches Fund.

Moulton St Michael or **Grea[t] Moulton** [16] The church is full [of] atmosphere inside, with goo[d] painting of 1909 over the chanc[el] arch and lively mediaeval carvin[g] on the jambs. Tower rebuilt 188[interesting Norman pillar pisci[na] and royal arms of James I an[d]

◁   **Morley** Old Hall (*above*);
The Old Parsonage, **Methw**[old]
(*below*)

Morston

George III. Near the church is an attractive villa in the style of Osborne.

Mulbarton [10, 11] Has one of the largest village greens in Norfolk and some Georgian houses; next to the church of St Mary Magdalen, the Old Hall of the Rich family still retains a shaped gable. The much-restored church contains some interesting memorials. Sir Edwyn Rich, 'who lov'd the poore', has an elaborate epitaph (1675) in which he describes himself as 'my own death's poett'. His rector, Daniel Scargill, put up a curious memorial to his first wife, Sarah, two copper plates hinged together so that they open in the form of a book; on the right-hand page Mrs Scargill's hand is beckoning from the clouds—'Deare Love, one feather'd minute & I come'; but the feather'd minute lasted 41 years, during which time Mr Scargill married again. He started his career by being ignominiously expelled from Cambridge for 'Hobbism and Atheism' but made a public recantation of his errors.

Mundesley [5] A pleasant little seaside resort which Cowper visited in his boyhood and again several times at the end of his sad life, staying at the little double-fronted Georgian house which is still called by his name. All Saints' Church was restored early this century after being ruinous for years; the Jacobean pulpit came from Sprowston.

Mundford [14] On the edge of Breckland with a Forestry Commission view of conifers, has cottages, built in the Breckland style with cut flint and blue pantile roofs, around a small green. St Leonard's Church has a superb rood screen and loft with crucifixion and saints, added to the remains of an old screen in 1911 by Sir Ninian Comper who also did the reredos, the chancel and the organ case.

Mundham [17] Has the remains of a ruined church, St Ethelbert, and some thatched cottages. The

113

church of St Peter has a Norman south doorway, a tower with prominent gargoyles, a rough 15th-century screen and an almost invisible wall painting.

Narborough [8] The estate was inherited from the Narborough family by the Spelmans in the 15th century, and the Hall includes Tudor brickwork. It was refaced, enlarged, and a castellated parapet added in the 18th century. It was later sold by the last of the Spelmans, the Revd Henry Spelman, under an Act of Parliament of 1773. Here lived the great antiquarian, Sir Henry Spelman, author of the *History of Sacrilege*. All Saints' Church contains wonderful monuments and brasses, mostly to the Spelman family. Sir John and his lady, 1607, with a little kneeling daughter and a baby in swaddling clothes; Sir Clement Spelman (1672), a standing alabaster figure of Cibber; very fine brasses from 1496 to 1581. Curious demi-effigy, 1293, north of the sanctuary.

Narford [8] The Hall, added to in the late Georgian period and again about 1860 by William Burn, has a magnificent early 18th-century core, and important frescoes by Pellegrini (1708–13) and Clermont (1740). St Mary's Church in the park has a monument to Sir Andrew Fountaine, the notable antiquary who succeeded Newton at the Mint, with bust by Roubiliac. The estate and Hall still belong to his family.

Neatishead [11] A pretty Broadland village with a creek running down to Barton Broad. The cottages and farms are scattered over a wide area but there is a compact village street with late Georgian houses. Only the chancel remains of St Peter's Church, which must have been a very large building. There is a 14th-century font and 16th-century pulpit. A winding road leads to Irstead, past many thatched cottages and a double-

fronted Georgian house with fan-light.

Necton [9] The tower of All Saints' Church has an attractive cupola which dates from 1865 but the church is mediaeval. There is a wonderful hammerbeam roof, whose wall-posts supporting the hammerbeams are carved in the form of niches containing figures. Good pulpit and tester (1636), altar table (1643), and several brasses.

Needham [17] The cottages with their steep-pitched roofs are well restored and cared for, as is St Peter's Church with its 15th-century brick porch and old benches.

Newton by Castle Acre [9] Has a little Saxon church of All Saints with central tower, one of the most attractive of the early churches of Norfolk untouched by the great rebuilding of the 15th century. Very simple and inspiring.

Newton Flotman [17] A village and bridge on the River Tas. St Mary's Church has 15th-century seats and remarkable brass plate erected in 1571 by Thomas Blondevyle.

Nordelph [7] In flat fens, and strung out along the banks of Well Creek. Has some cottages a century old or more but the brick church, Holy Trinity, was built in 1865. Bradford, poet of romantic friendship, was vicar here.

North Elmham [9] Once the centre of the Saxon diocese of the North Folk, but after the Danish invasions the See was re-established at Thetford and then transferred to Norwich in 1093. The substantial ruins of the Saxon cathedral can be seen near the great earthwork due north of the church. St Mary's Church, with tall west tower dominating this lengthy village, is mainly 14th century. There is a groined roof to the western

porch and remains of a 15th-century rood screen with figure paintings. The carved altar (1622) and pulpit (1626) were the work of Francis Floyd, parish clerk for 46 years; he was paid £1 15s 0d for the altar and £5 3s 4d for the pulpit. Vineyards flank the main Dereham road and produce an excellent wine.

North Pickenham *see* Pickenham, North

Northrepps [5] Gathers about the well-proportioned St Mary's Church, 1475–87; battlements 1520s. Very nice ironwork on the south door and a rood screen given by John and Constance Playford. The Hall has belonged to a branch of the Gurney family for the last century, and Verily Anderson's book, *The Northrepps Grandchildren*, describes the life there. On the road to *Southrepps* is a small estate which, though conceived and designed in the 20th century, is much more like the achievement of an 18th-century landowner. Templewood was designed in the 1930s by the architects, Seely & Paget, for Viscount Templewood (Sir Samuel Hoare), the famous politician and local landowner, who was a keen naturalist and planter of trees. He commissioned this single-storey house in the manner of a Palladian villa in order to enjoy the undisturbed wildlife of his sequestered woodland. The avenues of Spanish chestnut and ilex were planted ten years in advance so as to provide an established setting for the building, which incorporates stonework and other features salvaged from Nuthall Temple in Nottingham and from Robert Taylor's Bank of England in the City of London. Lord Templewood left the estate to his nephew, the distinguished architect, Paul Paget.

North Runcton *see* Runcton, North

North Tuddenham *see* Tuddenham, North

Saxon Cathedral, **North Elmham**

North Walsham [5] The 15th-century St Nicholas' Church of this little market town with its cross in the market place, is the largest in Norfolk after Yarmouth; the tower fell in 1724. Just to its north is the tower of the earlier Saxon church. The large bare interior has a splendid monument designed by John Key of London for William Paston (1608) during his lifetime; the arms board has the arms of the Commonwealth on one side and those of Charles II on the other. There is a fine restored 15th-century font cover, the base of a 15th-century painted screen, and an Edward VI altar table; the south porch bears the arms of Edward II and John of Gaunt. The Paston Grammar School, where Nelson spent some of his schooldays, is across the square from the church; it has Georgian buildings, with later additions.

Northwold [14] Here there is an outcrop of chalk, so the village has, as well as large 17th- and 18th-century houses, many delightful chalk-built cottages, some white, some colour-washed. St Andrew's Church tower has flint flush-work; the rest of the outside is plastered except for the clerestory where the inscription 'Pray for the sowle of John Sterling' is written under the westernmost window. Inside there are 13th-century arcades with alternate plain and carved capitals; a repainted roof with angels and flowers and a beautiful though very mutilated 14th-century Easter Sepulchre—the four figures of the Roman soldiers amongst the olive trees are unusual. At the west end of the church is a carved and painted wooden memorial (1727) to Robert Burhill, D.D., who took sanctuary in Northwold 'at ye breaking out of ye troubles in Oct. 1641'. He was an antiquary and poet and 'his learned works writ in Latin against the greatest champions of the Romish Church did great service to the Protestant Cause in general as well as to ye Church of England in particular.'

There are remains of painting on the wall of the north aisle.

North Wootton *see* Wootton, North

Norton Subcourse or **Soupecourse** [18] Has a big thatched round-towered church of St Mary, much restored but with good sedilia and east window tracery (Decorated); the contracts for new roofs survive from 1319–20 (although the roofs don't), so the Decorated fittings evidently date from that time.

Norwich [11] The city reveals itself from several directions as you approach it—as you breast the hill at Trowse or reach Boundary Road on the way in from Drayton, or from the famous viewpoint of St James's Hill on the very edge of Mousehold Heath. There are the landmarks—the cathedral spire, the castle on its mound, the City Hall, many of the 30-odd churches and a few prominent new buildings. Just as Norfolk is not flat, neither is Norwich, as any traveller who has carried luggage up from Thorpe Station to Castle Meadow will tell you. Early Norwich was settled on these slopes overlooking the river and much of this settlement was along the present King Street/Magdalen Street north–south axis and along the St Benedict's/Pulls Ferry east–west axis. The name Norwich probably derives from North-wic—*wic(k)* being a small settlement. By the time of the Domesday survey, Norwich was a borough with at least 25 churches, and although the Conquest produced chaos for a time, the building of the castle and the transfer of the seat of the bishop from Thetford to Norwich resulted in continued growth, with increased trade overseas, such as in the stone from Caen in Normandy that had to be imported to build the cathedral. The population grew more cosmopolitan, including not only Normans and other Euro-peans, but also the Jews who formed a distinct settled community; and the position of Norwich as the chief market town of one of the most densely settled areas in England meant that by the early 14th century it was the sixth richest town in England, with a population of some 6,000. The local textile industry, based particularly on worsted cloth (which took its name from the small Norfolk village of Worstead) brought Norwich to the position of an important city by Tudor times. Wealth was concentrated in relatively few hands; this was largely the cause of Kett's rebellion in 1549. Norwich had been a distinctly rough city in the Middle Ages, with anti-Jewish disturbances in 1144 and pitched battles between monks and citizens in 1271 as particular examples. The time of Kett's rebellion coincided with the Reformation and many churches were deconsecrated then; the decline in English church-going began in the reign of Elizabeth (and not, as many think, in the 18th century). Even so, Norwich has retained 32 of its mediaeval churches, whose future was the subject of a report by the Brooke Commission, appointed by Bishop Fleming in 1967, which concluded that 24 of these churches 'would seem no longer to be required for Church of England parish worship. Alternative uses for these churches have been hard to find, and several of them still stand lifeless and sad. The 16th century saw a further influx of 'foreigners', weavers for the most part, who had fled from religious persecution on the Continent, and Norwich remained the largest provincial centre until the Industrial Revolution meant the growth of the northern manufacturing towns. The increase in the size of Norwich was due to the employment offered to people from rural areas whose commons were being enclosed; yet Norwich, which lacked coal and fast-flowing rivers to turn machinery, could not compete with the northern textile mills—it had to diversify, as is still the situation.

Approaching the city from the west, one enters along St Benedict's, one of the earliest areas of settlement, and passes through some of the old walls. This part of the city is receiving welcome housing development, some of it centred round the Norman tower of *St Benedict's*, all that remains after bomb damage. Here, possibly better than anywhere else in Norwich, one sees signs of the old city in the narrow lanes leading up to Pottergate and St Giles Street. Here we meet that characteristic of Norwich, a rapid succession of churches, little towerless *St Swithin's*, for years a store, *St Margaret's* with its own little plain, recently closed despite an east window of 1967, and noble *St Laurence's*, in many ways the finest and saddest of the unused churches. It does not look its best from St Benedict's, but if you go down to Westwick Street, it is seen to be a really big 15th-century church. The tower, with a stair turret (probably 1893) is 112 feet high; the church is generally accepted as having been built in the present form 1460–72, although the tower and chancel may have been finished about 1500. It was this church which for some time during the incumbency of Edwin Hillyard (1860–76) was host to Joseph Lyne, Father Ignatius, who was attempting to re-start the Benedictine Order (in the Anglican church) at a monastery in Elm Hill. The interior retains some dignity; there are several brasses and also fine carvings of the martyrdoms of Saints Laurence and Edmund outside the west door. A little further along to the east, and on the other side of the road, is *St Gregory's*; an interesting feature is the way the east end is built up over an alley. The tower is partly Saxon and the interior light and airy; a fine but over-restored wall painting of St George is in the north aisle. The brass lectern was removed to St Giles's and the rare mediaeva knocker is now in one of the city's museums. Despite articulate protests by those wishing to use it for worship and related activities, it will probably become a branch of the Norwich Museums. Behind St Gregory's, in Upper Goat Lane, is the Friends Meeting House (1826, . T. Patience) where the Norwich Quakers met, including the Earlham Gurneys whose best known member was Elizabeth Fry. Another well-known Quaker who came here was Amelia Opie, wife of the painter; there is a nice little statue of her in Quaker dress above an insurance office where Opie street joins London Street. Continuing eastwards, we come to Charing (more correctly Shearing) Cross; to take our minds off the modern multi-storey car park which is on the site of the Tudor palace of the Dukes of Norfolk; this was extended in the 17th century, partly demolished in the 18th, and obliterated by bulldozers in the 20th) and the disused Anchor Brewery, there are three things of interest on the other side of the road. Strangers Hall is a particularly good Folk Museum, with rooms furnished in different periods; the building is worthy of the subject as the frontage is 1621 and the house behind it a mixture from about 1300 onwards, mainly 15th and 16th centuries. Behind this is the Maddermarket Theatre where the Norwich Players, started by Nugent Monck between the wars, still maintain a fine tradition. The names here are redolent of the old city—Shearing Cross, where the shearers worked, Pottergate, the potters' street, and Maddermarket, centre of the weaving trade where dye was sold. At St John Maddermarket church, notice the east window, possibly reset from a demolished chancel. Inside there is a most splendid 18th-century balachino, a west gallery, sundry monuments including one to Nugent Monck, who was churchwarden here, and the finest collection of monumental brasses in

Norwich, wall-mounted. St Andrew's is the next church one meets continuing east, the present building dating from 1478 to about 1520. The roof is a fine cambered tie-beam, and there are the Suckling tombs. Although most of the fittings are recent, the spaciousness of the church is impressive. Across the road is Garsett House, 16th century, and the big St Andrew's Hall, once the Blackfriars' church, which has had various uses since the Dissolution and now is used mainly for concerts, exhibitions and similar public events. At the north-east corner Becket's chapel has recently been excavated. The church of St Peter Hungate is now a very good ecclesiastical museum, containing many beautiful objects, among them the funeral pall from St Gregory's. Behind St Andrew's Church is the Bridewell Museum, devoted to local industry; the house was built c. 1370 and was lived in by William Appleyard, whose arms appear above the east window of St Andrew's Church. Continuing around to the right, we pass St Michael-at-Plea, which has a nice south porch and owes its name to the fact that the Archdeacon held his courts here. The mediaeval paintings this church once had are now in the cathedral; the church, though closed, is sometimes used for exhibitions. From here one could move to the east, to Elm Hill and the cathedral, but we can swing round through Bank Plain where the important Barclays Bank was built in 1929–31 by E. Boardman & Son, and Brierley & Rutherford, and come under the shadow of the great castle on its artificial mound. The present building, the Norman keep of c. 1160, was refaced by Salvin in the 1830s; part of it, designed by Soane, was used as the gaol; it has since 1894 been a museum and a very fine art gallery. The most recent addition has been a well-planned central rotunda; the museum has a splendid collection of Norwich School paintings and various collections covering the

archaeology, natural history and other aspects of Norfolk history and life. In fact, one use for some of the churches not needed at present may be to act as museums for certain specialities. One can cross from the museum to the market place by a number of routes—London Street, for example, which has become a pedestrian precinct, or by the Royal Arcade, a splendid entrance in the Art Nouveau style by G. J. Skipper, the prolific local architect. Norwich is most fortunate in its market place, full of stalls, surrounded on one side by the old Guildhall, on another by the modern City Hall, on a third by a great mediaeval church. The Guildhall was built in the 15th century and has a most attractive 16th-century east end with chequerwork. This is at the bottom of St Giles Street, once the medical quarter; along St Giles, there are openings to Pottergate; and occasional vistas like that down Fishers Lane where in line ahead one sees the 15th-century tower of St Lawrence's, the late 17th-century brick tower of St Augustine's, and the little Saxon tower of St Mary Coslany. St Giles is mainly a Georgian street, though it includes A. J. Skipper's Telephone House of 1906, rising up to the church of St Giles, with the churchyard (like the other city churchyards, well kept by the corporation) enclosed by splendid espaliered wistaria. Like most of the other city churches, St Giles' was rebuilt in the prosperous 'Perpendicular' days (the Victorian decorated chancel remedied a 300-year gap due to Dean Gardner's demolitions) and has a lovely, light, open interior with a very early hammerbeam roof (after 600 years the timbers are still in good condition). There are some good brasses, and the brass eagle lectern, formerly in St Gregory's, which was given by William Westbrook in 1493; after the passing of 500 years, the gospel is still read from it at High Mass. At the top of the hill, St Giles is in every sense the Highest

Castle Keep, **Norwich**

church in Norwich; the tower is 120 feet high, too. Just round the corner in Willow Lane is the former *Roman Catholic chapel* (1827, by J. T. Patience), which was actually built before the passing of the Catholic Emancipation Act. It was closed in 1894 when the present church of St John the Baptist was built and became a school until 1969. After ten years of uncertainty and neglect, it is now being restored under the supervision of the Norwich architects, Michael and Sheila Gooch, and will be used as an auc-

tion room. The Roman Catholic church of *St John the Baptist* by George Gilbert Scott and John Oldrid Scott, begun in 1882 and paid for by the 15th Duke of Norfolk, has recently attained cathedral status with the creation of the Roman Catholic diocese of East Anglia. It stands beautifully and is a most imposing building, in a very exact copy of the Early English style. It is rather lifeless inside except for the splendid stained glass by John and Dunstan Powell. Back within the old city

walls there are other old buildings to admire, such as Churchman's House (1750) opposite St Giles' Church, and Holkham House in Cow Hill by Matthew Brettingham, the Norwich architect. Certain parts of the city walls remain by Chapelfield, although the gate shared the fate of the other city gates around 1800. Chapelfield Gardens were the open space belonging to the College of St Mary, which stood near here until the Reformation. The Crescent here consists of nice Regency houses; further on is some of the new housing built since the war. Bethel Street, like St Giles, has some Georgian houses as well as a mental hospital founded in 1713. Going along Bethel Street or along Theatre Street, the central library is passed, built in 1960–2 by David Percival. Close by is the rather Swedish City Hall (1932–8, architects C. H. James & S. R. Pierce) with an imposing façade owing a lot to its position overlooking the market. Across the road from the Library there are the Assembly Rooms, built in 1754 by Thomas Ivory on the site of the College of St Mary-in-the-Fields, which are now used as a restaurant and meeting rooms. This very attractive building, which contains good plaster work, has been a dancing academy and a school. Oliver Messel, on a camouflage course in Norwich during the war, recognized its importance in spite of its dingy state and instigated its rescue. Its full restoration to much valued community use was made possible by the generosity of a local family. The church of *St Peter Mancroft* (correctly dedicated to Saint Peter and Paul) dominates the Market Place and is undoubtedly one of the finest mediaeval churches in the country. It was built in one stage between 1430 and 1455 and thus is entirely Perpendicular. Particular points to notice are the 15th-century font canopy, though this is largely a rebuild of 1887, over the defaced Seven

Norwich: (*above, left*) Norwich Union, and (*above, right*) entrance to the Royal Arcade, both by G. J. Skipper; (*below*) 19th-century warehouse

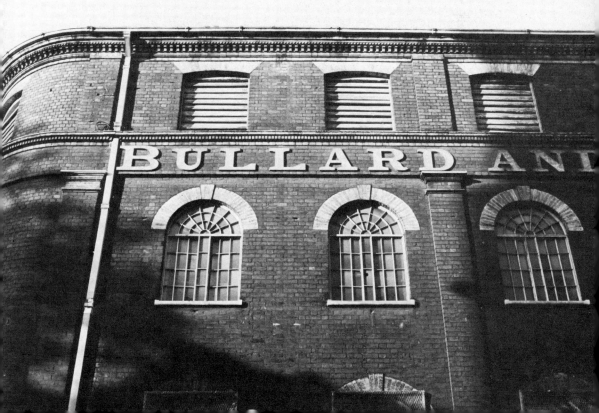

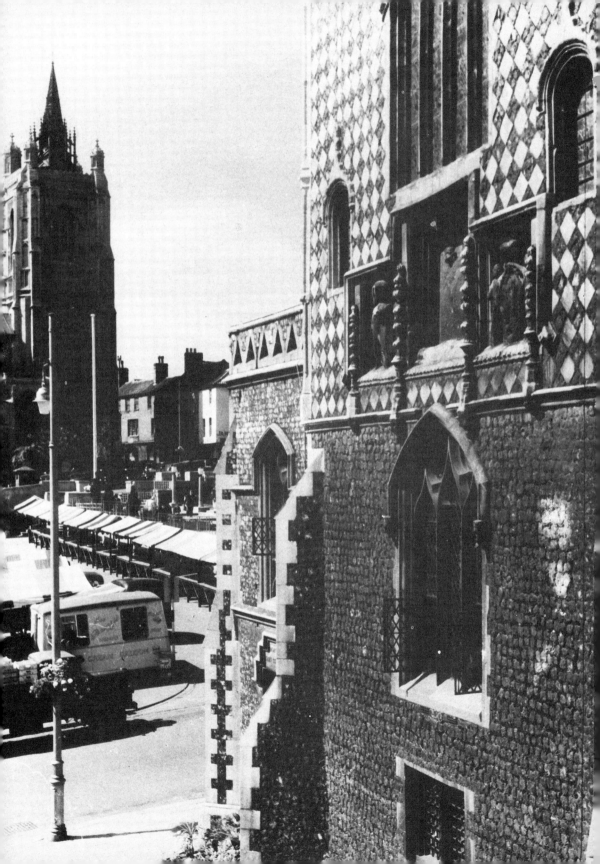

Norwich: (*left*) Market Place with the Guildhall and St Peter Mancroft; (*above*) St Giles; (*below, left*) St Andrews; (*below, right*) St Peter's Hungate

Sacrament font given in 1463, the hammerbeam roof with the hammerbeams concealed by false vaulting (as at Ringland), a considerable collection of the mayoral sword and mace rests so typical of the Norwich churches, and the reredos completed by Comper. The east window is particularly notable, being one of the finest collections of 15th-century glass in the country. The east window of the south aisle has attractive glass by H. Hendrie, 1921. Behind the altar is the sacristy which contains many relics of Mancroft's most famous parishioner, Sir Thomas Browne, who died in 1682. The sacristy is, like Browne's study, 'a cabinet of rarities', with a splendid collection of church plate, and beneath the kindly features of 'the most religious physician' (painted by H. Morland) are early editions of his works. Henry Pegram's statue of Sir Thomas Browne has, since 1905, looked down on the Haymarket, to the south-east of Mancroft. It shows him musing on a broken urn, and it is ironical that Sir Thomas himself suffered that 'Tragical abomination escaped in burning burials' when his skull was 'gnawed out of his grave' by a careless workman digging the grave of Mary Bowman in 1840. It has been put back in its proper place near his neat memorial in the chancel opposite to that of his wife, Dame Dorothy (a bright 'starre of pietye'), which holds the honoured dust of this kindly man who was known in his own age as the devoted practitioner ever solicitous for the welfare of his patients, Norwich's most illustrious citizen, physician, antiquary, poet, philosopher and lay divine, and the writer of a melodious prose in the baroque style unsurpassed in the English tongue. The other church by the Market Place is *St Stephen's*, at the top of Rampant Horse Street; the lowest stage of the tower also serves as the porch, and is the earliest part (14th century) of a building dating mainly from

St Peter Mancroft, **Norwich**

1530–50. Here, too, there is some fine stained glass (15th-century English, 16th-century German from Marianwald in the Ruhr, Victorian and later, including good windows by Kempe, Knowles of York and Alfred Wilkinson) and several good brasses and monuments. Many of the pews still retain the plaques marked FREE, a reminder of the days of rented pews. St Stephen's Street, which until recently was relatively unspoilt, has fallen victim to redevelopment, with a dual carriageway and undistinguished architecture which has no Norwich character. At the top of St Stephen's, Victoria Station once stood, on the site of a 19th-century pleasure garden. It was the terminus of the Eastern Union Railway's line from Ipswich. Relegated to the status of a goods depot about 1910, it remained a goods station though bombed in 1940, until a few years ago; with its domed roof, it was a good example of mid-19th century railway architecture. All Saints Green and Surrey Street

122

intersect each other and have some notable houses; there are still a good number of 18th-century buildings in All Saints Green, including Ivory House and St Catharine's Close, now the B.B.C., and in Surrey Street the Norwich Union building by G. J. Skipper (1903) is interesting outside and has an amazingly lush interior. *All Saints'* and *St John's Churches* (Timberhill) stand in close proximity; the former is now in the care of the Norfolk branch of the Mothers' Union. Its 15th-century font has gone to St Julian's Church. St John's has undergone an interesting rearrangement recently; it contains a fine German chandelier of c. 1500 and another one of about 200 years later; a very good carved and painted reredos and a statue of Our Lady and the Holy Child by Martin Travers. Timberhill remains quite an attractive street. Ber Street, opposite, once known as Blood and Guts Street because of its many slaughterhouses and butchers' shops, is separated from the River Wensum by King Street, where the breweries were. The church of *St Michael at Thorn* has gone, a victim of bombing (although material was reused at Hempton Church and the Norman door is in St Julian's), but a little of *St Bartholomew's*, one of the churches desecrated in the 16th century, survives. At the end of Ber Street stands *St John de Sepulchre*, in a splendid position; its great 15th-century tower a landmark, with a weathervane commemorating the Treaty of Utrecht (1713). Part of the screen is mediaeval, and there are several brasses, one a palimpsest. Quite a lot of recent housing development has gone on around here, particularly between Ber Street and Rouen Road. Continuing out of the city along Bracondale, there are plenty of fine old houses to see until one reaches the vast new County Hall (1968) by Reginald H. Uren and Anthony B. Levy. Between Bracondale and King Street are substantial remains

St Stephen's, **Norwich**

of the old walls, running down to the river by Carrow Hill. King Street has some fine houses spanning the period from the Middle Ages to the 17th century, including the Music House which in part goes back to the 12th century. There are three churches along here. *St Etheldreda's* is closed; it has a Norman tower and some other work of that period; nearby is *St Julian's Church*. Julian of Norwich was an anchoress here in the late 14th century in a cell attached to the chancel, and it was here that she wrote

Revelations of Divine Love, one of the great works of the mediaeval English mystical tradition. The church was damaged by bombs but part of the tower survived, along with much of the original Anglo-Saxon nave and chancel, and it was restored after the war when the Norman doorway from St Michael's at Thorn was inserted to form an entrance into the south chapel, probably on the site of Julian's cell. The 15th-century font recently came here from All Saints' Church. Sisters of the Community

123

of All Hallows, Ditchingham, are based here. *St Peter Parmentergate* is a large 15th-century church (called 'new' in a will of 1486), which has an attractive setting; it has a fine tomb (1623) to Richard and Elizabeth Berney in the chancel, and an interesting 18th-century painting of St Peter with the cock, by the waterman painter Joseph Brown, which may have been part of an earlier reredos. Although the other fittings are of no great merit, it is a good building, but has now been closed for worship. It is down King Street that one realizes that Norwich was a port with a considerable coasting trade, and large boats occasionally come up the Yare and through the swing bridge at Carrow near Carrow Abbey. This is a fine 19th-century house built into the remains of the 16th-century prioress's lodgings. The remains of the Benedictine nunnery, founded in 1146, can be traced in the grounds. Up at the top of Rouen Road is the new (1969) headquarters of the Eastern Counties Newspapers by R. H. Sims and W. J. M. Haines of London, in a fine position looking out to the castle. Much of the old Cattle Market is now a car park. At the top of Prince of Wales Road, built in the mid 19th century to link Thorpe Station with the city centre, is the impressive former Post Office, built as the Crown Bank in 1865. Sir Robert Harvey-Harvey, senior partner in the bank, gambled away much of the bank's money and shot himself in the garden of Crown Point Hall (now Whitlingham Hospital). Soon after this the bank became the Norwich G.P.O. Now this building and the Agricultural Hall (1882) are competently joined together to make the new headquarters for Anglia Television by Feilden & Mawson of Norwich. King Street and the continuation through Tombland and Magdalen Street is the surviving early (possibly Roman) north–south route through the city, and some of the most notable build-

ings in the city come in the next part; Upper King Street emerges into Tombland, the market place of the early city, where George Borrow saw the old men take off their hats to the great trotting horse, Marshland Shales. Behind Queen Street is the church of *St Mary the Less*, which had a colourful history after the Reformation as it was successively the place of worship of the Walloons, Swedenborgians and the Irvingites, but now it is a furniture store and very hard to find. *St George Tombland* stands at the junction with Princes Street, mainly 15th century, having a fine 18th-century pulpit and reredos, and a 17th-century font cover and dole table by the font. Particularly interesting is the early 16th-century sculpted plaque of St George and the Dragon in the north aisle. Princes Street affords an interesting contrast between more of the seemingly inevitable prestige offices on the south side and a splendid sequence of old buildings to the north. By the end is the top of Elm Hill, about the most photographed part of Norwich, with its cobbles and timber-framed houses. It seems amazing that forty years ago much of it was planned for demolition. It was finally saved by the efforts of the very effective conservation group, the Norwich Society, which has played a very important part in influencing the development of Norwich. At the foot of Elm Hill is the church of *Saints Simon and Jude*, now used as a Boy Scout hall but containing three fine Pettus memorials. Among the buildings may be noted the thatched Britons' Arms—now a restaurant—and nearly opposite, the house where Father Ignatius spent two of the most turbulent years of his vigorous life's work of re-founding the Benedictine rule in the Church of England. Back in Tombland facing the cathedral are the 17th-century Samson and Hercules house, which has two extraordinary statues guarding its entrance, and Augustine Steward house (now the Tour-

ist Information Centre), a delightful Tudor building named after the mayor who built it. And now for the cathedral, the most splendid building in the city; the Close may be entered through the tall arch of the Erpingham Gate or beneath the vaulted roof of the Ethelbert Gate, beautifully embellished on the outside with flint flushwork in geometrical designs. The Cathedral Close retains some of its former atmosphere despite the encroachments of the motor car and the conversion into offices of many of the stately 18th-century houses, as well as the Deanery itself built on much of the conventual buildings. In the Upper Close, the 14th-century Grammar School is overlooked by a figure of its most famous pupil, Nelson, who, however, left at the age of 11 to go to the Paston School in North Walsham. This building, now the Chapel of Norwich School, is raised up on a vaulted undercroft, once the enormous charnel vault for all the city churches of Norwich. The Lower Close, quieter and more retired, leads down to Pull's Ferry with its picturesque staithe and archway through which supplies were brought from the river to the cathedral monastery. The *Cathedral Church of the Holy and Undivided Trinity* is one of the most splendid of English cathedrals, sturdily English but, as behoves the great mother church of all East Anglia—'different'. Norwich retains its pulpitum between nave and choir with a beautiful modern organ and organ case upon it. So it remains as a great cathedral church should be, namely two churches; the choir for the capitular body where the worship of God is daily offered; the nave, a great congregational meeting place for all the parishes of the diocese. In the nave and transepts the solid Norman of Bishop Herbert de Losinga's cathedral rises to a superbly beautiful vault where all the colouring of the bosses has been restored—a marvellous series of carvings representing the story of man and his salvation—this won-

Norwich: (*above*) Elm Hill
(*below, left*) Tombland; (*below, right*) The Close

derful roof having been added by Bishops Lyhart and Nix in the 15th and 16th centuries after the destruction of its predecessor by fire. In the choir are the lovely stalls, justly described as some of the best in the world, and, beyond, the Norman presbytery retains its apsidal shape with the altar standing in the chord of the apse with the ancient bishop's throne directly behind. Norwich is the only cathedral north of the Alps to retain this primitive arrangement, largely because there was no popular local cultus to displace it. Above the presbytery is Bishop Goldwell's soaring clerestory rising to a vaulted roof which, like Bourges and Beauvais, leaves one amazed at the beauty, originality and structural daring of the Gothic age. A great Gothic cathedral is like a forest glade in stone, and especially so at Norwich with this tremendous vault held in place by the immense trunks of the flying buttresses which have made this cathedral famous and which look, as Percy Lubbock said with regard to another great Gothic church, like enormous handles by which some giant descending from the skies might lift the whole edifice into the air. Norwich Cathedral is famous also for the spire, second only to Salisbury in height. Present-day problems of structural repair have revealed the abandon of the 13th-century builders who put such a thing on top of a Norman tower that was never intended to carry it. But the fact that it *has* carried it, and after extensive restoration, will continue to carry it for centuries to come, shows how wonderfully and with what a huge margin of strength the Normans built. Like any great Gothic church, Norwich Cathedral does not reveal itself all at once but leads one on from room to room. In the north ambulatory is the reliquary bridge, now housing a collection of church plate drawn from all over the diocese (another collection is in the Castle Museum). Going round the east

end are two rounded Norman chapels, St Luke's on the south side having a 15th-century Seven-Sacrament font—for it serves as the parish church for the Lower Close. At the east end is a 20th-century addition in St Saviour's chapel which contains magnificent panels with figure paintings (c. 1380–1440) brought from the church of St Michael-at-Plea. The reredos in St Luke's chapel is a great treasure of mediaeval art known as the Norwich Retable, and the Bauchun chapel of Our Lady (once used as the Consistory Court) has a magnificent vaulted roof. The mediaeval stone altar of the Jesus Chapel is still in use, whilst under the crossing is a Flemish pelican lectern c. 1450. Then on the south side of the nave come the cloisters, the biggest in England. Beginning with the east walk and going round, one sees in the changing window tracery the development of the Gothic style during the 13th and 14th centuries. Against the south wall are some rather garish poster-like coats of arms, being a restoration of the armorial achievements of the descendants of those courtiers who waited upon Queen Elizabeth I when she dined there in 1578. The monuments of Norwich Cathedral are neither so numerous nor impressive as might be expected. Bishop Goldwell has a fine canopied tomb beneath his glorious vaulted choir, Dean Fairfax is commemorated in the nave with a fine wall tablet by William Stanton. The works of the Norwich sculptors of the 18th century are well represented in mural tablets in all parts of the building, and in the north transept the brooding and bewigged figure of Bishop Bathurst (1805–37) is the latest work of Sir Francis Chantrey. There is a particularly attractive and colourful 17th-century memorial near the high altar to Bishop Overall (the author of the second part of the Catechism), erected by his *secretarius domesticus*, John Cosin, a Norwich boy who was to become

Bishop of Durham; and just opposite, a chaste memorial to Bishop George Horne (1792). In the north transept is a rare memorial to a bishop's secretary, Bishop Pollock's 'Sweetest Vi' (Violet Morgan), by Derwent Wood, 1921. South-east of the cathedral, past the grave of Nurse Edith Cavell, the Close continues down to the river with very attractive houses of all dates; little 16th-century cottages, fine 18th-century houses, and Victorian ones. After heading north across Fye Bridge one comes to Magdalen Street, with *St Clement's Church* where Matthew Parker Queen Anne Boleyn's confessor and her daughter Elizabeth's Archbishop of Canterbury, was rector. Magdalen Street still has some good houses but has been ruined by the flyover for the Inner Link Road and gross shopping development, in spite of being one of the first places to have a Civic Trust face-lift in 1958. But there are still nice old yards and courts leading off the street, including Gurney Court where Elizabeth Fry and Harriet Martineau were born in a fine old house. Along Colegate however, the picture is brighter with energetic efforts being made at conservation and *mirabile dictu*, new housing. For it is residential accommodation that the city needs in order to live, and Friars' Quay and other new building is a sign that Coslany ('over the water') and other parts of Norwich are moving in the right direction. In Colegate the mediaeval and the Georgian jostle each other, and here are four of the most interesting buildings in Norwich. The 17th-century *Old Meeting House*; John Ivory's super *Octagon chapel* (1754–6), called by John Wesley 'the most elegant Meeting House in Europe', but by other clergymen 'the devil's cucumber frame'; *St George's Colegate*, a fine 15th-century church in which John Crome lies buried, still furnished in the classical and wainscotted style of his time, with the recent addition of a copy of

pp. 128, 129: **Norwich** Cathedral
nave; *pp. 130, 131:* Cathedral
from the west and from the east ▷

Dali's greatest work a happy centre
to the reredos. And then the lofty
west tower (bequests in the 1420s)
and the marvellous flushwork in
flint and stone (the chancel work a
fine Victorian copy of the Thorpe
Chantry) of *St Miles-in-Coslany* is a
fitting end to the street. Here is
good conservation of old houses, as
well as interesting new development. *St Mary's Coslany* has a pre-
Conquest round tower (the rest is
15th century) and contains a
memorial to one of John Crome's
most famous pupils, the Revd E. T.
Daniel, who died at Adalia in Asia
Minor in 1843; and in St Augustine's with its 17th-century brick
tower lies Matthew Brettingham,
the Norwich architect. In *St Augustine's* parish are the restored cottages of the Gildencroft, a quiet
corner that was once the city's Jew-
ish quarter, and where there is also
a Quaker burial ground where
Elizabeth Fry's relations were
buried. On the other side of Magdalen Street development is taking
place, and, as elsewhere, there are
disused churches: *St Saviour's*, *St
Edmund's in Fishergate*, and *St James
in Pockthorpe*, now a successful puppet theatre. This much-loved
church was closed in 1969 and
some of its fittings can be seen in *St
Mary Magdalene's* (1903), at the top
of the hill in Silver Road; these
include some mediaeval English
and 16th/17th-century Continental
glass, a fine 14th-century font with
a gallery of saints round the bowl
and stem and the mediaeval screen
panels (money was left to paint
them in 1479) with saints, including Zita, Blide and Walstan. Along
Barrack Street, Cow Tower is the
finest of the towers on the old wall,
by the sharp bend in the river;
further along is the 14th-century
Bishop Bridge. Do not cross the

Norwich; north-east door into the cloister, detail

127

bridge, but turn left up the hill to Rosary Road; almost at the Thorpe Road end is the little Gothic lodge of the Rosary cemetery, opened as a speculation in 1819 where persons of all denominations might be decently buried. It is a lovely place, with beautiful trees and fascinating monuments; one, a portrait bust in a Gothic canopy, commemorates

John Barker, a steam circus proprietor accidentally killed on Norwich Market, April 1897, and there is a headstone for Arthur Cupper, locomotive engine driver who died in an accident at Thorpe (Norwich) Station in 1889. Much Norwich history is here, and it has an elegance lacking in the large municipal cemetery. Over Bishop Bridge one

comes to the Great Hospital founded by Walter de Suffield in 1249. This is the most extraordinary and fascinating building in Norwich; originally a hospital and almshouse for poor priests and laymen, *St Helen's Church* is at its centre, and there is a charming little cloister of 1450. At the Reformation the chancel of the church with its wonderful roof painted with 252 black eagles, was divided horizontally into two wards, as was the western part of the church. The middle remains, with the parish altar in the south transept beneath a magnificent lierne vault embellished with gorgeous bosses. Behind the altar is a Georgian reredos, and opposite it a Gothic pew, the work of the Ivory family who also built the Georgian house across the courtyard. Bishopgate widens out into Palace Plain with the church of *St Martin-at-Palace*; there is still some Saxon work in its chancel, around which a battle raged at the time of Kett's revolt. A tablet on a nearby house marks the place where many men were slain. On Palace Plain is the fine entrance to the Bishop's House, a building in the Georgian style by James Fletcher-Watson, 1959. The great 13th-century portico stands in the garden; nearby is a lovely chapel with 14th-century windows, reconstructed after the Restoration by Bishop Reynolds, author of the General Thanksgiving. The old Bishop's Palace, now part of the Norwich School, is by Ewan Christian, 1858–9. Norwich has some of the best parks and open spaces of any city, exceptionally well designed and maintained by the Corporation, who also look after the churchyards. The roundabouts on the ring road are prettily

planted and admired even by those who hate municipal gardening. The diarist Evelyn, visiting Sir Thomas Browne in 1671, remarked on 'the flower gardens which all the inhabitants excel in'. George Borrow, more than 200 years later, called Norwich a fine old city, and said that her children 'are proud of her and offer up prayers for her prosperity'. Finding a place to offer up prayers is not as easy as it was, but Norwich people are still rightly very proud of their city; much has been lost, of course, but good things have been added, too; and it still has its own very strong character.

Outside and inside
St Miles-in-Coslany,
Norwich

Overstrand Hall

Old Hunstanton *see* Hunstanton, Old

Ormesby [12] A seaside village with caravan camps along the shore; some nice 18th- and 19th-century houses. There are two churches. St Margaret's, which has a 15th-century tower (1492) with flint flushwork and a tomb recess in the chancel; and St Michael's, recently restored and given a thatched porch, mainly 14th century, with a simple 15th-century arch-braced roof, with bosses recently recoloured. Several of the Pilgrim Fathers came from here. To the north are Scratby Hall (c. 1750 with additions) and a few cot-tages; to the west are the peaceful Ormesby and Rollesby Broads; Ormesby Hall is a Georgian house with Gothic additions of 1810.

Oulton [4] A small village having a 13th-century church dedicated to St Peter and St Paul with later additions. Traces of a wall painting survive. On the road to Ittering-ham is a pleasant little 18th-century Congregational chapel, retaining many original fittings; the chapel is charmingly grouped with the former minister's house. These Nonconformist places of worship are as vulnerable as the churches and every effort must be made to save them.

Outwell [7] Lord Orford sailed with a fleet of nine ships through Outwell and Upwell in 1774 and described them as 'populous towns'. There are delightful houses on either side of the River Ouse, and the large church of St Clement, with 13th-century tower, looks very fine beside the river. There is some 16th-century stained glass, and 18th-century wrought-iron gates.

Overstrand [5] St Martin's Church, which contains interesting 19th-century memorials to the Buxton family, including the Liberator, was largely rebuilt in 1911. There are two interesting houses by Sir Edwin Lutyens, the Pleasaunce (1897) and the Hall (1899). The Hall was built for Lord Hillingdon and is now a convales-cent home, the Pleasaunce is a holiday home owned by Christian Endeavour, but was built for Lady Battersea who was born a Rothschild.

Ovington [9] St John the Evangel-ist's Church has a Norman door-way and a 14th-century font which was once in Watton Church nearby.

Oxborough [8] *Oxburgh Hall* is the most exciting mediaeval house in Norfolk. Built of brick in 1482 by Sir Edmund Bedingfeld, it sits squarely round a courtyard sur-rounded by a rectangular moat, a Catholic fortress in these Protes-tant parts, because neither at the Reformation nor since have mem-bers of the Bedingfeld family (who happily still live there) altered their faith. Inside the magnificent Gate Tower, and shown to the public, is the King's Chamber, where Henry VII stayed. There are exquisite hangings embroidered by Mary Queen of Scots and Bess of Hard-wick (Elizabeth, Countess of Shrewsbury, wife of the Queen's custodian). The embroidered panels show very attractive animals based on contemporary woodcuts, and mottoes referring to

he two embroideresses. There is a Roman Catholic church by A. W. N. Pugin (1835) in the gardens, with interesting furnishings and glass; but the superb terracotta tombs of the Bedingfelds are, with other good monuments, in a chapel attached to the parish church of St John the Evangelist. The church itself, consisting of chancel only, has some 15th-century glass. The steeple fell in 1948 and destroyed the nave; luckily it missed the Bedingfeld Chapel entirely.

Oxnead [11] Only one wing remains of the splendid mansion where Charles II and Queen Catherine of Braganza were magnificently entertained in 1671 by Robert Paston, first Earl of Yarmouth. Traces of the gardens and terraces can be seen near the bank of the Bure, and in St Michael's Church is a bust of Lady Katherine Paston (1636) by Nicholas Stone. In the sanctuary is a table tomb with effigy of Clement Paston (1597). The great estates of this senior branch of the Pastons were sold after the second Earl's death and largely acquired by Lord Anson, the circumnavigator.

Oxwick [3] This hamlet, now part of Colkirk, has a small ruined church (All Saints), probably 14th century.

Palling see Sea Palling

Panxworth [11] The mediaeval tower of All Saints' Church is an attractive landmark. The nave, rebuilt in 1847 by James Watson, is now closed and the prey of vandals and, if 'no acceptable alternative use' can be found—and this seems likely—it will be demolished except for the tower.

Paston [5] The original seat of the Paston family was here. There is a

Oxburgh: (*above*) Hall; (*below*) Bedingfield tomb ▷

Ranworth screen

fine thatched barn (1581) built by Sir William Paston. St Margaret's Church (also thatched) contains some wall paintings including the Three Living and Three Dead. Nicholas Stone designed monuments to Dame Katherine Paston (1629) and her husband, Sir Edmund; the wording on Dame Katherine's tomb is said to have been written by John Donne. Stained glass window (1917) in the south of the nave shows a naval destroyer of the period.

Pentney [8] Amongst meadows and woods is a wayside cross and a flint gatehouse, sole remnant of the 12th-century priory of Augustinian Canons. The church has fragments of Norman arcading.

Pickenham, North [9] The much-restored church of St Andrew has a nice window by Powell, 1864. The north transept is old, but the rest of the church was rebuilt by D. Male in 1863.

Pickenham, South [9] The round-towered 13th-century church dedicated to All Saints has a wall painting and painted frieze below the roof, organ case by Pugin (originally at West Tofts) and a Jacobean pulpit from Stoke Edith in Herefordshire. The church has an attractive setting and is particularly well cared for. The Hall, built in 1829 by Donthorne, was replaced in 1903 by a house by Weir Schultz.

Plumstead [4] (by Holt) A very small village with a few brick and flint cottages and farmhouse gathered round St Michael' Church, which contains a pleasing little memorial to Theophila Fleming (1723) and a royal arms board for Elizabeth II.

The **Plumsteads** [11] (by Norwich) *Great Plumstead* St Mary has tower of 1711 and most of the rest was rebuilt in 1875. Plumstead Hall, 1889, is now a hospital and but it is *Little Plumstead* church, the only one in England dedicated to Saint Gervase and Protase. The round tower may be Saxon and most of the rest is Norman.

Poringland [11] Used to consist of a long street, but the village has been spoilt by haphazard growth. The round-towered All Saints Church has no aisles and yet there are clerestory windows on both sides of the nave. There is some 15th-century glass in the east window and an Italian triptych over the Lady Altar. The White House at the end of the village, is the residence of the R.C. Bishop of East Anglia.

Postwick [11] The church has been well restored; some of the nave may be 11th century. There is good 13th-century piscina and an interesting font.

Potter Heigham [12] The yachting centre has created a new village near the bridge over the Thurne. The old village nearly a mile to the north has a mainly 14th-century church with a circular tower and 15th-century belfry. There is painted screen and some wall paintings including the Seven Works of Mercy; the mediaeval rood beam remains but the really unique feature is the 15th-century brick font. A local garage proprietor, Sidney Grapes, who died 1958, wrote superb letters in dialect signed 'The Boy John', which appeared in the *Eastern Daily Press* and were later collected and published as small books.

Rushford church and college

Pudding Norton [3] A hamlet whose church—*St Mary's*—was 'dilapidated' before 1602; all that remains of it now is part of the tower, with a top like a broken tooth, and a base worn into hollows by cattle. At the end of a fine avenue is Pudding Norton Hall, an old house refronted and rendered; with, unusually, a clock in the south wall, facing the farmyard.

The **Pulhams** [16, 17] Two very attractive villages in the Waveney Valley. *Pulham Market* (or Pulham St Mary Magdalene) is a village of plaster and colour-washed houses with high-pitched roofs surrounding a wide green. The 15th-century church has been rather tastelessly restored, but there is an arch-braced roof in the north aisle. The adjoining parish to the east, *Pulham St Mary the Virgin*, is a smaller township with the houses standing among a grove of trees. In the middle of the village stands Pennoyer's School, in which one of the classrooms is built inside the old 15th-century Guild Chapel of St James, very similar to the Chapel of St Thomas à Becket at Wymondham. An avenue of limes leads down to the church, which stands high above the roadway. It is a magnificent 15th-century building very well restored by G. F. Bodley. There is a splendid south porch with the Annunciation in the spandrels and, under canopies, angels with musical instruments. Bodley's restored screen, organ case and font cover are excellent. There is much 15th-century glass. Arms for Charles I. At the northern extremity of the straggling parish of Pulham Market is the Manor Farm, which is an excellent example of the way in which an old 17th-century building was rescued from a state of almost complete decay and restored, retaining all its old features for no greater cost than an entirely new house.

Quarles [3] 'Chantrey Hills' here are named in memory of the place where the sculptor, Sir Francis Chantrey, killed two woodcock with one shot. The woodcock have a marble monument at Holkham Hall, made by Chantrey himself.

Quidenham [16] The church has a Saxon round tower with 15th-century belfry and spire. It has been heavily restored within. There is a poorbox of 1639 with three locks. Quidenham Hall is mainly Georgian with later additions and is now a Carmelite monastery. It was formerly the seat of the Keppels, Earls of Albemarle.

Rackheath [11] The early Victorian Hall was the home of the Stracey family, whose 19th-century monuments with 17th- and 18th-century Pettus memorials adorn the early 14th-century All Saints' Church. There are nice quatrefoil clerestory windows, and the charm of the church lies also in its surrounding landscape and its interesting churchyard. The church is redundant, though valiant efforts are being made to revive it, with the help of the parish and of the American Pettuses. There is also a mission church in the new development in the village, a rather stark place, by H. Truman, built in 1959. The rectory, on the Norwich road, is an early work (1911) in the arts and crafts tradition of Cecil Upcher, a well-known Norfolk architect—very attractive.

Ranworth [11] St Helen's Church has what is probably the finest rood screen in England, with beautiful figure painting, particularly the glorious figures of St George and St Michael on the projecting wings, one of the most remarkable examples in England of the work of

138

Raynham Hall

the mediaeval artist, dating from c. 1450. The 'Sarum Antiphoner', probably given to the church in 1478 by William Cobbe, was removed about 1550, and bought back in 1912; it is a splendid piece of illumination. Near the screen is a 15th-century lectern used by cantors, with mediaeval texts painted on it. The chancel roof was thatched until it caught fire in 1963; mercifully no damage was done to the interior. From the top of the tower one gets a magnificent view. The Old Hall, of about 1600, was built by the Holdich family and later passed by marriage to the Sidleys. The wild Colonel Sidley vanished here, summoned from a party by a stranger said to be the Devil, on a stormy night in 1770.

aveningham [18] The Hall, ome of the Bacons, premier Baronets of England, is Georgian with additions, and contains a fine collection of pictures including watercolours by Cotman, Turner, Cozens, Girtin etc., not normally shown but frequently lent to exhibitions. The Bacons inherited the estate from the Castells who were here from Henry III's reign. St Andrew's church in the park has a large marble monument to Major Edward Hodge, killed at Waterloo.

The **Raynhams** [3] *East*, *South* and *West Raynham* lie around the park of Lord Townshend's splendid house, red brick with stone dressings built early in the 17th century by Sir Roger Townshend, the design being variously attributed to Inigo Jones, Roger Pratt or, as seems equally likely, to Townshend himself and William Edge, his master mason, who is buried in *South Raynham* churchyard. The inside is authentic Kent. *East Raynham* St Mary's Church in the park was rebuilt in 1868 (architects Clark & Holland) and retains from the earlier church a most opulent Easter Sepulchre willed by the widow of Sir Roger Townshend in 1499. Townshend family pew and good carved arms. *South Raynham* St Martin is unspoilt. Victorian text over the door, some Victorian glass, and a 13th-century altar slab. *West Raynham* church has been disused since the 18th century.

Redenhall [17] In the 15th-century church of St Mary the family chapel of demolished Gawdy Hall contains an 18th-century monument, and there are others, of the 17th and 18th centuries, in the nave. The imposing tower with octagonal buttresses and much flushwork (rather in the Suffolk style) was built between 1460 and 1520, and there is a

139

mediaeval brass lectern with, uniquely, a double-headed eagle; the font is probably a very good Victorian copy of the 15th-century Norfolk style, with the Instruments of the Passion and the Five Wounds of Christ. A most interesting church.

Reedham [12] In wide, watery scenery. St John the Baptist's Church was gutted by fire in 1981; most creditably, restoration work started immediately. The 15th-century tower was being built in 1466 when Margaret Paston gave 8s 4d towards it.

Reepham [10] Parson Woodforde did his shopping (as did Whitwell Elwin a century later) in this mellow brick town which gives the impression of an 18th-century prosperity not yet passed away. In the market place is a fine brewery house with sundial, built in 1729, and subsequently acquired by the Birchams, who owned it until 1972. It is now a restaurant and hotel. The two churches of Reepham and Whitwell are joined by a passage from the chancel of Whitwell to the nave of the larger church of Reepham. The stone cross with figures built into the west pillar of the north arcade marks the place where the parish boundaries of Whitwell, Hackford and Reepham meet—doubtless the reason for the unique situation of three parish churches in adjoining churchyards. *Reepham* St Mary has a very fine canopied tomb in the chancel showing a knight in full armour—probably William, second Lord Kerdeston, who died in 1361—lying on a bed of pebbles. There is also a fine brass to Sir William de Kerdeston (son of William the Elder) and his wife Cecily, 1391. Stained glass by O'Connor, c. 1870. *Whitwell* St Michael has a tower for which money was left in 1441 and a good Jacobean pulpit. The nave is used for community purposes, whilst the chancel is still furnished and used for worship—a commendable

solution to the problem of what might have been considered a redundant church. *Hackford* church was destroyed in a fire of 1543; the tower was demolished in 1790 and there are slight remains to the south-west of Whitwell church. *Kerdiston* contains the site of the manor house of the Kerdeston family, and of a church nearby.

Repps-cum-Bastwick [12] St Peter's Church has a Norman round tower with a fine 13th-century top; the brick chancel is a 19th-century rebuild. Bastwick Church has been a ruin since the late Middle Ages.

Reymerston [10] A scattered village whose church, St Peter's, approached by an avenue, dates mainly from the 13th century. There are an imposing 17th-century three-decker pulpit, box pews, a Jacobean poorbox, and 17th-century Flemish altar rails. There is 16th-century Flemish glass in the east window. The Old Hall was built in 1620, and the present Reymerston Hall is Georgian.

Riddlesworth [15] The Hall is of white brick and was built by Thomas Leverton in 1792. It is now a school. It was burnt in 1900 and rebuilt to the same design by J. H. Green. St Peter's Church beside it in the park has a good wrought-iron weathercock on its little tower. Inside is a fine monument to Sir Dru Drury (1617) with angels holding back the curtains round his kneeling figure. Notice the floor slab inscriptions. The present chancel was probably added at the 1856 restoration; there is a Jacobean pulpit and royal arms of Charles I from the ruined church at Knettishall, just over the Suffolk border.

Ridlington [5] Scattered in a bleak district; St Peter's Church has a 13th-century font and a 15th-century tower.

Ringland [10] An attractive village with its street rising up towards the magnificent St Peter's Church containing a fine single hammerbeam roof with the hammerbeams themselves enclosed in vaulting. The glass, mainly in the clerestory windows, is mostly mid 15th century and includes whole figures of the Virgin and Child, the Holy Trinity, St John the Baptist and the Annunciation. Screen base with painted figures. To judge by the iron-bound door, the 13th-century tower was once the village strongroom. Ringland Hills, the heathland above the village, gives a broad view of the Wensum valley.

Ringstead [2] From the village a grass road leads to Ringstead Downs, a valley with steep chalk sides covered with short grass, at the end of which, still quite unspoilt, is one of the prettiest places in the county, Barrett Ringstead Farm, with an old house of brick and timber barns, and a chalybeate spring which bubbles through a rusty old pipe into a pond fringed by ash trees. It looks (except for the TV aerial) like an 18th-century picture. Ringstead has one much-restored church, St Andrew, and the remains of another, St Peter.

Rockland All Saints [15] (near Attleborough) All Saints' Church has considerable remains of pre Conquest long-and-short work at the west end of the nave and a very ancient (also probably pre Conquest) sepulchral slab which has been reused as a gravestone for a Mr Mansfield. *Rockland St Peter's* Church has a round tower and small transepts; and the remains of the screen have been re-erected at the west end. The Jacobean pulpit and reader's desk, mediaeval screen and splendid benches came from Tottington, in the Military Training Area. In this peaceful place, it is difficult to envisage that two mediaeval incumbents of All Saints were imprisoned, one for breaking and entering; and that in 1608, Leonard James, the rector of Rocklands St Peter, was murdered by his curate, Lowe, with the connivance of James's wife, for which crime Lowe was drawn and hanged and his mistress burnt ('consumed to ashes', as a contemporary account puts it). St Andrew's Church, near All Saints', is a ruin.

Rockland St Mary [11] An attractive village whose church is on a rise above farm buildings. It has a 15th-century font with restored and painted figures on the stem. Once there were two churches in the churchyard—some of St Margaret's still remains to the east of St Mary's.

Rollesby [12] As so often with the Broads, one has no knowledge of their existence until one is actually on them, and here the main road to Yarmouth passes between two of the largest of them—Ormesby and Rollesby Broads—but affording only a glimpse of either on the bridge between. The round-towered church of St George, mainly 14th century, has a curious cubicle in the south-east corner of the chancel and an interesting monument to Rose Claxton (1601): Her Bewtye Love and Gracefull modestye in her freinds hartes shall yve eternallye. Her Soule redeemed from sinns captivitye in Heaven lyves crownd wth immorallitye.' Porch of 1496.

Roudham [15] Is a small Breckland village. The ruined St Andrew's Church, a landmark to travellers on the railway, was in use until about 1740 when a workman repairing the tower knocked out the ashes from his pipe onto the thatched roof.

Rougham [9] A neat village. An avenue of trees, whose planting is mentioned in John Evelyn's diary, lead up to the Hall (reduced from its original size but dating from 1693 onwards). Since the 17th cen-

tury it has been the seat of the North family, by whom St Mary's Church has been excellently restored. There is a rare stone rood over the west door and under the tower an engraved set of the Ten Commandments and a mediaeval altar stone. There are many good brasses and on the south side of the chancel wood carving which once formed part of a larger memorial to a vicar who died in 1499. In the churchyard, notice the aeroplane depicted on the gravestone of Thomas Keppel North (d. 1919), who was the Superintendent of Vickers and designed the first aeroplane to cross the Atlantic Ocean.

Roughton [5] The gaunt tower of a windmill rehabilitated by local Boy Scouts and Girl Guides stands on Roughton Heath from which runs the long village street to St Mary's Church, which has a fine Saxon round tower.

Roydon [16] (near Diss) A Suffolk-like village with much new housing. St Remigius' Church has a round tower with an octagonal top copied from Rickinghall Inferior in Suffolk, put there c. 1850 by G. E. Frere, who also rebuilt the south aisle in 1864. Unusual window on the north side of the nave, said to have been put in to give more light to the rood. Much-altered royal arms. Nice 15th-century porch, and a Jacobean pulpit.

Roydon [8] (near Lynn) The village straggles round a large green with willows and a duck pond. All Saints' Church was rebuilt by G. E. Street in 1857 in what was, for him, uncharacteristic Norman style, keeping two original Norman doorways.

The **Rudhams** [3] *East Rudham* is the larger of the two villages and has a wide green surrounded by many well-proportioned 18th-century houses and shops. On the

gateposts of the house usually occupied by the local vet are two charming foxes. St Mary's Church was much rebuilt in 1876 when the tower collapsed and destroyed a good deal of the nave. The 14th-century porch has a good vaulted roof. There is a Norman pillar piscina with interlacing on the cap and some fragments of alabaster, probably from a reredos. The more interesting of the two churches, *West Rudham* St Peter, is mainly 13th–14th century, but there is evidence that an earlier 12th-century aisle was extended during the later work, when the unusual windows with attached shafts were put there. Most curious 13th-century arcade with an additional half-bay at the west end with carving; at the east end of the arcade, a strange recess, possibly the site of a heart burial, or a shrine. Arch-braced nave roof with carving, and grotesque carving on corbels in aisle, traditionally supposed to be Henry VIII, Jane Seymour and Edward VI. Late Georgian screen and doorway under tower. 17th-century benches with poppy-heads. Some beautiful stained glass (c. 1430–40), recently exhibited at the Victoria & Albert Museum, is at present stored, hopefully awaiting replacement. The most interesting figure is Christ displaying His wounds. This church was closed for some years and is currently undergoing restoration. It will be maintained by the Norfolk Churches Trust and used for occasional services.

Runcton, North [8] Once a very pretty village, now a dormitory suburb of Lynn. Still some interesting 17th/18th-century houses, though the Hall, largely rebuilt by Anthony Salvin and standing in a pretty park, has been demolished. However, nothing can diminish the attraction of its classical church, All Saints, finished in 1713 by Henry Bell, replacing the former church whose tower fell on 15 August 1701 and irreparably damaged the remainder ('beaten down flat to the ground' runs the contemporary record). The influence of Wren is evident. Notice the big Ionic columns and domed vault, and the elegant tower with spirelet and corner urns. The reredos contains Florentine paintings set in a surround designed by Bell for St Margaret's, Lynn, in 1684, which came here in 1901. Many monuments to the family of Daniel Gurney (Elizabeth Fry's youngest brother) who owned the Hall, including one with a long poem written to his bride by William Cowper, son of Lady Palmerston.

Runcton, South [8] A small village with a Norman revival church, St Andrew's, by John Brown of Norwich, 1839, which incorporated some genuine Norman work.

Runcton Holme [7] Is a pretty, unsophisticated village with trees and St James's Church, with Norman tower and doorway, a Jacobean pulpit and 15th-century screen.

Runhall [10] A small village having a round-towered church, All Saints, without a chancel. Victorian text over the altar. Important early wrought-iron work on the door.

Runham [12] This small village looks over much Broadland and St Peter and St Paul's Church has a Perpendicular tower (c. 1501). After a period of closure, it is hoped to reopen it.

The **Runtons** [5] The caravan sites in these villages provide an opportunity for people to enjoy the excellent beaches and pretty commons. On the coast road, the Village Inn next to *West Runton* church is by Temple Moore. Holy Trinity Church is in a mixture of styles and has some mediaeval glass in the chancel. There is a little Victorian school under the railway viaduct in *East Runton* which has been reconstructed as a church. The charm of these villages is their large greens with streams and ducks. Runton Old Hall is a nice Jacobean building, and on the road inland there is a charming 18th-century farmhouse.

Rushall [16] Attractive village with several pleasant houses. Round tower (possibly Saxon) to St Mary's Church, unusual prayer desk, and two 13th-century lancets in the east wall of the chancel.

Rushford [5] Here is a college, founded in 1342 by Edmund Gonville, with two sides of its quadrangle and some old windows. St John the Evangelist's Church faces it with a noble tower. The whole place is attractive and unexpected. Shadwell Park was rebuilt by Teulon in 1857–60 for the Buxton family who had owned it since the 16th century. Rushford Hall stands across the river in Suffolk, but the parish now includes Snarehill House, formerly extra-parochial.

Ryburgh, Great [3] The village is built on a long street and has a most interesting church, St Andrew's. The lower part of the round tower is Saxon, topped by a 14th-century belfry; the most unusual feature is that the body of the church is cruciform, nearly a Greek cross, with a short nave and long transepts. There is a good modern screen to the south transept; the church was restored by Comper in 1912 and is beautifully kept. Note memorial to Fr F. H. Tatham.

Ryston [7] The Hall and the church are close together in the park. St Michael's Church has a 14th-century east window and priests' door; neo-Norman tower of 1858. Sir Roger Pratt, the squire, one of the pioneers of Renaissance architecture in England, built the Hall between 1663 and 1672 but not much of his work survives. It was altered for his descendant, Edward Pratt, by Sir John Soane in 1784, and again later. It still belongs to this family.

Saham Toney [9] The tree-surrounded mere is one of the most attractive in Breckland. The red-brick Georgian rectory has connections with New College, Oxford the patrons of the living; the Fellows have memorials in St George's Church, which has 15th-century woodwork and a grand tower (c. 1490). St George fights the dragon in the spandrels of the west door, and there is a fine canopied niche in the porch. The font cover was given by John Ives in 1632. The neo-Georgian Hall was recently destroyed by fire.

Salhouse [11] A scattered village above a Broad bordered with trees All Saints' Church has an hour glass stand on its 17th-century pulpit and, most unusual, a sanctuary bell above the screen. The Hall was built c. 1860–70.

Sall or **Salle** (pronounced as in *Saul*) [4] Is a very small village with the most glorious church (dedicated to St Peter and St Paul) in the county, whose size is due to the munificence of the great local families, the Briggs, Fountaine and Boleyns. The soaring west tower, 111 feet high, dominates the countryside. Feathered angel swing censers in the spandrels c the west doorway. Inside, a grea feeling of spaciousness and change lessness—no drastic restoration here. Seven-Sacrament font with contemporary pinnacled cover suspended by a beam and pulley in the tower gallery. Two-storied porches to both aisles; that on the north was a chapel and has fin re-coloured bosses. The slender columns of the nave rise to a soaring clerestory and arch-braced roof, like so much of this church textured by time. The 15th-century pulpit was made into a three decker in 1611, and there are many old benches. The transepts and

chancel keep their old roofs, too, the latter having most wonderful carved bosses of the Life of Christ. Excellent 15th-century glass, particularly part of the nine orders of angels in the chancel and figures of donors in the south transept. Fine Victorian Jesse window in north transept by Heasman. The base of the 15th-century screen backs on to traceried return stalls fitted with misericordes, and there are some good brasses. A magnificent church, epitomizing the finest things that the 15th century could provide. Salle Park was built in 1761 by Edward Hase and continued in his Jodrell descendants until acquired at the end of the 19th century by the White family, who still own it. Ann Boleyn's ghost is said to walk Bullen's Lane.

Salthouse [4] Has suffered many inundations from the sea, the most terrible of which was on 31 January 1953. The church of St Nicholas is a magnificent example of the very late 15th-century style and was

built by Sir Henry Heydon of Baconsthorpe Castle between 1497 and 1503. His wife was Anne, daughter of Geoffrey Boleyn, Lord Mayor of London; hence the arms of Heydon impaling Boleyn above the arches of the south arcade. On the mutilated screen (1513) are figures of the apostles. On the backs of the parclose screens are mitred 'Ns' for St Nicholas, together with crude drawings of the sort of ships that inattentive choir boys in the 17th century would have seen in Salthouse Mayne Channel, for Salthouse was once a port with access into the Glaven estuary near the Cley haven.

Sandringham [2] This spick and span estate was bought in 1861 for King Edward VII, then Prince of Wales, by his mother Queen Victoria. On the whole it is sandy heathland (hence the name, originally Sand Dersingham) with conifers and silver birches, and there is also marshland and arable farmland. At the main entrance to San-

dringham House, note the Norwich Gates, good wrought-iron designed by Thomas Jekyll, made in Norwich by Barnard, Boulton & Barnard, and given to the Prince of Wales (Edward VII) as a wedding present by the County of Norfolk. The present Sandringham House was enlarged by Colonel Edis (who later built the Great Central Hotel in London); many of these additions have now been pulled down. The house was bought from Mr Spencer Cowper, whose wife, Lady Harriet, was the daughter of Lord Blessington and had been the wife of Count Alfred d'Orsay, who had been her stepmother's lover. After much private unhappiness, Lady Harriet spent many years in charitable works, including the establishment at Sandringham of an orphanage for the children of soldiers who had fallen in the Crimean War. Outside the royal stables is a life-size bronze statue of Persimmon who won the Derby in 1896 for his master, King Edward VII. The church of St Mary Magdalene is a small carrstone building restored by Teulon in 1857, and by Blomfield in 1890. It is the home church of the Royal Family and contains many private memorials to them from—and including—Queen Victoria. In the west window one detects the features of the Duke of Clarence. There is more interesting early 16th-century glass in the nave, possibly made at Lynn. The silver altar was a gift from an American, Rodman Wanamaker. Sandringham House is open to the public. Crowds gather outside the church on Sundays when the Royal Family is in residence.

Santon [14] The little church of All Saints belongs to the parish of Santon Downham in Suffolk. The nave was rebuilt in 1628 and in the cha-

cel (added in 1858) is an early 18th-century organ.

Saxlingham [4] (by Holt) St Margaret's is one of several local churches restored by Sir Alfred Jodrell, the rich and pious squire of Bayfield. It retains the continuous arch-braced roof, and some old glass. The ruined manor house east of the church was a home of the Heydons, one of whom, Sir Christopher, erected an extraordinary monument in the church to his first wife, Mirabel Rivett (c. 1593). This monument took up so much space in the chancel that one could hardly walk round it; a pyramid on a square base was surmounted by a flaming urn, reaching nearly to the roof. The surface of the pyramid was covered with emblems and astrological hieroglyphics (a passion of Sir Christopher's). The monument was removed early in the 19th century, and all that survives is an Elizabethan figure and a tiny alabaster Bible, with a text from Job, in the transepts. It is sad to have lost the rest, though it was clearly inconveniently placed.

Saxlingham [17] (south of Norwich) *Saxlingham Nethergate* has a 16th-century half-timbered house and a parsonage by Sir John Soane, with recent additions by Fielden & Mawson. St Mary's Church with a 15th-century tower has a most important collection of Norwich glass of the 13th to 15th centuries. *Thorpe* is a hamlet whose ruined church is in a grove. *Saxlingham Green* has reed-thatched cottages along the edge of a wide common. The timbered Old Hall, by the church, passed through the families of Gawdy, Suckling, Tuttle and Mingay in the 17th century.

Saxthorpe [4] A potentially pretty village divided from Corpusty by a river. St Andrew's Church is well restored, with unusual 17th-century altar rails with very big knobs on the posts. These knobs are said to have been confirmed several

times by short-sighted bishops. Very fine arms of Queen Anne with Commandments and texts (1711) under the tower.

Scarning [9] The 'Arcady' of Dr Jessopp, the Norfolk historian who was rector here 1875–1914. Spacious church with a tower built in the 1520s. Very good contemporary screen. There is a square late-Norman font, and a tablet (with alabaster effigy) in the chancel to Edward Games (1623) who died 12 hours after birth.

Scole [16] The thing to see here is the White Hart Inn (1655), the most important coaching inn between Ipswich and Norwich. St Andrew's Church, rebuilt in 1963 after being destroyed by a fireraiser, has an exciting east window by Patrick Reyntiens.

Sco' Ruston [11] Roadside church, dedicated to St Michael, of a hamlet. The tower has long been a ruin, and the rest of the church bids to join it. The south door (probably early 16th century), a gift of Stephen Bolte and his wife Eleanor, has been removed for safekeeping.

Scottow [11] Much housing for those working on the aerodrome. Secluded 14th- and 15th-century church of All Saints. Nice 17th-century font cover with dolphins, and much carving worked up into the organ case (organ given in 1844 by Sir Henry Thomas Durrant) and lectern (given in 1876 by Lady Lamb). The rood beam remains; there are 10 hatchments in the chancel and good royal arms for William and Mary 1696 and Elizabeth II 1953. Huge monument in the chancel by George Storey to Davy Durrant 1759; slabs to the Durrant family, too. The Georgian Hall, partly Gothicized, is near the church.

Scoulton [9] The attractive mere encircles a large island, breeding ground for many rare birds. Holy Trinity Church stands apart from the village; it has a 14th-century tower with octagonal top, a Jacobean pulpit, and a curious niche in the chancel with five deep holes, possibly for cressets.

Sculthorpe [3] A vast American aerodrome covered many acres here in the war, and some activity still remains. The large church of All Saints was rebuilt in 1847 by R. & J. Brandon and then by Jekyll in 1860. It contains many good things—a famous Norman font with the Adoration of the Magi, a Snetzler organ of 1756 with a very fine case, and good Morris and Burne-Jones glass. There are brasses of 1470 (Henry Unton) and 1521 (John Humpton) and many monuments to the family who lived at Cranmer Hall, an 18th-century house nearby, which was built in 1721 and acquired in 1751 by the Jones family who owned it until after World War II. A younger son, the Revd Herbert Jones, was incumbent here 1859–89, and his wife wrote very interesting topographical books, worth searching for.

Sea Palling [6] Palling has become a pleasure resort with rows of bungalows and shacks. The village was much damaged by inundation from the sea in January 1953 and is still one of the danger spots along the coast. Marram grass is being planted to encourage a further row of sand dunes, which is the best—and in fact the only —defence against the sea. In St Margaret's Church even the base of the 15th-century screen has been varnished and grained; there are a few bench ends and a 14th-century banner stave locker at the northwest angle of the nave.

Sedgeford [2] The village is built in a tiny valley, the church is mostly 13th century with a round 11th-century tower having a later octagonal top. There is interesting glass and a 1914–18 war memorial in the chancel. The Hall is an attractive Queen Anne house built of yellow brick. On some cottages there are terracotta plaques made by the gifted Lady of the Manor at the end of the last century, and on the road just outside the village is the hamlet of Littleport is the Magazine House used by the Royalist, Sir Hamon L'Estrange as a store for ammunition during the Civil War.

Seething [17] Is as nice as its name. The church is dedicated to St Margaret and St Remigius. Across wide fields one sees it, with its flint tower, little lead spirelet and thatched nave. It contains a screen with 15th-century painted base and a top carved by a local man in 1898. There are restored wall paintings including a giant St Christopher, and a Seven Sacrament font.

Setchey or **Setch** [8] Has cottages and a little toll-house made of brown carrstone with red pantiles and an 18th-century red-brick house by the bridge. The small church (1844) is built of carrstone.

Sharrington [4] The late mediaeval Hall, seat of the Daubeney family, c. 1360–c. 1600 was added to in Tudor times and has a forecourt flanked by farm buildings. All Saints' Church has lost the aisles it once had but has curious heads on the corbels and fine brasses to the Daubeney family. The finest is ascribed to John, killed by a crossbow dart defending Caister Castle in 1469 though the style of the brass is of 1445.

Shelfhanger [16] All Saints Church here has a nice timber porch and the font bears the arms and initials of Adam Bosville, patron of the living c. 1370. In the chancel are very fine late 13th-century frescoes of the Adoration of the Magi, discovered in 1965.

Shernborne font

Shelton [17] A marvellous Perpendicular church dedicated to St Mary, built of red and blue brick in 1480–90 by Sir Ralph Shelton, except for the earlier tower. Inside, continuous nave and chancel, the clerestory almost all glass. Good monuments in the chancel particularly Sir Robert Houghton. Much beautiful 15th-century glass including two big kneeling donors. Fine carved royal arms for William III and unusual sacristy at east end.

Shereford [3] A small village with a delightful little church dedicated to St Nicholas, pre-Conquest round tower and window in nave. A late Norman door has been inserted into the original Saxon south doorway. There is a circular Norman font with scalloped bowl and an interesting 14th-century east window.

Sheringham [4] A cluster of old cottages, some with lofts for mending nets, are reminders of the old fishing village. With the coming of the railway, Sheringham became a popular seaside resort; it is neat and well planned with a splendid golf course along the cliffs and a nice promenade. To the south, the ground rises steeply to a stretch of beautiful heath and woodland; from the spot called (somewhat inadequately) 'Pretty Corner', there is a superb view of the countryside. The old railway station has

Shingham

been taken over by the North Norfolk Railway Company who have reopened the line to Weybourne; two of the last steam engines to be run by B.R. in Norfolk are among their stock. The interesting Roman Catholic church is by Sir Giles Gilbert Scott, but much attractive Edwardian architecture, such as the Grand Hotel, has vanished. St Peter's Church, 1895, by St Aubyn & Wadling, is of flint and red brick, not exciting.

Sheringham, Upper [4] The Hall was built in 1812–17, and the park most beautifully landscaped with a lake and wonderful views of the sea, by the Georgian gardener-architect, Humphry Repton. He laid out the estate for Abbot

Upcher, whose descendants still own the house and whose monument by J. Bacon and S. Manning is in All Saints' Church, which also has a fine 15th-century rood screen and loft, a painted beam with pulley for raising the font cover, very good bench ends, including a mermaid, and a Victorian portrait in the south-west window. Sheringham Park contains a famous collection of rare and beautiful rhododendrons, and is open to the public on certain days.

Shernborne [2] A Sandringham estate village. The moated house with a gable end with angle shafts is part of the earlier house of the Shernborne family. St Peter and St Paul's Church, largely rebuilt in

1898 through the generosity of the Prince of Wales, has a very good Norman font and brasses of 1458 for Sir Thomas Shernborne and his wife. An attractive village.

Shimpling [16] The moated Tudor 'Place', formerly the seat of the Shardelows, looks fine across the fields. St George's Church, with round tower and little lead spire, 1863, is charmingly placed with a sloping view to woods, like a Gainsborough landscape; it has some mediaeval glass and benches

Shingham [8] The little hamlet church of St Botolph, a popular Norfolk dedication, is still like Cotman inside, with pale brick floor and 15th-century benches

148

Jacobean pulpit and altar rails, and Norman door. It is closed for worship but cared for by a local landowner.

Shipdham [9] The long village street thickens about the church with a number of late Georgian houses. All Saints' Church was much restored by the Victorians, but has a 15th-century lectern, nice Commandment boards of 1630 and a lovely lead cupola on the tower.

Shotesham [17] *All Saints* stands above a winding stream with little white bridges. There are willow trees and cottages with curly Dutch gables, a William and Mary house, a nice Regency stucco one and an excellent modern Georgian one by a local architect, James Fletcher-Watson. All Saints' Church stands on a hill with a view of village and valley; the tower has a curious iron staircase outside. It contains wall paintings and 18th-century monuments; the oil lamps have wisely been retained and electrified. The Hall was built c. 1785 by Sir John Soane for the Fellowes family. The design is restrained, with giant pilasters and entablature set against an unadorned brick wall with, on the ground floor, three Venetian-type windows confirmed as blank arches, and separated by two narrower niches. *Shotesham St Mary* has a ruined ivy-clad tower (of the old St Martin's Church) with the 14th-century church above it in a very pretty churchyard. There is a 16th-century brass in the chancel. You can see the old village street as a hollow way in the fields. St Botolph's Church nearby is, like St Martin's, a ruin.

Shouldham [8] Once had a Gilbertine Priory, a large grammar school, and a famous spring called the Silver Well; it was a market town and had two annual fairs. Now it is a pleasant, quiet place with old houses, some thatched, some with red and others with blue

pantiles, grouped around a green; above, on a hill, a big flint church of All Saints with embattled tower and a roof with carved hammer-beams. Recent excavations suggest Shouldham has been inhabited for at least 2,000 years.

Shouldham Thorpe [8] Has an 18th-century house by a pond and little St Mary's Church, rebuilt in 1858 but with a real Norman west door and a 17th-century monument with kneeling figures of three children. 'Toombers Wood' indicates the site of Toimere, or Toombers, one of the lost villages of Norfolk, which Blomefield says was standing about the reign of Henry III.

Shropham [15] St Peter's Church with a 15th-century tower and a good 13th-century north door. There is an arch above the sedilia and a squint from the north aisle; the screen across the aisle has an inscription (possibly from a pew) set in, asking for prayers for the welfare of Thomas and Catherine Beny, 1527. The Hall is a Georgian building of five bays and two storeys, with a three-storey central block with pediment. Shropham House is a square four-bay late-Georgian house of two storeys.

Sidestrand [5] Clement Scott gave to this village some fame as 'Poppyland' and the old churchyard on the cliffs he called the 'Garden of Sleep'. The repose of the forefathers of this particular hamlet was perhaps disturbed by their remains being washed away by the sea. The last fragments of the old church went 'down cliff' in 1961, but the rest of St Michael's Church had been moved stone by stone and rebuilt in its original form a third of a mile inland; it was consecrated in 1881. Most of the later work there, e.g. the War Memorial, is by Seely & Paget.

Sisland [17] St Mary's Church was built in 1761 in Gothick style

but with Georgian columns, west gallery and bell turret. A sweet little church.

Skeyton [5] All Saints' Church is a 12th-century building with an asymmetrically placed tower. The charming setting of the church is spoilt by a rubbish dump to the north. The Goat Inn is a nice building.

Sloley [5] St Bartholomew's Church, alone in the fields, has early 19th-century box pews and two-decker pulpit; but the feature is a 15th-century Seven-Sacrament font with marvellously preserved carving—note particularly the Confirmation panel. Good modern hatchment in north aisle. The Hall was occupied for the first time the night before the Battle of Waterloo while the dancing was going on in Brussels. It was designed by the Revd William Gunn. The Old Hall, built by the Le Gros family in the 16th century, is a pretty old house with stork gables.

Smallburgh [11] A straggling village on the edge of Broadland, with Low Street running down toward the Ant; St Peter's Church has 15th-century figure paintings on the screen. An attractive village street leads towards Dilham with pleasant brick and flint houses. The four-bay Hall was built in 1837.

Snetterton [15, 16] The old aerodrome near this hamlet is now a motor track, whose noise is scarcely less hideous than that of jet aircraft. The mediaeval church of All Saints, vested in the Norfolk Churches Trust and now a small monastery, has a repainted screen (Thomas Gifford bequeathed to the 'edifying' of the screen in 1479) and fine 13th-century double piscina and east window of c. 1300 in the chancel. It lost a good deal of mediaeval glass at the Victorian restoration; there are signs that there may still be wall paintings by the chancel arch.

Shotesham

Snettisham [2] Is a large village, built mainly of local brown carr-stone, which straggles from the magnificent St Mary's Church (with one of the very few mediaeval stone spires in Norfolk) down to the Wash through a market place and past several fine old houses. Behind a high wall bordered by lime trees is the Old Hall, a William and Mary house with Dutch gables, once the seat of the Stylemans, and now a Sue Ryder Home. The huge 14th-century church has a west front with triple porch and a magnificent west window; the chancel has gone. There is a very interesting alabaster monument to Sir Wymond Carye (1612), and several brasses including a palimpsest in the south aisle and a remarkable one to John Cremer, his wife, six sons and daughter (1610) in Jacobean dress in the north aisle. Mediaeval brass eagle lectern. The Cathedral of Fredericton in New Brunswick,

Canada, is modelled on this church. There is a curious ghost story (1895) connecting the church and an old house in the village. Ken Hill (the new Hall) was built in 1888 to the design of J.J. Stevenson for Sir Edward Green, whose family still owns it. Snettisham Park, formerly called Cobbe Hall, belonged to the Cobbe family, Lords of Ingoldisthorpe Manor in Snettisham from the 16th century. It is a fascinating old house, with most interesting out-buildings and a crinkle-crankle wall.

The **Snorings** [3] St Mary's Church in *Great Snoring* has Commandment boards with figures representing the Four Last Things—Heaven, Hell, Death and Judgement—flanked by figures of Moses and Aaron. 14th-century chancel with good sedilia, handsome black-and-white marble paving and good monuments to

Fellows of St John's College, Cambridge, patrons of the living. To the west is the magnificent Old Rectory (1525), formerly the manor house, built by Sir Ralph Shelton and embellished with carved brickwork like the neighbouring Thorpland Hall. John Pearson, born at the rectory in 1612, later became Bishop of Chester, and his book on the Creed was the standard work for many years. In *Little Snoring* St Andrew's Church has an early round tower, with an attractive red cap, which is detached from the rest of the church; it is one of the unsolved riddles of Norfolk as to why a church appears to have been demolished within a century or so of its building, and replaced by another church a few yards away. There is a fine late-Norman doorway and circular font, as well as the only set of the arms of James II in Norfolk; in the chancel is a ledger slab to Mr Benjamin Lane (1744),

151

Old Rectory, **Great Snoring**

'As good a parish priest as perhaps ever lived.'

The **Somertons** [12] At *West Somerton*, St Mary's Church is a 13th/14th-century building with 15th-century screen and pulpit, and many faded wall paintings. In the churchyard is buried Robert Hales (1863), the Norfolk giant who was 7 feet 8 inches tall. St Mary's Church, *East Somerton*, takes a bit of finding—it is hidden in a wood and in ruins. But the walls stand up to roof level and there were fine 15th-century windows. Burnley Hall (formerly Somerton House) is a handsome seven-bay house of about 1700.

Southburgh [9] St Andrew's Church in this small village was much rebuilt, particularly the tower and spire, about 1880; it has an interesting stained glass window (1935) by Leonard Walker.

Southery [13] A sizeable Fenland village; the mediaeval church of St Mary was allowed to fall into ruin when the present tidy carrstone building with a broach spire was erected in 1858, designed by Higham & Robinson. A dark but attractive interior.

South Pickenham *see* Pickenham, South

Southrepps [5] The restored S James's Church has a lofty (114 foot) tower (built c. 1448) which has much flushwork and carving at the base, including scallop shells signifying St James; it is the mos prominent landmark in the district Although reduced in size in 1791 the interior is impressive. Lovely little mediaeval angel in low side window in chancel. Bucklands Farm, 1744, is a pretty house nea the church.

South Runcton *see* Runcton South

South Walsham [11] Has two churches, St Laurence (burnt in

1827) whose tower fell in 1971, and St Mary's, of the 14th and 15th centuries, with good mediaeval screen and benches and an Annunciation over the porch. In St Mary's, notice the window in the south aisle representing Astronomy. It is by R. O. Pearson, 1907.

Southwood [12] St Edmund's Church is a ruin, the tower being the most prominent part. A late 17th-century summerhouse survives at the Hall.

South Wootton *see* Wootton, South

Sparham [10] St Mary's Church was built in the 14th century but much altered in the 15th, when the three western arcades of the nave were replaced by two much wider ones, and the clerestory raised and rebuilt. The arch-braced roof, the east, west and most of the aisle windows are also of this date. The tower stands about 90 feet. Four extraordinary and fascinating panels from the base of the rood screen survive, including one representing the donors as skeletons, but fashionably dressed, and another, a shrouded skeleton beside a font. The 15th-century pulpit has been restored. The brass to William Mustarder, rector (1493), survives, but that to Robert and Alice Giggs (1534) has gone. The Hall is an irregular ten-bay house, built in 1856 with recently added shaped gables, standing on the site of a manor house of the Mautby and Paston families which was the subject of much discussion in the *Paston Letters*. Sparham House, a five-bay Georgian house built c. 1820, stands near to the site of Stewk Hall, a manor house of the de Stiffkey family. The five-bay Georgian Old Rectory was built c. 1775 by the Revd Edward Atthill.

Spixworth [11] An outlying suburb of Norwich. St Peter's Church has a slender square tower (round inside) at the south-west

corner, a Norman tub font, and in the chancel a rather extraordinary monument to William and Alice Peck (1635). It is by Edward Marshall, a pupil of Nicholas Stone, who was Master Mason to the Crown in 1660. The Hall was largely rebuilt by William Peck in 1609 but was later demolished.

Sporle [9] A long, attractive street with flint and brick cottages and here and there a bigger 17th/18th-century house. St Mary's Church has 13th-century arcades and in the south aisle a series of paintings showing the life and martyrdom of St Catherine. To the north are the decayed villages of Great and Little Palgrave (which once had a chapel), and which have dwindled to isolated farmhouses on what are apparently moated sites. Of recent years Great Palgrave has received a few modern houses. Blomefield says, 'It never had any church that I have met with.'

Sprowston [11] St Mary and St Margaret's Church of this Norwich suburb is on the edge of the country, much restored, but with several fine 17th- and 18th-century monuments, mainly to Corbets and Micklethwaits, one (1757) by Robert Page; much nearer the city is the Lazar House, now a branch library but originally a hospital founded by Herbert de Losinga.

Stalham [6, 12] A pleasant little Broadland town of one street containing some Georgian houses and with a lane to the River Ant and Barton Broad. The restored St Mary's Church is remarkable for its 15th-century font, with the Baptism of Christ, the Trinity, and groups of saints. Mounted on the wall of the chancel are five panels of the rood screen, including the rare plague saints, Roch and Sebastian. The Hall was built about 1670.

Stanfield [9] A scattered village with its cottages dotted about along the lanes and in the fields. The very

atmospheric St Margaret's Church has a 17th-century pulpit and font cover, a mediaeval screen and benches, and unusual windows.

Stanford [15] Now in the Stanford Military Training Area. All Saints' Church has an early round tower with 15th-century octagonal belfry.

Stanhoe [2, 3,] A large straggling village, at the west end of which is a beautiful early 18th-century house, once lived in by Fanny Burney's half-sister Maria Allen, who married Martin Folkes Rishton in 1772. The well-proportioned 14th-century All Saints' Church has numerous memorials to the Hoste family, of whom William Hoste was one of Nelson's most valued captains. East window by Kempe, 1879. Note pathetic tomb in churchyard of Mrs Hollway, 1856.

Starston [17] Stands among big trees on a stream beside which is an old farmhouse and the large Georgian rectory. St Margaret's Church has a chequer-work tower parapet and some fragments of wall paintings. There is a memorial in the chancel with a kneeling figure of Bartholomew Cotton (1613); in a niche on the restored porch is a modern statue of St Margaret and the Dragon. Starston Place, built c. 1840 by Samuel Taylor, was a model farm.

Stibbard [3] A very compact village gathered about All Saints' Church attractively placed in a pine grove. Originally 14th century, it has been drastically restored, but contains 15th-century bench ends, many of which have figures carved on the arms. The front of the rood loft remains. Remains of the screen tracery are worked up into the pulpit. There are a few scraps of ancient glass.

Stiffkey [3] A coastal village with brick and flint cottages along a narrow street which follows the winding course of the river. In July the

153

marshes are purple with sea lavender. Stiffkey is famous for its cockles called 'Stewkey Blues', which find their way onto the market stalls of towns all over England. The church of St John the Baptist stands at the east end of the village with the ruins of St Mary's in the same churchyard. Stiffkey Hall stands to the south of the church and consists of one wing of the great quadrangular house built by the Bacon family whose arms can be seen over the gatehouse on the south side. The towers at the corners of the house remain, as well as the ruins of the Great Hall. The former rectory is a surprisingly grand flint house, Georgian, with elaborate plaster ceilings. It is famous as the home of its rector of the 1920s and 1930s, the Revd Harold Davidson.

Stockton [18] Has several 17th- and 18th-century houses, pretty cottages and barns and fine trees. The thatched St Michael's Church has a gabled porch with a sundial and a little lead spire on its round tower; the spire was added by an 18th-century parson, Valentine Lumley, so that he could see the church from his Bungay vicarage. Inside the church are remains of mediaeval glass, including a Virgin and Child, and Victorian texts.

Stody [4] A very pretty village. The church, strikingly sited above the stream, has an early round tower and 15th-century nave, chancel and transepts. A lovely contemporary roof and fragments of 15th-century glass. Stody Lodge, built by the 1st Lord Rothermere, has a very pretty water garden with good azaleas and rhododendrons.

Stoke Ferry [8] Has two Methodist chapels and All Saints' Church, largely rebuilt in 1848. There are some old houses in the town, but the centre needs new life. The red Georgian Hall, opposite the west end of the church, is late 18th century.

Stoke Holy Cross [11] Has a large white weatherboarded mill in watery meadows, a chapel with tin texts, a lot of new houses and the 13th-century Holy Cross Church (15th-century tower). The churchyard and the park of the demolished Hall, with cypresses and poplars, show the taste of the last squire, Geoffrey Birkbeck, an artist who died in 1953. Blackford Hall incorporates the remains of the chapel attached to the former manor house of the Blackford family.

Stokesby [12] Another remote corner of Broadland at the end of a long lane which runs down to a staithe. St Andrew's Church has an unbuttressed 13th-century tower, some 14th-century ironwork on the south door, and 15th-century bench ends with figures, including a nun at prayer with her rosary. Several good brasses. Memorial to the Revd William Taylor Worship—'Reader, offer, if not a prayer, at least a kind wish for the welfare of his soul.'

Stow Bardolph [7] The planting of cedars, ilex and copper beeches, the vistas through the park (the Hall was rebuilt in 1873, keeping the high castellated garden walls and outbuildings of an earlier house), the cottages, almshouses and general layout of the village mark it as a place which has been cherished by a family with money and taste for 400 years. Part of the tower of Holy Trinity Church is Norman, but the remainder was heavily restored by Raphael Brandon in 1848–9. On the north side is the brick Hare chapel, dated 1624, containing many excellent monuments. The most beautiful and elaborate is that of Ralph Hare (1623), who was knighted at the coronation of James I; there are swags of fruit and flowers and a canopy with columns. The most extraordinary is revealed on opening a mahogany cupboard in which Sarah Hare, dying in 1744, directed

her effigy should be kept. There she is, life-size in wax, with curly fair hair, staring blue eyes, a white tucked silk dress and red cloak and hood, peering out from behind white curtains in a truly fearful way. The story is that she died from a pricked finger, a punishment for sewing on Sunday. Her father, Sir Thomas (1693), is also life-size, but he is in marble and dressed as a Roman; there is also a monument to Susanna Hare (1741).

Stow Bedon [15] A typical Breckland village with its mere. The restored St Botolph's Church has remains of a rood screen, a mediaeval altar stone and some early tombstones in the chancel.

Stradsett [8] The church is mainly 13th century but much restored. It includes a window of south German glass of 1540, a memorial to Thomas Bagge (1823), and two charming embracing angels of 183_ who commemorate Grace Bagge both by Westmacott. The Hall, originally Elizabethan E-plan, has a late Georgian front and a large lake in the grounds. The Bagges still live there.

Stratton, Long [16, 17] Consists of one long wide street with timber framed houses round the centre and pleasant houses and villas towards the south. St Michael's Church at its northern extremity has an early western tower and is very atmospheric inside. Some 17th-century altar rails now form the front of the choir stalls. St Mary's Church at the opposite end of the village has a round tower, 17th-century pulpit and font cover, 15th-century screen base, some 14th- and 15th-century glass in the east window, and chancel monuments. The sexton's wheel (of which there is only one other known example) is supposed to be a sort of revolving calendar indicating festivals and fasts. South Norfolk House, the District Council's offices, designed by Norwich architects, Lambert, Scott & Innes, received Civic Trust Commendation in 1980.

Stratton Strawless [11] St Margaret's Church, with exceptionally wide 14th-century tower, is mainly 15th century. The south aisle, which has plaster vaulting, was rebuilt in the 17th century as a mortuary chapel to the Marsham family and contains two very fine monuments, Thomas Marsham (1638) in shroud (notice the grave-digger's tools), and Henry Marsham (1629) with his wife and small son of 12, who is shown in the costume of the Bluecoat Boys. There is also very fine 15th-century glass, some of it from a bequest by John Marsham in 1473. Few of the trees planted by the great naturalist, Robert Marsham (1707–97), a correspondent of Gilbert White, still survive, but among them is an aged cedar. The Hall is a six-bay Georgian building, recently lowered in height, acquired from the Marshams at the end of the 19th century by the Keppels and from them soon afterwards by a branch of the Birkbecks. W. J. Birkbeck, the scholar, High Churchman, and great friend of the Russian Orthodox Church, who bequeathed the famous morse and cope to Norwich Cathedral, lived here, dying in 1916.

Strumpshaw [11] St Peter's Church has a lofty 15th-century tower (c. 1487), a coloured screen of that period and 13th-century piscina. There is a banner stave locker.

Suffield [5] St Margaret's Church in this scattered village has a 13th-century chancel, 14th-century north aisle and 15th-century tower. There is a painted screen with grotesque carvings of animals and birds above its panels; the saints depicted include Jeron and John Schorn. Monument to John Symonds, 1584.

Surlingham [11] The upper part of the village consists of groups of cottages near St Mary's Church, which is up a little lane that soon becomes a path leading to another church, St Saviour's, ruined since the 17th century. St Mary's has a round tower with 14th-century octagonal belfry, a nice 15th-century font, and a wooden eagle lectern with an owl at the bottom. The rood stairs are unusually low and there is a west gallery. The lower part of the village on Surlingham Broad is in a wide bend of the Yare and there is a ferry across the river to Postwick. A good place for botanists and bird watchers. Ted Ellis, the famous naturalist, lives here.

Sustead [5] St Peter and St Paul's Church, mainly 14th century, has beautiful window tracery, that in the chancel having capitals decorated with oak leaves and acorns. The 17th-century pulpit is charmingly primitive. The nave windows have fragments of mediaeval glass. The sedilia and font are fine. The former rectory, to the west, is 17th century and so is the Hall, with later additions. It must look much as it did when the Revd Patrick St Clair and his daughter, Elizabeth, whose correspondence has been published as *Country Neighbourhood* by R. W. Ketton-Cremer, lived there in the 1740s.

Sutton [12] The Broad is weedgrown. The restored 14th-century church of St Michael has 15th-century bench ends.

Swaffham [8, 9] A beautiful 18th-century market town with a fine market place, in which stands a classical market cross surmounted by a figure of Ceres with a sheaf of corn, built by Lord Orford in 1783. Hamond's Grammar School is an 18th-century house, and opposite stands the Assembly Room, for Swaffham was a winter assembly town for the neighbouring gentry. The magnificent 15th-century

church of St Peter and St Paul has a hammerbeam roof; the rebuilding began in 1454 at the instigation of the rector, Dr John Botright, chaplain to Henry VI, and it finished in 1510 with the tower. There is a parochial library in the chamber above the sacristy on the north side of the chancel; it includes the famous Black Book, which has a list of benefactors to the church, dating from Botright's time. There is a mediaeval legend of how the pedlar of Swaffham, walking on London Bridge, met a stranger who told him to return to his home town of Swaffham and search for treasure which was buried there. The pedlar became a wealthy man and built the north aisle of the church. John Chapman (a pun on pedlar) was a rich man, at all events.

Swafield [5] St Nicholas' Church stands on a rise overlooking this small village. Like most of the church, the wide thatched nave is 15th century. It is well lit by tall windows, and retains its original arch-braced roof. The original knocker remains on the south door, probably contemporary with the 14th-century tower. 15th-century screen base with painted Apostles. The Hall has stepped gables.

Swainsthorpe [11, 17] Angels in roof of St Peter's Church and a good monument of 1765. The Vale Hospital, former workhouse, 1836, by John Brown.

Swannington [10] The church of St Margaret is Decorated and Perpendicular, much restored, with a very fine porch (for which money was left in 1452 and 1457) with the legend of St Margaret in the spandrels. A pillar piscina has 12th-century carvings of St George and the Dragon. Swannington Hall is a much altered Tudor house within a moat. Swannington Manor, formerly Court and originally the Lawn, has an interesting collection of mediaeval stained glass, and much early woodwork from various sources. The rectory incorporated the 17th-century parsonage of the Royalist, Edmund Duncon, friend of George Herbert.

Swanton Abbot [5] St Michael's Church has an interesting nave with both Decorated and Perpendicular windows, dating from the period of transition between the two styles. Monument to Elizabeth Burke (1821) who died shortly after her wedding ('May the useful lesson which her death inculcates not be lost upon us'), and a nice brass to Stephen Multon (1477), the rector, who probably gave the screen, for the initials SM appear on it. Though heavily restored, it still has panels of the apostles. Door knocker on south door, possibly 13th century.

Swanton Morley [10] Has connections with Abraham Lincoln's family. There is a large aerodrome here, used by the American Air Force in the last war. The big church was begun in the 1370s and has a fine west tower inset into the nave. Carving on the chancel roof and west door shows swan and tun, a pun on the village's name. Fine square-headed windows with charming tracery below the transoms light the lofty interior. There is a crypt below the chancel. Good royal arms for Anne. Both the Mill House and the White House, on the river, are very attractive indeed.

Swanton Novers [4] Set amid woodlands noted for the profusion of lilies of the valley. St Edmund's Church has been much restored.

Swardeston [11] Nurse Edith Cavell, who was born here, is commemorated in St Mary's Church by an east window by Bryans. The church has been well restored; there are curious low recesses on each side of the nave. The village has an attractive green. Gowthorpe Hall was built in the 16th century by the Styward

family, and Mangreen Hall is an Elizabethan or Jacobean house built by the Aldrich family, which now has a front of about 1700.

Syderstone [3] Is a long village of brick and flint houses. St Mary's Church has an early round tower with 12th-century west door. Only the arcades of the north and south aisles remain, the south arcade being of 12th-century work with very wide capitals to the columns. The church has been somewhat heavily restored with barrel roofs in nave and chancel. In the chancel a neat memorial of coloured marbles for the Revd George Jacob, 1739, and one to the Revd. G. Hall, 1605. It is said that Amy Robsart was born in the former Syderstone Hall. To the south-west of the village is the wide common, a lovely place when the gorse blooms.

Tacolneston [16] An attractive long village on the New Buckenham road; thatched cottages with high-pitched Suffolk roofs stand among the trees. The Hall is a fine half-moated Queen Anne house, probably built by Edward Knipe and standing on the site of an Elizabethan building. The Old Hall to the south of the church was erected by Sir Robert Baldock, who defended the Seven Bishops against James II; only one wing of the house survives. There is a 16th-century manor house further towards Buckenham; the Dairy Farmhouse, also probably once a Hall, has some pargetting, unusual in Norfolk. There were three manors in the parish, all probably having Halls, and there is even another Hall site at the moat a quarter of a mile north-west of All Saints' Church, mainly 15th century, which has a good Jacobean pulpit and two screen panels (c. 1510) showing the Annunciation and Temptations of St Anthony.

Tasburgh [17] Rainthorpe Hall was built by Thomas Baxter who died in 1611. The house post-dates

Amy Robsart who is said to haunt the gardens one night in August and was a connection of the Appleyards, earlier owners of the manor. There is a most interesting collection of mediaeval stained glass in many of the windows; much of the woodwork and panelling belongs to the house, but some was collected from elsewhere. The romantic garden, through which the River Tas runs, includes a very pretty knot garden (open to the public). St Mary's Church has an early tower and beautiful modern book bindings, a Jacobean font cover, interesting glass and monuments. The new church hall is very well designed and attractive.

Tatterford [3] St Margaret's Church in the middle of this small village was rebuilt in 1862 by W. Lightly, and has a pleasant interior. Some 18th-century tablets survive from the old church. In the rectory, now the centre of a new development, the Revd. W. T. Hand had a seminary between the Wars.

Tattersett [3] All Saints' Church in the fields is mainly 13th century with unusual south porch. The brick alcove in the chancel is probably 16th-century sedilia. There are wall paintings of a particularly horrid subject—bowels of a saint being wound out on a windlass. Coxford Priory was a house of Augustinian canons; fragmentary remains survive of the house in a large meadow opposite Tattersett Church. Pynkney Hall was originally Georgian but was substantially altered by Ewan Christian in the 19th century.

Taverham [10] An over-rapid development has spoilt this once tiny village. There is an early round tower and Norman doorway in St Edmund's Church, a very fine font with saints round the stem, and a mediaeval screen. The communion rails have splendid tracery underneath which once formed part of

Tattersett church (*above*) and Coxford Priory (*below*) ▷

Terrington St Clement

the screen at Booton; also 15th-century glass. The Hall, built in neo-Tudor style in 1858–9, by the Micklethwait family, was owned by them until this century but is now a preparatory school.

Terrington St Clement [7] Is a large, prosperous marshland village with rich farmland and market gardens. Nice Victorian shopfronts with cast-iron pillars. St Clement's Church is splendid outside, with dressed grey stone, detached tower, west window flanked by niches and turrets and a large south porch. The excitement of the interior is in

the fittings—Georgian screen at the west end, huge elaborate Jacobean boards with the Commandments and Lord's Prayer, and best of all, the fantastic 17th-century font cover with classical pillars surmounted by high Gothic top—all painted blue and white and opening to reveal charming rustic paintings of scenes from Our Lord's life, including the Temptation, with a hook-nosed Devil crowned and in scarlet. There are fine 16th-century sedilia and double piscina in the chancel, which has a vault under the high altar. Lovell's Hall is an early

Tudor brick and stone house, tra ditionally dated 1543, long after th Lovells had sold the manor.

Terrington St John [7] Ha several nice 16th- and 17th-centur houses. The slender church tower i linked to the nave by a priest' house containing rooms and staircase going up to the top, afford ing access to the nave roof; th church is full of box pews and has faked classical chancel arch of plas ter, a clerestory with alternat round and pointed windows, a hex agonal tiled floor, and at the we end a beautiful little wooden figure probably the Virgin of the Visitation, English work dating from the third quarter of the 15th century. Font of 1632. There are Tables of Affinity on a board.

Testerton [3] St Remigius' Church is a ruin, only part of the tower surviving. Testerton House, late Georgian, was built c. 1802.

Tharston [17] 14th/15th-century St Mary's Church with old benches and many Harvey memorials, including a mausoleum (1855) in the churchyard. The Hall is a pretty Jacobean house of brick, with patterns, and a two-storey porch.

Thelveton [16] The church of St Andrew is much restored; it has a brick south porch, nice 15th-century font, and a pillar piscina. The fine Elizabethan Hall was built in 1592 by the Havers family. There is a monument in the church to Thomas Mann (1868) who 'died from his horse falling with him'.

Themelthorpe [10] Straggling village with an early church, St Andrew's, although most datable work is 13th century. Some old poppy-heads.

Thetford [15] The capital of Breckland, Thetford was a most important Saxon settlement, for it was the seat of the bishopric from 1075 to 1094. There were 13 churches in the 11th century and for two centuries it had its own mint. Before then it had been a focal point at the confluence of the Little Ouse and the Thet; the Icknield Way passed through Thetford. It remained significant through the Middle Ages but at the Dissolution it gradually lost its importance and became a quiet country town. Its Georgian parts still manage to retain the gentility from the time when attempts were made, albeit unsuccessfully, to transform it into an East Anglian Cheltenham. Prosperity came in the form of light

industry, but only for a while; the second period of industrialization followed the choice of Thetford as a recipient for London overspill in 1959. Within 20 years the population has quadrupled from 4,500 to over 17,000; new industrial and housing estates have sprung up round the outskirts of the old town. The effect on the centre of the town has been mainly a proliferation of car parks and the provision of pedestrian precincts in the shopping centre, though how much longer the present situation can continue is perhaps questionable; the overspill policy was unpopular and is no longer to be pressed. Like many mediaeval towns, Thetford grew up round its castle; the great mound was raised after the Conquest, probably on top of earlier defences. It was surmounted by a keep, probably of wood, demolished in 1173. Near the river on the Brandon road are further earthworks and ramparts called the Red Castle, part of the Saxon defences. The settlement was sacked by the Danes under Sweyn in 1004. The mediaeval ecclesiastical buildings are considerably depleted. There are three mediaeval churches still intact, only St Cuthbert's being in regular use. St Cuthbert's has been much rebuilt—the tower, after falling, in 1851 and the north aisle in 1902. St Peter's is now used as a church hall; it is mainly a 15th-century building, with a flint tower rebuilt in 1789, and some nice flushwork and stone carving. St Mary's has a fine tower (bequests 1427–51) and white brick chancel. It contains the monument to Sir Richard Fulmodeston (1567), the greatest benefactor of Thetford. The earliest ecclesiastical building is the Benedictine Nunnery of St George on the south side of the river near Barham Cross Common. Founded as a monastery in 1020, it was refounded in 1176; all that remains is a fine Norman arch leading into the former south transept. The house standing in the ruins has some Elizabethan work and was

occupied by Sir Richard Fulmodeston, or Fulmerston. There are considerable remains of the monastery of the Canons of the Holy Sepulchre near the Brandon road, and just off the London Road are the substantial remains of the Cluniac priory (like the Cluniac house at Castle Acre, one of the most substantial monastic ruins in Norfolk). There is a big 14th-century gatehouse of three storeys. The tombs of the Howards were in the church here originally, but at the Dissolution the Duke of Norfolk obtained permission from Henry VIII to transfer them to Framlingham in Suffolk, where a new chancel was built to accommodate them. Probably the best-known building in Thetford is the Bell Hotel, standing at the corner of King Street and White Hart Street. This is a mediaeval building in origin (there was an inn on the site in 1493); the present half-timbered building has an Elizabethan front and some interesting contemporary wall paintings in a first floor room. Just the other side of King Street (now a pedestrian precinct) from the Bell is the King's House, a pleasant mid-18th-century building by Thomas Wright, standing on the site of an earlier one, which was used as a hunting box by James I (hence the royal arms in the centre of the front parapet). In front of the house is a statue of Tom Paine (by Sir Charles Wheeler). Born in a house in White Hart Street in 1737 (a plaque marks the house at the top of the street), he wrote the controversial books *The Rights of Man* and *The Age of Reason*. Also in White Hart Street is a half-timbered house of about 1500 known as the Ancient House; it is a museum with a fine collection of antiquities relating to Thetford and Breckland. In the market place is the Guildhall (1900), which has a selection of Norfolk and Suffolk portraits bequeathed in 1926 by the local antiquary, Prince Frederick Duleep Singh (son of 'Queen Victoria's Maharajah'), and the Vic-

torian 'Shambles', a covered shelter with cast iron pillars. The stocks and pillory, first erected here in 1581, are now in Cage Lane opposite the entrance to the Carnegie Rooms in Tanner Street (the name came from the former tannery). The old market place is further to the east; the market was held here until 1786. Here is the Dolphin Inn (1649) and the former gaol (1816) with barred top windows and panels carved with chains. One can cross the river here to see Spring Walk, a promenade laid out in 1818 past the former Pump Room. Bridge Street, still unspoilt, has Fulmerston School (formerly the Grammar School) which was founded before the Conquest and refounded by Sir Richard Fulmerston in 1566, having been under church control until then. Among its *alumni* are Thomas Howard, second Duke of Norfolk and the victor of Flodden; Francis Blomefield, the historian of Norfolk; Tom Martin, the antiquary; Tom Paine; and Roger North, the biographer. Further down is the Roman Catholic church of St Mary and priest's house (1829); the contemporary Methodist church (1830) is in Tanner Street. In November 1979 a man with a metal detector discovered a remarkable treasure of gold jewellery and silver spoons, thought to be the hoard of a jeweller and dated to the end of the 4th century A.D. Unfortunately the spot where these wonderful objects were found is now beneath the premises of Travenol Laboratories.

Thompson [15] Has a large and attractive mere. The church of St Martin is a splendid 14th-century building with most beautiful flowing tracery in the chancel windows. A conservative restoration preserved the flavour of the interior, full of excellent woodwork of two ages; mediaeval font cover, roofs, choir stalls, benches, and screen, and Jacobean three-decker pulpit, family pew and altar rails. Finely carved sedilia. There are original

consecration crosses on the walls and the old floors remain. Painting (c. 1790) *Joseph's Coat* on the south wall of the nave by Giacomo Berger, whose patron was the celebrated Frederick Augustus Hervey, builder of Ickworth. Thompson was a collegiate church served by a college of priests, founded by the Shardelowe family in 1349; the Shardelowe Arms can be seen on two misericordes in the chancel. Some remains of the college survive in College Farm, a quarter of a mile to the south.

Thornage [4] The 11th-century All Saints' Church, enlarged and restored, has a table tomb to Sir William Butts, physician to Henry VIII, and an incised slab (Lady Anne Heigham, 1590) under the tower. There is also a rare organ of 1812. Thornage Hall, with a big square dovecote, is part of a former grange of the Bishops of Norwich, probably dating from the 15th century. There was a forge here throughout the 19th century, and though it was mainly for repair of agricultural implements, there are still reminders in the shape of bits of ornamental ironwork on cottage walls.

Thornham [2] To the south-west of this coastal village, off the Ringstead road, are remains of a small fort dating from A.D. 40–60. The village is built mostly of the local pink and white chalk, with a little flint. All Saints' Church tower is partly Norman but was ruined until restored in 1936; the chancel was renewed in 1877. The chancel screen is unusual in having twelve Old Testament Prophets; it was given by John and Clarice Miller about 1488. There are several interesting mediaeval bench ends, including a fox preaching. Note the memorial lych-gate. The village school (1858) can hardly be missed. Just outside the village, towards Hunstanton, is a red-brick early 18th-century house with a prim front garden; at the back it turns

out to be a much older house, with a little window high in the roof to watch for the ships that once came into the little harbour in the marsh. The Hall is Georgian. There was a famous lady blacksmith in this village, Mrs Ames Lyde, who died in 1914. Her forge made much ornamental ironwork, including garden gates for the Prince of Wales (Edward VII) at Sandringham, and lamps and brackets for local churches, as well as elaborate gates shown at both the Paris Exhibition of 1900 and the Brussels Exhibition of 1911.

Thorpe Abbotts [16] All Saints' Church has a round tower. There is a Tudor porch and two early doorways; inside, remains of 15th-century screen and a well-preserved font with evangelists. The rest of the village is up the hill, with a little group of chestnut trees, and seats round a rustic well cover given in 1867. Thorpe Abbots Place is a large Italianate mansion built in 1869–71, and beyond it is a charming brick house (1677).

Thorpe Market [5] On the village green stands a 16th-century house and east of it a long avenue of trees leads to the Gothick St Margaret's Church (1796) with its porches and turrets, and inside, its screen, woodwork, glass and plaster—a charming light-hearted contrast to all the splendid mediaeval Gothic of the churches round about.

Thorpe-next-Haddiscoe [18] St Matthias' Church has a Saxon tower with Norman top, Norman doors and font and a chancel rebuilt in brick (1838). Black Letter Bible (1617) and monument to Thomas London, 1661. Early 18th-century Hall.

Thorpe-next-Norwich [11] A riverside suburb much painted by the Norwich School, with many old houses and two churches; the old one is in ruins beside its handsome Victorian successor, St Andrew's, by Thomas Jekyll, 1866. The best view of the fine riverside buildings is from the Cromer–Norwich railway line, and it includes the very sad sight of Thorpe Hall, an early 17th-century house, almost completely derelict, for whose preservation a long battle has been fought.

Threxton [9] In this attractively sited hamlet, the little church of All Saints in a farmyard is full of interest and atmosphere; the tower is Norman, and part of the nave is Saxon. All the glass is very pretty except for the east window of 1865; some in the north aisle is mediaeval. Simple 17th-century pulpit and desk, original painting on arcade, and 14th-century font.

Thrigby [12] Hamlet near Filby has a Victorian Hall (1876) with attractive gardens; an over-restored but mainly 14th-century church of St Mary, with atmospheric greenery growing all over.

Thurgarton [5] Thatched church of All Saints, with no tower, contains 15th-century bench ends carved with figures, one of them an elephant with a howdah. In 1981 the church is in disrepair, especially the roof, but rescue is at hand.

Thurlton [18] All Saints' Church has a Norman south door and 15th-century screen, wall painting of St Christopher, and north door with censing angels in the spandrels. Contemporary tower with nice base.

Thurne [12] St Edmund's Church is mostly 14th century and has a 17th-century altar table and rails. St Benet's Abbey can be seen through a squint in the west wall of the tower.

Thurning [4] St Andrew's Church here is a perfect example of an unrestored Georgian interior with three-decker pulpit, handsome box pews in the north aisle, hat pegs on the north wall, and some panelling round the Communion Table, which is surrounded on three sides by very fine communion rails, some of which came from the Chapel of Corpus Christi College, Cambridge, when that chapel was rebuilt in 1825. There are interesting memorials to the Elwin family who lived at the Georgian Hall standing squarely above the river.

Thursford [3] The Victorian Hall of the Chad family (who owned the estate from 1753 to c. 1919) has been demolished, apart from the kitchen wing. It replaced the Elizabethan house of the Guybon family. St Andrew's Church in the meadows nearby was restored by W. Lightly in 1862. He built the chancel and south chapel, the latter containing a family pew. There is a fine monument to Sir Thomas Guybon by William Stanton but the feature of the church is the

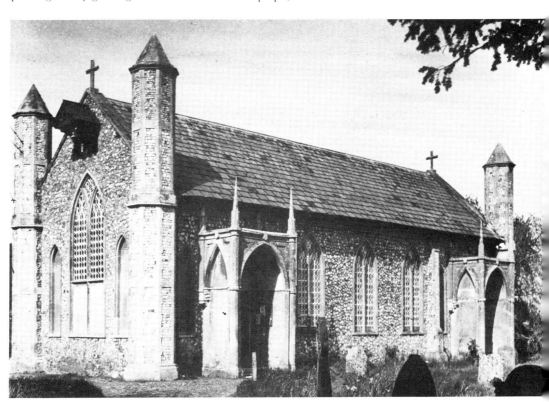

Thorpe Market church, outside and inside

The Royal Arms, **Tivetshall St Margaret**

stained glass, some of the best Victorian glass in England. The north and south chancel windows have figures drawn by Wooldridge for Powell, and the east window, with a Virgin and Child, Crucifixion and Ascension above two tiers of apostles, was designed by the incumbent, the Revd Arthur Moore, in 1862. Arms of Elizabeth I (1579) in glass in the vestry. Candlelit, partly by coronae. A wonderful church, well worth the effort to get to it.

Thurton [11, 17] St Ethelbert's Church has a very fine Norman south doorway, thatched roof, and some mediaeval glass as well as a good deal of 17th-century French glass, possibly from Rouen. The

inn is an old house with a carved sign of St George and the Dragon. The small late 17th-century Hall was from the early 18th century part of the Langley estate. There are good new houses, well laid out, by Tayler & Green, whose work is always distinguished.

Thuxton [10] Small village with St Paul's Church, which has a curious tower; an octagonal top is linked to square bottom by a broach. Circular Norman font bowl and Jacobean pulpit.

Thwaite All Saints [5] (between Erpingham and Alby) On this Holt–North Walsham road is a string of good churches and pretty

Old Rectories, standing isolated from their villages. Thwaite church has a round tower; inside, a Jacobean pulpit with canopy (1624), crude benches which may be contemporary, and the base of the mediaeval screen. Nice old floors. Brass to John Puttok (1442) who is said to have built the aisle in which he is buried. An interesting feature of the church is the school room of 1835 on the north side of the chancel, with old lettering and coat pegs on the wall.

Thwaite St Mary [17] (between Loddon and Bungay) Mainly 14th-century church with a late Norman south doorway. The chancel was built 1737 but Victorianized.

164

Tibenham [16] A pretty South Norfolk village of cottages with steeply pitched roofs. All Saints' Church has a tower with chequerwork but the real excitement comes inside—about the most 17th-century in atmosphere of any Norfolk church. There is a carved and gilded pulpit with tester, a four-sided reading desk, an altar table, and the double-decker family pew of the Buxton family erected in pursuance of a faculty granted by Archbishop Laud himself in April 635 (a translation of which hangs on the pew). A hatchment, a beautifully carved and painted achievement, and the arms of George I, are all there, while bits of the mediaeval screen can be found round the organ. Channonz Hall was built by the Buxtons traditionally in 1569. It became a tenant farmhouse as a result of the Buxtons concentrating on Shadwell as their seat, and only one wing remains.

Tilney All Saints [7] Has a 16th-century brick Hall with thatched roof. The church, one of the most splendid in the county, has a 13th-century tower with 14th-century top and stone spire; inside, a high nave with solid Norman arcades and double hammerbeam roof. 15th-century parclose screens and stalls with misericords; Jacobean chancel screen (1618), communion rails, reredos, and curiously inscribed font of this period. At the west end of the north aisle is a very big coffin lid thought to belong to the tomb of Sir Frederick Tilney, who was killed at Acre.

Tilney cum Islington see Islington

Tilney St Lawrence [7] The church was largely rebuilt in 1846 and the chancel is loftier than the nave or the mediaeval tower. Whitewashed wine-glass pulpit, good 18th-century tablet, arms of James I and nice atmosphere. The Coach and Horses Inn is 17th century.

Titchwell [2] Between main road and marsh, has cottages of local chalk and a wayside cross, or rather pillar, with no inscription. St Mary's Church, away from the village, with round tower, possibly Norman, and little lead spire, is very pretty, with good 1897 glass.

Tittleshall-cum-Godwick [9] Godwick Hall (now ruined), an E-shaped house in fields, was a home of the Cokes before Holkham was built; the ruined tower of Godwick church still stands, and Godwick is one of the best examples of the 'lost' villages in Norfolk. Tittleshall church, mainly 14th century, is remarkable for the Coke monuments by Nicholas Stone, Roubiliac, Nollekens and Atkinson. The inscription to Lord Chief Justice Sir Edward Coke (1634) says he 'was so compassionate that while the prisoner heard the sentence passed on him dry-eyed, never did this judge pronounce it save with tears'.

Tivetshall [16] The church of St Margaret has huge arms for Queen Elizabeth I in the tympanum of the chancel arch, said to be the finest in existence, and a repainted screen. St Mary's Church fell down recently and is now a most romantic Piper-ish ruin, with interesting tracery in the east window. There were proposals to demolish what is left (although Sir Henry Morse, who spent his childhood here, may be buried nearby), but the ruins have now been stabilized through joint efforts of the local authorities and the Norfolk Churches Trust.

Toft Monks [18] Rather scattered village with some nice old houses. St Margaret's Church has a good 13th-century octagonal tower, which may once have been round, some Norman work, and modern glass in the east window. The Elms belongs to the Freeland family who gave it a Georgian front of five bays (including two bow windows) on acquiring it about a century ago,

Trunch font

but at the back it incorporates a three-storey porch with stepped gable of Elizabethan or Jacobean date.

Toftrees [3] The church of All Saints has recently been restored through the efforts of villagers and friends. There is a magnificent Norman font with geometrical designs in high relief.

Topcroft [17] St Margaret's Church has a brick chancel rebuilt in 1712, a round tower and a 1637 monument. Interesting old houses in the village.

Tottenhill [8] A derelict post-mill and St Botolph's Church, isolated from the village for the good reason that the church of Tottenhill has vanished and this was the church of the 'lost' hamlet of West Briggs. There is a Norman doorway (unusual tympanum), a Norman chancel arch, 18th-century chancel slabs, and a monument of 1882 which displays very little Christian resignation.

Tottington [15] This village is now in the Stanford Military Training Area; the church of St Andrew is 14th/15th century.

Trimingham [5] A seaside village whose church, dedicated to St John the Baptist's Head, has a 15th-century painted screen (including St Petronilla) with restored loft and much carved wood by a former rector, the Revd Reginald Page, including illustrations of parables.

Trowse Newton or **Trowse** [11] The much-restored St Andrew's Church has a 15th-century vaulted porch and a most amazing pulpit erected in 1902, with huge figures of King David and angels. There are paintings of the Ascension and the four evangelists from St Michael Coslany; the tracery of the east window has been dated to 1282. Crown Point (now Whitlingham Hospital) was built about 1865 by H. E. Coe. It was owned by the Colmans, for whom Boardman enlarged it in 1904. It has a splendid conservatory. The fortune the Colman family made from mustard has been most generously spent on acquiring a very fine collection of Norwich School paintings, bequeathed, with a fine gallery, to the Norwich Castle Museum.

Trunch [5] The glory of this small village is the 14th/15th-century St Botolph's Church at its centre, with lofty tower, hammerbeam roof, and a magnificent canopy over the font, standing on corner posts (c. 1500). There is also a mutilated but very interesting screen (1502) and a

priest's door with buttress porch. Horatia, daughter of Nelson and Lady Hamilton, married Philip Ward, one of the family whose monuments are in the chancel.

Tuddenham, East [10] Pretty church of All Saints in meadows with unusual 15th-century porch (Annunciation in spandrels) and effigy of Sir Edmund Berry, holding his heart in his hands. East window by L. Walker (1952), mediaeval benches, and an early 13th-century circular font. Berry Hall is a good Georgian house, formerly the rectory; its name comes from the former manor of the Berrys. In 1754 the site was bought by the church for Parson Woodforde's friend, Mr Du Quesne, then the incumbent.

Tuddenham, North [10] Scattered village with fascinating large 14th/15th-century church dedicated to St Mary. Incredible interior due to the Revd Robert Barry (rector, 1851–1904) who lined the walls with shiny red tiles as far as the base of the windows, and stencilled the rest; except for the east wall, the stencilling has now been covered over. He also found a collection of 15th-century Norwich School glass lying in a Dereham builder's yard and installed that; some is at present (1981) awaiting restoration, but there are two exquisite panels of the life of St Margaret and one of St George and the Dragon in the tower. There are two sets of screen paintings, the panels in the rood screen (painted c. 1499) including the rare saints, Geron and Roch, and a collecting shoe. Two good Skyppe monuments in the chancel. The parishioners successfully resisted proposals to close or partly demolish this church, and it is in regular use.

Tunstall [12] Small remote village where St Peter and St Paul's Church is in ruins except for the chancel, which was repaired in

1705 by Mrs Elizabeth Jencenson and Mrs Anne Kelcall (*sic*); and again in 1980 by the Norfolk Churches Trust.

Tunstead [11] Is such a scattered place that it is hard to realize that it was a thriving weaving village which built a magnificent church late in the 14th century. St Mary's is 140 feet long and, unusually, has a windowless clerestory. There are arch-braced roofs, fine 14th century ironwork on the south door, a rood screen painted in the late 15th century (bequest 1470–90) with the apostles and Latin Doctors, and above this the mediaeval painted rood beam. In the chancel are fine sedilia and the unique feature of this church, the stone platform behind the high altar, which runs the width of the chancel. It has steps leading up to it on one side, and on the other side steps run down to a chamber beneath the platform. The purpose of the platform is unknown, but it may have been for exposing the Blessed Sacrament.

Tuttington [5] An attractive group of cottages around the church of St Peter and St Paul. The house close to the west tower has Flemish gables, and north of the church is good 17th-century farmhouse with great thatched barn. The church itself has a round tower of unusual design with a deep band of flint about the centre. Inside are splendid 15th-century bench ends with rich variety of subjects, a Jacobean pulpit (1645) and hourglass stand and font cover (1638).

Twyford [4, 10] The attractive little St Nicholas' Church has a late 16th-century porch with turret and wooden cupola. The Hall is a pretty house of several dates, whose park adjoins the churchyard.

Upper Sheringham *see* Shering ham, Upper

Upton [12] Most of the village gathers round Upton Green. There

Tivetshall St Mary

is another collection of cottages at Gargate Green. St Margaret's Church is mainly 15th century with a well-proportioned arcade, a 14th-century font with well-preserved figures around the stem, a painted screen (c. 1505) and a mediaeval pulpit. The tower was rebuilt in 1928 after long being a ruin; in the churchyard is a tomb-stone with a wherry on it.

Upwell [7] Continuous with Out-well, the two villages spread along either side of the old course of the Ouse, the houses on the east bank of the river being in Norfolk and those on the west, in Cambridge-shire. With its riverside houses and windmills, Upwell presents an essentially Dutch landscape. Along the river bank and crossing to the Norfolk side in Upwell itself was the tramline from Wisbech along which a steam tram plied until the early 1950s. St Peter's Church has a good angel roof and many memor-ial brasses including a quadrangu-lar plate in the chancel showing Mr Sinulphus Bell and his family kneeling in prayer; Mr Bell was indeed fortunate, as Mrs Bell 'never delayde by deeds and good usage to give him content'. Close to this is a mid-19th-century memor-ial to a number of people 'who died in this Rectory' of the cholera. (The incumbent of the time was using the word 'rectory' in its legal sense, meaning the whole parish.) The church, with its galleries and pews filling even the central alley of the nave, presents the most crowded seating that could be found any-where. The brass eagle lectern is mediaeval; in the well-kept churchyard are some very fine 18th-century headstones.

Wacton [16] It is pleasant to find in this round-towered, slate-roofed

All Saints' Church (near a nice old house) beautiful 14th-century windows, sedilia and piscina, and 17th-century altar rails and table. Complete rood stairs and a 15th-century font, having a 17th-century cover bearing a text (John 3:5). The Hall, a six-bay two-storey wood-and-plaster house, has a good three-storey brick porch with angle shafts and pinnacles in relief over pilasters, is a very old house, probably 15th century, and is moated on three sides.

Walcott [5] All Saints' Church in this somewhat bleak village has a 15th-century tower with an attractive parapet and unusual stair turret (built 1453–74) and nave windows (c. 1427). Much of the Victorian restoration was the work of the Revd Horatio Nelson William Comyn (godson of the Admiral, baptized on board H.M.S. *Victory*) who raised much money by selling tobacco, sweets, etc., which he carried in his pony and trap; he is even said to have done this when preaching at neighbouring churches. Doubtless this seemed more unusual to the Victorians than to present-day church restorers. The Presbyterian divine, Dr John Collinges, is buried in the chancel here.

Wallington [7] Only the tower remains of St Margaret's Church, which was profaned by Judge Gawdy, who depopulated the village; justly, when he died of apoplexy, he was consigned to anonymity in an unmarked grave at Runcton. The Hall is an Elizabethan brick building, with a fine porch of about 1525, and a large entrance gateway carved with bells, probably a rebus on the name of Bell, the family who built the house.

Walpole St Andrew [7] Nice brick tower with a curious cell in the west face, possibly used by an anchorite. The whole church is 15th century; a bequest of 30 stones of lead in 1504 may mark the completion of the

building. Green glass in the clerestory and bare patches of yellow stone on the nave pillars give exciting light to the spacious interior. There are twin turrets for rood stairs, and a most unusual stone pulpit bracket. The Jacobean pulpit itself is fitted with an hourglass stand complete with glass; over the pulpit hangs a painting of Christ and the Two Marys by Sebastiano Ricci.

Walpole St Peter [7] The 15th-century church of this charming village of old footpaths, old cottages, and trees is said by many to be the most beautiful church in England. The strong Marshland light pours through the clear glass windows onto the grey-brown carved benches, 17th century in the nave and 15th century in the aisles. In the splendid chancel, the rows of richly canopied niches have not been improved by the insertion of later monuments, although some of those are good in themselves. The painted saints on what is left of the screen are undefaced and include, uniquely, St Gudula. A mediaeval brass lectern, and an enormous brass chandelier (1701) and several smaller ones increase the effect of richness and light. There is a Jacobean pulpit (1620) and, at the west end, a Jacobean screen, font cover, and poorbox (1639) and a 'hood' or sentry-box to shelter the parson at funerals. The font was given in 1532. Over the south door are two casket slabs of 1825. The stepped-up chancel is explained if you look outside; a foot passage runs under it. St Godric, the 12th-century hermit, was born in this parish; he had power over wild animals and the knowledge of distant and future events usually associated with holy men such as the Orthodox *starets*.

Walsingham [3] In 1061 the Lady of the Manor, Richeldis de Fauvraches, saw in a vision the Blessed Virgin who instructed her to build at Walsingham a replica of the Holy House at Nazareth. Two

springs of water appeared in the place where the vision was seen, and close at hand the Holy House was built in the form of a wooden hut surrounded by a flint and stone building; it was a pilgrimage centre of European reputation during the Middle Ages. The Canons Regular of St Augustine were the guardians of the shrine and the arch surrounding the great east window of their church can be seen in the Abbey gardens which are approached through the 15th-century gateway in the village street. Part of the conventual buildings are worked up into the 18th-century house, known as Walsingham Abbey, adjoining which are considerable remains of the refectory with its stone pulpit. The mediaeval shrine, which was north of the nave, has long since disappeared, but the new shrine church was built (mainly 1931–8) on what is claimed to be the original site. This shrine church is in communion with the Church of England, while the directions on signposts usually marked with the papal arms indicate the Roman Catholic shrine in the next village of Houghton St Giles. An impressive recent addition to the Anglican Shrine of Our Lady of Walsingham is the chantry chapel of St Michael and the Holy Souls, designed by Laurence King. Little Walsingham with its Common Place retaining its mediaeval pump, 15th-century Guildhall, now a little museum, High Street, and Friday Market Place is one of the most delightful of all the small Norfolk market towns. The houses in the High Street on the east side back onto the precinct wall of the Priory. There is a fine Georgian house in the Friday Market and a well-proportioned late Georgian Methodist Chapel. At the southern end of the Friday Market a lane leads towards the ruins of the Franciscan Friary, where there are considerable remains of the Great and Little Cloisters and the Pilgrim's Hall. The church at Little Walsingham, a spacious 14th/15th-

Walpole St Peter,
outside and inside

century building, extensively
restored by G. E. Street in the
1860s, was entirely gutted by fire in
1961; it has been rebuilt by Mr
Laurence King. One of the finest of
the East Anglian Seven-Sacrament
fonts was saved, but its Jacobean
cover was lost, as was some
interesting late mediaeval glass and
woodwork. A large 17th-century
tomb survives in part. John Hay-
ward's new east window relates the
story of Walsingham and includes
the figures of Henry VIII, who
destroyed the shrine, and Fr Hope
Patten, who did more than anyone
else to revive devotion to Our Lady
of Walsingham. The reredos in the
Guilds Chapel was designed by G.
F. Bodley in 1889. St Peter's, *Great
Walsingham*, though it has lost its

chancel, is a most beautiful 14th-century building with exquisite window tracery. The 15th-century seating and arch-braced roof have gone a silvery grey colour with age. The bells cast by William Silisden c. 1330 are reputed to be the oldest set of three in Britain. They are still in use. There is a recent Roman Catholic church of the Annunciation in the Friday Market. The former railway station has become the Orthodox chapel of St Seraphim of Sarov, a gilded dome has been added, and the iconostasis divides the old waiting room. It works well; and the Orthodox in the region, English as well as foreign, flock there on feast days.

Walsoken [7] The lovely late-Norman arcade in All Saints' Church has a 15th-century clerestory above and a roof with remains of colour. Notice two wooden figures, one above the Norman chancel arch and the other over a painting of the Judgement of Solomon. There is a fine 13th-century tower with 14th-century spire, a Seven-Sacrament font (1544), some good screenwork, a heart shrine, and a stone Gospel lectern in the south chapel.

Walton, East [8] A hamlet with chalk farm buildings and St Mary's Church which has all its Georgian fittings—three-decker pulpit, box pews, and chancel arch with fluted pilasters—all plain, unspoilt and dignified in the light that floods in through large Perpendicular windows.

Walton, West [7] St Mary's is the finest 13th-century church in Norfolk, surely the work of a cathedral builder. The tower is detached and complete; the church, in spite of ugly buttresses stuck onto its west end and a replaced east window, is very thrilling. The arcades with detached Purbeck shafts are superb; so are the stiff-leaf capitals and other mouldings. There are 17th-century

wall paintings and some old inscriptions commemorating the Great Floods of the 17th century.

Warham [3] This pretty village, with interesting early 19th-century flint cottages as well as earlier brick ones, three very nice Georgian farmhouses (one, north of the church, a former rectory), also has a most interesting Iron Age fort with very high banks and ramparts. This is an attractive place where recent excavations have been carried out. In the small village itself are two mediaeval churches. All Saints' at the south-east end of the

village has lost its tower, but it is still a very interesting church with a fine stone effigy of a civilian holding a roll, of the early 14th century, in the sanctuary. It is mysterious to find three fonts; that in the north transept is a very fine Norman one. This shows the Labours of the Months, and at one point there is a hare playing a zither. Perhaps this font came from the other church in the village, St Mary Magdalen's, at the north-east end of the village, which has a blocked Norman doorway in the north wall. The interior is purely Georgian with box pews and a towering three-

West Walton, outside and inside

decker pulpit under a plastered ceiling. On the north side of the chancel is the Turner chapel, built of brick in the 18th century when the Turner family moved to Warham from Lynn, where they were merchants, and patrons of the architect, Henry Bell. In the Turner chapel are nine black ledger slabs to Turners and their wives, including Dame Mary, wife of Sir Charles Turner and sister of Sir Robert Walpole, the builder of Houghton. The church also contains some very good glass; in the window nearest the pulpit is 15th-century Norwich School glass, with three pieces which are 100 years earlier—Eve spinning, Adam delving, and the Angel of the Expulsion. But the major part of the glass in the church is foreign; much of it came from the German monastery of Steinfeld and was probably imported by a Norwich dealer, J. C. Hampp, who sold it to the Revd Wenman Langton whose monument is in the church which he 'adorned with painted glass'. It is an exceptionally interesting church, nearly closed in 1959 but rescued by local 'Friends' and still in weekly use.

Waterden [3] A large farm, a former rectory, and a few cottages lie around the 11th-century church of All Saints, which is in the middle of fields. It has lost its tower and has a little bellcote; it has two Norman doorways, and windows which look even earlier. There are low box pews, and a text over the chancel arch. Still a parish church, it is a very atmospheric place and the occasional services are very well attended.

Watlington [7] A village of attractive farms. The 14th-century church of St Peter and St Paul with later brick stair-turret has a fine 15th-century font with 17th-century pelican cover, carved benches, and a Jacobean pulpit (1616). The Hall was recently rebuilt after a fire.

Watton [9] A small country town consisting of one wide street of late 18th/early 19th-century houses. St Mary's Church stands up a lane to the east, somewhat apart. It has a round tower with 15th-century parapet, and inside is a poorbox in the shape of a bearded man. The words, 'Remember the Poore 1639', are written across his chest; he stands with open palm for coins which slide from his hand through a slot into his body. Rokeles Hall was built in 1653, and was refronted in the 18th century.

Waxham [6] Gaunt and weather-beaten with a ruined chancel, St John's Church stands close to the sand dunes. The tower was built c. 1436; the porch of 1477 has tracery in spandrels and an elaborate frieze above. Inside are a banner stave locker and a magnificent tomb for Thomas Wodehouse (1571) whose family lived at the manor, now a farmhouse which, with its outbuildings, forms such an attractive group. They stand within an enclosing wall with turrets at the corners, and a fine 15th-century gateway on the east side.

Weasenham [9] Both churches, St Peter's and All Saints, were extremely well restored in the 19th century, All Saints being almost completely rebuilt; it has an attractive porch. *Weasenham St Peter* is the more picturesque village, with the cottages gathered about the village green. The Hall was built in 1905 in Elizabethan style. The New Wood is a fine and well-known example of irregular uneven-aged forestry.

Weeting [14] This place of bungalows and Nissen huts lies in the earliest inhabited part of Norfolk. Up a rough track in the heart of Breckland, amongst bracken, silver birches and Scots pines, are Grimes Graves, thirty-four acres of underground pits and tunnels, of about 2000 B.C. This is where prehistoric men mined the precious black floor

flint which was so hard and strong that it could be made into axes for their big task of deforestation. There are miles of low, dark tunnels all interconnected, where the black flint gleams in the light of torches and candles; some hollowed-out lumps of chalk have been found whose sooted edges show that they were used as lamps. There were also numerous flint tools of many types, and antler picks, used to prise out the flint; some of these are shown at the site. One of the pits—No. 15—contained no floor flint; in propitiation, an altar was built, flanked by two pedestals, one bearing a grotesque chalk figure of a vastly pregnant woman, the other, a symbol of male fertility. There are also the remains of a moated late 12th-century Hall, where Hereward the Wake is said to have spent some time in disguise; Bromehill Priory was a 13th-century house for Austin Friars. There is a ruined church among trees and another, St Mary's, with a modern tower and a fine chancel with three 14th-century windows.

Welborne [10] In a somewhat scattered village, behind an attractive lychgate, is All Saints, a round-towered church. There is some mediaeval glass in the porch and a well-restored screen. 'A sweet little church ... restored with taste', wrote Parson Armstrong in 1878; it still is.

Wellingham [9] A charming little church in a small village, dedicated to St Andrew; mainly 13th-century with 15th-century additions. Its great feature is the mediaeval screen base with most vivid paintings; one panel is dated 1532. On one panel, St George is fighting the dragon, watched by a kneeling princess, with the king and queen and their courtiers looking on in the background from a palace. The landscape also contains spires, birds, and a lamb. Another panel shows the Instruments of the Passion, and water being poured

Waxham remains

over Pilate's disembodied hands. A church not to be missed.

Wells-next-the-Sea [3] Is the most considerable of the North Norfolk ports, still having a certain amount of coasting trade up to its broad quay, which was developed by the Great Eastern Railway. The town consists of a number of narrow streets around St Nicholas' Church (entirely and very well rebuilt by H. J. Green after a fire in 1879 and retaining a mediaeval eagle lectern and a chest, 1635) and the open green, originally the Buttlands for archery practice, from which streets run down towards the quay. There are many fine Georgian houses in these little 'lokes' or lanes. Of recent years Wells has been developed as a seaside resort, its beach nearly a mile away, and with a boating lake known locally as 'Abraham's Bosom'. The town

was badly flooded in 1953 and 1978. There are garish amusement arcades on the quay, but these are balanced by the public house called the Fleece, a fine 17th-century building.

Welney [13] A Fenland parish nearly into Cambridgeshire which has an important refuge run by the Wildfowl Trust, visited by large numbers of migratory birds, and the breeding ground for over 60 species. St Mary's Church was rebuilt in 1848 by J. C. Buckler. It has a good east window by Wilmhurst and a west gallery, and retains some parts of the earlier building, including a nice 18th-century monument.

Wendling [9] Now bypassed, using the track of the old Lynn–Dereham line; the church of St Peter and St Paul, just by the

new road, has a curious Norman head above the south door and a locally carved Seven-Sacrament font. Jacobean carving in choir stalls and book cupboard. The Premonstratensian Abbey, of which nothing remains above ground, stood about half a mile away to the east on what is now Abbey Farm.

Wereham [8] Village full of pretty houses; St Margaret's Church by the duckpond has a 1779 monument.

West Bilney *see* Bilney, West

West Dereham *see* Dereham, West

Westfield [9] Straggling village with an isolated 14th-century St Andrew's Church without a chancel. Nice Jacobean pulpit and communion rails.

Wells-next-the-Sea

West Harling *see* Harling, West

West Lynn [7] Has some pretty cottages, a canning factory and a distressing view over the Ouse to King's Lynn. St Peter's Church, whose tower and lead spire are a feature of the view the other way, also has a sanctus-bell turret complete with bell, a roof with the apostles carved on canopied wall posts, and a Jacobean table.

West Newton [2] Part of the Sandringham estate. Carrstone church of St Peter and St Paul, thoroughly restored by the Victorians; many of the houses here were built by Edward VII when Prince of Wales.

Weston Longville [10] Parson Woodforde's rectory and Squire Custance's house have gone, the latter demolished in 1926. The present Weston House is built out of the former stable block. The lodges survive, with attractive Venetian windows and small columns. All Saints' Church has a very fine Tree of Jesse wall painting, 15th-century screen, a memorial to Woodforde, whose portrait by his nephew hangs by the tower, and a 16th-century brass to Elizabeth Rookwood. The church has recently undergone a most thorough restoration and is excellently cared for. Weston Old Hall, home of the Rockwoods, has a

16th-century porch, most of the res being early 18th century, thoug there is a fragment of a 14th century house.

West Tofts [15] In the Stanfor. Military Training Area. St Mary is an important church. The towe has an inscription to the 'begyner of the work', including Sir Joh Vyse, Rector 1451–86; four wil between 1482 and 1518 left mone to its building. It is most importar though for the rebuilding of th chancel and transeptal chapel b Pugin in 1849–50. The chapel wa designed as a memorial to Ma Elizabeth, wife of the Rector, th Revd Augustus Sutton. Pugin pr

174

vided a painted organ case (now at South Pickenham), painted ceilings, encaustic tiles, screens, and stained glass (made by Hardman to Pugin's design). Now it is gently decaying, with many of the fittings stacked on the floor. The Hall has been demolished but the stables with a horseshoe door remain.

West Walton *see* Walton, West

Westwick [5] A fine pedimented arch across the main road near the entrance to Westwick Park was demolished in 1981. The Georgian house overlooks the lake which comes close to the road at its south-west extremity. It was built by the Berneys and was inherited in the 18th century by the Petre family, the present owners. At the other end stands St Botolph's Church; the tower was built in 1460 when John Batalye left 10s to the new' tower and other bequests were made up to 1473. There is a good base course with the Sacred Heart in a Crown of Thorns, and flushwork in the buttresses and parapet. Inside, 15th-century screen with paintings of the Apostles and some interesting Victorian glass bought by the Revd H. J. Coleman with 'honey money' in 1885. Several Berney and Petre monuments, that to John Berney, 1730, is particularly good. Petre family pew in chancel.

West Winch *see* Winch, West

West Wretham *see* Wretham, West

Weybourne [4] The beach, called Weybourne Hope or Hoop, shelves so rapidly that it is possible to bring a large ship within a hundred yards of the shore; hence the local adage, He who would Old England win, must at Weybourne Hoop begin.' It has accordingly been heavily defended, in 1588 against the King of Spain, in 1914, and again in 939—such threats have left their mark on Weybourne in the form of an army camp. The priory of

Wheatacre

Weybourne was an Augustinian house which was dependent on the much bigger priory at Westacre. The Augustinian canons took over and extended the old Saxon parish church, the tower of which survives to the north of the chancel of the parish church. All Saints' Church is mainly 15th century; money was left for the tower in 1442. There is a nice two-storeyed porch and a Jacobean pulpit.

Wheatacre [18] Is on the wide Waveney marshes, very moist and green, good for hydrangeas and cottage gardens. The church of All Saints has a curious chequer-work tower, with squares of flint and brick, and inside a riot of woodwork, some 1885–6 and some later, 1900. The 15th-century font has remains of colour.

Whinburgh [9, 10] A tin plate over the chancel arch of St Mary's Church announces that 'beauty is in His Sanctuary'. The church is of good proportion, with solid tower (minus its top storey and parapet) at the south-west corner. The Old Hall which is Jacobean has a stepped gable and a pretty doorway.

Whissonsett [9] The village encircles St Mary's Church, rather thoroughly restored, which has

inside an Anglo-Saxon cross with circular head and interlace work.

Whitwell *see* Reepham

Wickhampton [12] St Andrew's is a wonderful church, attractively sited by farm cottages. Nice tower, 'new' in 1436; the chancel is reached, unusually, by a step down from the nave and contains, in two fine canopied recesses in the north wall, the tombs of Sir William Gerbygge and his wife (c. 1270) probably about the earliest three-dimensional effigies in a Norfolk church. Sir William holds his heart; his wife wears a wimple. There are very interesting wall paintings in the nave, of the Three Quick and Three Dead, and the Seven Works of Mercy, as well as the more usual St Christopher. Fine 17th-century pulpit. It is a remote church, but *must* be visited.

Wicklewood [10] The church of St Andrew and All Saints has a tower at the south-west corner. It contains a good monument to Bartholomew Day (1780), a physician from Wymondham, by the Norwich sculptors, Stafford and Athow. Near the church to the west stands the 1834 Poor Law Institution with good pedimented east front. Wicklewood Hall has a pleasing high-pitched roof and a two-storey porch.

Wickmere [4] The well-restored church, St Andrew's, which has an early round tower, has a 15th-century screen and an impressive modern table tomb by Esmond Burton for the 5th Earl of Orford. Wolterton Hall in this parish, built in 1741 by Horatio Walpole, who employed Thomas Ripley as his architect, is a fine red-brick house which looks much as it did in the 18th century. The State Rooms contain famous pictures and Gobelins tapestry. Wolterton church is a ruin in the park opposite the Hall.

Wilby

Wiggenhall St Germans [7] Here in the Fens, beside the wide Ouse, is a church with an intensely mediaeval atmosphere. The nave is full of dark carved 15th-century benches, very elaborate and heavy. The backs are all pierced and carved, as well as the ends; and there are the vices in the jaws of Hell, the figures of the apostles with their special symbols, and the usual contemporary figures of monks, etc. In the aisles are modern copies, and the pulpit, table and clerk's desk and chair are all 17th century. Outside the village is a red-brick Tudor house called Fitton Hall. St German's Hall is late 17th century.

Wiggenhall St Mary Magdalen [7] The light and noble church is, unusually for Norfolk, mainly brick; it has very fine 15th-century glass in the north arcade, a few painted panels of the old rood

screen and some fragments of parclose screens, and an 18th-century monument in the chancel. There is Jacobean panelling behind the high altar and some 18th-century box pews; turrets surmount the stairways to the rood loft and roof. Crabhouse nunnery was in this parish, although nothing of it now remains. Magdalen Road railway station has recently been reopened, after a successful campaign by residents.

Wiggenhall St Mary the Virgin [7] The 13th/15th-century church is full of splendid fittings, pride of place belonging to the carved benches, c. 1500, said to be the finest in England; as at St German's, they have saints in niches and traceried backs. The base of the mediaeval screen remains with colours still bright, and there is a parclose screen in the

Wiggenhall St Peter

south aisle, sheltering a beautifully painted alabaster tomb, with life-size effigies of Sir Henry Kervil, his wife Mary, his daughter Mary and his son Gervase in swaddling clothes, with ornaments and arms (1625). There is a Jacobean pulpit with hourglass stand, poor box, and pelican font cover (1625); also an eagle lectern (1518) and fragments of mediaeval glass. This church has recently been made redundant and thus its future is in question; it is surely an important enough building to be vested in the Redundant Churches Fund. Across the fields one sees the tall chimneys and castellations of St Mary's Hall, the home of the Kerviles until the 17th century. It was, however, rebuilt in 1864.

Wiggenhall St Peter [7] A splendid roofless ruin by the bank of the Ouse, this church was abandoned between the Wars but is now being maintained in its present condition. The tower, 15th century like the rest of the building, contains a good deal of brick—there is a bequest to the chancel in 1421. The church once had a south aisle, demolished in 1840. Note the corbels in the nave.

Wighton [3] A village of 300 with a message of hope for all Norfolk churches. A gale blew down the tower of All Saints' Church in 1965 but thanks to the generosity of Mr Leeds Richardson, a Canadian whose ancestors came from Wighton, the tower was rebuilt and dedicated in 1976. Well-proportioned nave strongly lit by 15th-century windows; a font of the same date with the Instruments of the Passion, and evangelists' symbols. Some excellent figures o

Wiggenhall St Peter

saints in mid-15th-century Norwich School glass in aisle windows. There was once a sacristy below the east window of the chancel outside. There are fine, large, old brick houses in the street running up to the church; a very pretty village.

Wilby [16] Is a small village with a few thatched cottages, 17th-century almshouses now being restored, and All Saints' Church entirely refurnished after a fire in 1633 and full of atmosphere. Excellent benches, box pews, and three-decker pulpit, the latter halfway

down the nave in the 17th-century 'preaching' position; altar rails and table all a pale grey colour. A poor-man's box with three locks (1638), a west gallery (1637) and an old chest; huge arms for Charles I over the south door. The nave is unspoiled 17th century except for the floor. Ledger slab in the chancel to Robert Wilton (1658) and small tablets on the walls painted with his arms and those of his three wives. The fine early 17th-century Hall of six bays and three storeys has a stepped gable over each bay and a pediment over each window. In the

1880s Samuel Colman, who lived here, was one of the eleven brothers who formed a famous cricket eleven.

Wimbotsham [7] Lies off the main road with nice cottages and gardens; St Mary's Church has two Norman doorways and a chancel arch of that period. Most of the apsidal chancel is a restoration (1853) retaining the original corbel table. The attractive bench ends show animals, including pigs, and a man praying with a rosary. Some of the others may be Victorian.

Winch, East [8] All Saints' Church restored in 1875 by Sir Gilbert Scott, has royal arms for George III over the tower arch, a Black Letter Bible dated 1611, a Norman pillar piscina, some old benches, and remains of a painted screen. Behind the organ a monument to William Barnes, J.P. whom 'noe allurements or threats from Him who usurped ye highest power could seduce him from his constant adherence to his Abandoned Prince and ye persecuted Church of England'. Poor Mr Barnes received no earthly reward for his fidelity, as he died in 1657. The Hall belonged to the Lancasters from 1900 to 1925 and Sir Osbert Lancaster is still Lord of the Manor here.

Winch, West [8] Amid the ribbon development are a few good cottages. St Mary's carrstone church has the Cholmondley arms on the tower and some flint ornamentation and there are two large niches on the west front. The late 17th-century altar rails have four carved figures holding Eucharistic symbols; Elizabethan altar table.

Winfarthing [16] Magnificent trees round here mark an ancient forest. St Mary's Church has a 12th-century font. It once possessed the Winfarthing sword, a mysterious object possibly left by a thief who sought sanctuary here, later known as the 'Sword of the Good Thief' and venerated by ladies who wanted to get rid of their husbands. Now it is lost, but commemorated in a modern stained glass window. Memorial to John Edwards (1784), 'Sleep on in silence never more to wake Till Christ doth raise ye and to glory take.'

Winterton [12] The splendid early 15th-century tower of Holy Trinity Church, 132 feet high, is a landmark for miles along the coast; the fine south porch is thought to have been built by Sir John Fastolf. The interior has a strong atmosphere; note the Fisherman's Corner, everything in it—ropes, anchor,

nets etc.—having been to sea, set up by the Revd Clarence Porter who was drowned saving a choir-boy from the sea. See also the statue of Our Lady of Perpetual Succour by M. Dupon of Bruges.

The **Witchinghams** [10] St Mary's, *Great Witchingham*, remote from the 'new' Witchingham, Lenwade, is a fine 14th/15th-century building surrounded by trees. Notable porch (Annunciation in the spandrels) and Seven-Sacrament font, the latter retaining much of its original colour and detail, such as the chalice and sacristy bell in the Mass scene. The eighth panel of the font shows the Assumption, a rarity. *Little Witchingham* church, dedicated to St Faith, ruinous for 30 years, has been totally restored recently; it has an early mediaeval carving of the Crucifixion set in the outside wall of the chancel and some magnificent 14th-century frescoes. The 14th-century font came from Whitwell. In the Wildlife Park, reached from the Norwich road, is a fine collection of exotic pheasants and other birds and animals. Great Witchingham Hall is largely a spectacular Victorian/Elizabethan rebuild of 1872, built by the Viscounts Canterbury who had inherited from the Tompsons. The latter had built the south wing in 1812, but the house also includes the south front of a 16th-century manor house. The late 17th-century squire was Oliver Le Neve, the duellist, and another of the family was Peter Le Neve, Norroy King of Arms and first President of the Society of Antiquaries. The Hall belongs to Bernard Matthews, the turkey farmer. Little Witchingham Hall is a small Georgian house built in 1819 by William Howard.

Witton [5] (near North Walsham) The round tower and north wall of the nave of St Margaret's Church are Saxon; there are good 13th-century sedilia and 16th-century arch-braced roof. Old bench ends

and box pews; monument to Ann Norris—'a woman of excellen sense, strictest principles, and fer vant piety'—whose inscription should be read in full.

Witton [11] (near Norwich Several good houses, particularl Witton House, grey, c. 1800. Th Green and Penrice families wer among the 19th-century owners The church of St Margaret has a octagonal turret capped by curiou battlements. A brass to Dam Julian Anyell, c. 1505, shows her a a vowess. One window, by War rington, of 1859, and a monumen of 1844.

Wiveton [4] Once a considerab port on the Glaven estuary but no a small village. At its southern en is a green, on which stands th splendid St Mary's Church. Part o the tower and flushwork-panelle chancel survive of the 14th-centur church that was substantiall rebuilt a century later, when i 1437 John Hacon bequeathed to 'y makyng of a nowe churche i Wyveton'. Good arch-braced roof arcaded aisles with seat altogether an airy interior. Ther are several good brasses to mem bers of the Brigge and Grenewa families. The road to Cley passe over a high mediaeval bridg Wiveton Hall, north of the coas road, is a flint house built by Joh Gifford of Gloucester in 1653, look ing over the marsh to Cley. It built of flint and brick, with curve gables, and a porch on the east sid It is a very romantic place. Gu Dawber, the architect, added wing early this century; quite we done.

Wolferton [2] This village, sep arated from Sandringham b several miles of road heavily bo dered by rhododendrons, is bes known as containing the forme Royal Station, now a private hous and museum, a neat affair wit much thick gravel, and crowns o the lamp-posts. The carrston church, St Peter's, has 14th- an

Wood Rising

15th-century screen work including parcloses in both aisles, mediaeval benches, a much restored painting over the chancel arch, and a lectern presented by Princess (later Queen) Alexandra, originally, to Sandringham church.

Woodbastwick [11] A lovely Broadland village with many thatched cottages; the church has a 15th-century screen and was restored rather thoroughly by G. G. Scott in 1878. It has a unique dedication to St Fabian and St Sebastian.

Wood Dalling [4] The 14th/15th-century St Andrew's Church has a lofty west tower (bequests 1486–1512), 13th-century chancel, several brasses, and a recumbent effigy in the north aisle. The good, remotely sited 16th-century Hall was built about 1582 by the Bulwer family.

Wood Norton [4] All Saints' Church is well kept; the tower has a brick top dating from a 1700 rebuild. Octagonal font with curious bulged faces and 17th-century cover. There are fragments of mediaeval glass in the tower window and an east window by C. A. Gibbs, 1875. There is a fine Georgian rectory and a Hall which, though Victorian, may incorporate fragments of an older house.

Wood Rising [9] The pleasant little church, St Nicholas, of this riverside hamlet has a barrel organ (1826), Jacobean pulpit, and Commandment boards with the figures of Moses and Aaron. Tomb in the chancel to Sir Robert Southwell (1563) with two helms above it. The bell is under a thatched canopy in the churchyard.

Woodton [17] A rather scattered village with a round-towered church, All Saints', standing alone; Norman font, Jacobean pulpit, and several monuments, one to Anne Suckling (1653), 'whose parentage was as honourable as ancient'. The Hall was built by the Sucklings in 1694, but it was demolished about 1839.

Wootton, North [2] A suburb of Lynn now, with a church, All

181

Saints', built by Salvin in 1852. Next door is a charming house, The Priory, 1718. And there are other old houses scattered amongst the new development. It was once a pretty village.

Wootton, South [8] The church has a curious Norman font. Between two villas in South Wootton, a turning leads off the main road to Reffley Wood where, beside a spring, a temple was built by a Friendly Society called the Reffley Brethren in 1789. Flanked by sphinxes, and with an obelisk over the fountain, and seats all round, the little temple was used by Lynn people for parties and *fêtes champêtres* under its big copper beech trees; the original Lowestoft punch bowls and churchwarden pipes were kept in the temple, until recent vandalism destroyed this charming and historic place.

Wormegay [8] With rich soil and prosperous-looking farms, this village has the large grassy remains of a motte-and-bailey castle. The carrstone St Michael's Church —up a long uneven track— has a 15th-century tower and a nave rebuilt in 1893.

Worstead [5] St Mary's, one of the finest of the spacious 15th-century Norfolk churches, was commenced in 1379 and finished about 1485. The tower screen was erected in 1501 at the cost of 'ye bachellers' and the rood screen, with saints including William of Norwich, and Uncumber, in 1512 by John Arblaster and his wife, Agnes. In 1831 the tower screen was given copies of Sir Joshua Reynolds' New College windows; there are some box pews and a magnificent font cover. Over the last ten years a large (and urgent) restoration programme has been carried out; this parish of some 500 people has raised £100,000 by various means, including an annual fair at the end of July. Looms now stand in the north aisle, for the weaving industry which

Wroxham, south door, detail

built this church has come back in the form of a Guild, and it is possible to see the weavers at work at certain times. North of Worstead is Meeting Hill, an early 19th-century Nonconformist settlement with church (1829), minister's house, and nice cottages, although its original character has been adulterated by new housing.

Worthing [9, 10] Hamlet which is almost part of Elmham; tiny appealing St Margaret's Church with round tower and Norman door. Very pretty niche in the east wall.

Wortwell [17] Has no Church of England church but a Congregational one (1773), yellow-washed and with Norfolk pantiles and some original fittings; next door is the minister's house of the same date. The part of the village called Low Street has picturesque cottages by the Waveney water meadows, and a former Baptist chapel standing under a horse chestnut tree in its little churchyard, which was built in 1822 and contains original galleries, panelled pews and baptistry. The pretty timber-framed Hall by the river was presumably the home of the Warners, who had the manor by 1428, and from whom it was inherited in 1546 by the Hollands.

Wramplingham [10] A very pretty village. Church of St Peter and St Paul has a Norman round tower and a very fine 13th-century chancel.

Wreningham [16] Pretty village, being developed. All Saints' Church is mostly 1852.

Wretham, East [15] Right on the edge of the Stanford Military Training Area. The church of St Ethelbert, rebuilt 1865 by G. E. Street, has a saddle-back roof to the tower, and retains a Norman door. Interior is a bit gloomy but has character. There are 18th-century monuments and early 20th-century

glass. Nice square flint-built Old Rectory of 1810.

Wretham, West [15] The Hall was rebuilt about 1912 after a fire in 1906, but has since been demolished. The church of St Laurence is a ruin. Obviously not a lucky village.

Wretton [8] Joins Stoke Ferry by a winding lane with some very pleasant cottages and gardens. All Saints' Church is of various periods, with several benches dated 1627, including one with the churchwardens' names. Nice 18th-century pulpit and fragments of 15th-century glass in the nave. Monument to William Harpin who died in 1851 on the way to Natal 'And was committed to the deep Lat. 36° 28′S, Long. 2° 43′W'. Appropriate text, Rev. 20:13.

Wroxham [11] The Broadland 'shopping centre', which is really one shop, Roy's, once the largest village store in the world. The beautiful broad is a very popular holiday place. St Mary's Church is mainly 15th-century with a good tower, but the south doorway is a magnificent piece of Norman carving—'barbaric and glorious' (Pevsner). Curious heads carved on the capitals, and the doorway stained a peculiar blue colour. Over the porch is a statue of the Virgin and Child, c. 1500. Many excellent memorials and in the churchyard to the north-west is the Trafford mausoleum (1831), Salvin's first ecclesiastical work. The manor house, one of a number of old buildings near the church which probably formed the original village centre, is dated 1623.

Wymondham [10] A market town on the road from Norwich to Thetford, now provided with a bypass, with a good view of town and abbey for those who wish to avoid the tortuous narrows of Bridewell Street, Market Street and Damgate. There are some fine 18th-century houses

in Middleton Street and on the Market Hill, where there is a market cross built in 1615, after a fire when most of the town was destroyed. A quiet little square called the Town Green has more Georgian houses, as also has the adjoining Cock Street. Vicar Street (leading from the Town Green to the Abbey Church) has a row of half-timbered cottages at one end, and graceful 18th-century façades at the other, and in the centre a small Queen Anne vicarage—all with the dignity of a cathedral close. In Church Street stands the 14th-century chapel of St Thomas à Becket (now the Norfolk County Library) and next door is the Green Dragon, an attractive half-timbered mediaeval house. By far the most splendid building in the town is the Abbey where, as at Binham, the nave has been preserved as the parish church. The parishioners built the west tower about 1450. The other tower, now ruined, was built by the monastery, not over the crossing as was usually the case, but two bays westward. This tower has been carefully restored and the magnificent eastern arch shows the great height of the choir roof. The extent of the choir itself can be seen in the churchyard, and standing by itself, to the south, is the eastern gable of the Chapter House. Inside, the Norman arcades and triforia rise to a splendid 15th-century clerestory and hammerbeam roof. There is another hammerbeam roof in the north aisle, and the south aisle was put together after the Reformation out of fragments of the conventual buildings. In this south aisle can be seen traces of the earlier Norman aisles which preceded the present ones. The majesty of this great church, which should be considered among the great conventual churches of England, has been wonderfully enhanced by a most beautiful reredos and tester, the work of Sir Ninian Comper, a memorial to the men of Wymondham who fell in the 1914–18 war.

Wymondham, inside and outside

The organ, in a fine 18th-century case, stands at the west end in a gallery set within the tower. There are also many memorials by the Norwich sculptor, Rawlins, and Thomas and Francis Stafford, and south of the high altar is a terracotta memorial supposedly to Elisha Ferrers, the last abbot, but more likely a re-assembly of an earlier tomb. At the time the textile industry was flourishing in Norwich, Wymondham had a considerable trade in bombazines and crêpe. In many of the old streets and in the back yards are rows of cottages, as in Rattle Row near the Town Green, with long windows against which a small loom could be erected. Cavick House, west of the Abbey, was mostly built by John Drake about 1720, and has a fine Rococo drawing-room. Burfield Hall is a Queen Anne house of 1709 about a mile and a half south-west. Gunvil's Hall is a Tudor manor house with 17th-century and 18th-century additions. Stanfield Hall is an early 19th-century Gothic house designed by William Wilkins. It was the scene of the infamous Rush murder of 1848 when Isaac Jermy, Recorder of Norwich, and his son and namesake, were foully murdered by their bailiff. Wattlefield Hall was built in aggressive mid-19th-century Gothic by John Mitchell, a solicitor, and passed in 1869 to his cousins and partners, the Clarke family, who owned it until 1973. Their proprietary chapel at Spooner Row is built in the same style; the architect was John Buckler (1843). This has now become a private house.

Yarmouth, Great [12] The slow-flowing rivers of East Anglia find it difficult to reach the sea, and at the very end of their courses are extremely hesitant about leaving the land. The Yare, strengthened by the Waveney, makes a little sea of its own in Breydon Water until, pushed by the Bure, it makes its way through the narrow channel of the port of Yarmouth, a channel which is a good three miles long before it reaches the sea at Gorleston. It gave the townsmen no end of trouble, for it was for ever silting up with shoals and sand banks until Joost Jansen, the Dutch engineer, straightened its course and deepened it in the 1560s. At the very outset it is as well to distinguish between Yarmouth Roads and Yarmouth Rows. The Roads is the name given to the quiet water between the beach and Scroby Sands (high and dry at low water), and a most welcome haven in which shipping can stand to in heavy weather. The Rows were narrow courts and alleys with their medley of mediaeval, 16th-century and more recent houses, all huddled together and, until the destruction of the late war, they still represented one of the most remarkable built-up areas of any town in England. The Rows were huddled together, for mediaeval and 16th-century Yarmouth was built on the strip of sand between the river and the sea and within a strong fortification with fifteen towers, three of which remain. But though Yarmouth has outgrown its defences, and roads and streets and a wide promenade have covered the sand and shingle, the sand itself is not very far below the surface. Going southwards past the Royal Naval Hospital (now the Barracks), an interesting group of buildings made to the design of William Pilkington in 1810, the distance between the channel and the sea narrows and becomes the long flat sandy peninsula of the South Denes. Dominated by the Nelson Monument, designed by William Wilkins of Norwich, and surmounted by an enormous figure of Britannia supplied by Mrs Coade's artificial stone manufactory at Lambeth, are the caravans which have replaced the fishing nets which used to be spread out to dry here. The very lie of the land makes Yarmouth a long narrow town. Towards the north, on the North Denes, the racecourse and the golf links and the Newtown Building Estate are fitted in on the narrow strip of land between the sea and the marshes of the Bure. Further south the town thickens about the huge Market Place. At one end stands St Nicholas', the biggest parish church in England destroyed by fire during the war and now magnificently restored by Dykes Bower. The restoration has included the reconstruction of the arcades and the entire refurnishing of the whole building; the Georgian pulpit, and the seating in the nave were brought from St George's. St Nicholas' is one of the most splendid of post-war restorations, in which it has been possible to preserve the very fine Norman work in the central tower and the Early English west end. Close by, and no doubt once joined to the church by cloisters, is the very fine 13th-century Priory Hall, once the refectory and now the assembly hall of the Priory School. Not far away is a half-timbered house, the birthplace of Anna Sewell (the author of *Black Beauty*) and the neat façade of the vicarage, 'built by the Corporation 1718' and repaired by 'Wm. Fisher Mayor, 1781'. Behind the vicarage is Priory Plain with the Corinthian splendours of the Methodist Temple, 1875, and hard by the beautiful quadrangular block of the early 18th-century Fisherman's Hospital. The Market Place narrows towards its southern end and is surrounded by the flashy façade of the multiple stores, but further on is a most delightful little square in the middle of which stands St George's. Built by John Price, in 1714, it was a most superb example of the Georgian church complete with galleries, contemporary organ case, wide plaster ceilings and western steeple, which suggest

that Price was influenced in its design by Wren's steeple at St James', Garlickhithe. This church is no longer used for worship but is to become an arts centre and has inevitably lost much of its furnishings. Joseph John Scoles was responsible for St Mary's Roman Catholic church and also for an unsuccessful suspension bridge over the Bure, which collapsed on 2 May 1845. In St Nicholas' churchyard, near the south door of the church, is an exceptionally vivid headstone to George H. Beloe, a small boy who was one of those who perished in this disaster. Carved in high relief, the bridge is shown parting asunder, the passengers on it falling into the foaming river beneath, the trees on the river bank bending in the storm, and high above, looking out of a cloud, is the All-Seeing Eye of the Almighty. Scoles also designed St Peter's Church, which is now the Orthodox church of St Spyridon, a most satisfactory alternative use for a redundant church. A better 19th-century Gothic church is St James' by J. P. Sedding. St Andrew's was built in 1859 to the designs of the curate-in-charge, John Gott (afterwards Bishop of Truro) as 'the Wherryman's Church', while St John's was built in 1857 for the use of the fishermen who at that time drew up their boats on the beach nearby. St

Luke's on Cobholm Island, which was damaged during the war and by the floods of 1953, is being rebuilt in a simple neo-Georgian style. Though severely damaged by bombing, and threatened by the demolitions of the planners, The Rows and the old houses on South Quay are best visited and studied as a separate town in themselves. Many of them contain much exquisite plaster and timber work, as for instance No. 4 South Quay. The Rows themselves are numbered. In No. 57 lived Sarah Martin, the prison reformer, and No. 91, now Middlegate Street, has considerable remains of the Franciscan Friary, together with one of the oldest Nonconformist places of worship in England in the Middlegate Congregational chapel. At the northern end of the Quay, near the modern bridge, stands the rather aggressive 19th-century town hall, which replaced an earlier one built by John Price in 1715, and near at hand is the Tollhouse, now a museum, but extensively damaged by bombing. Yarmouth is a market town and a port, was once one of the largest centres of the fishing industry in England, and is still a pleasure resort. The late-Victorian and Edwardian visitors who came for a family holiday by the sea were responsible for the neat rows of terraced villas, parks and wide promenade. These

change beyond the Wellington Pi into a good mile of fun fair wi those mechanical amusemer required by the 20th-century d tripper. On the other side of t river, a strip of the county Norfolk includes the residential d trict of Cobholm Island, liable flooding when Breydon Wat overtops its banks. Southtown co sists of one long street leading to t separate township of Gorleston.

Yaxham [10] A compact little v lage gathered about St Peter Church, which has been we restored. The round tower is Saxe and there is a splendid 14t century font (copied in the 19 century at Cromer); some goo screen work, old and new. In t chancel is a monument to the Re Dr John Johnson, Cowper's cous and protector during the last s years of his life, and called by hi 'Johnny of Norfolk'. In many wa a perfect village church.

Yelverton [11] A long village wi St Mary's Church dating back the 11th century. There are ange on the screen, and monuments Humphrey and Anne Rant insi (1661) and to William Hood ou side. 'His breath is fled and Body dead. But yet shall rise again A live above where Angels love Fr from disease and pain.'

Index

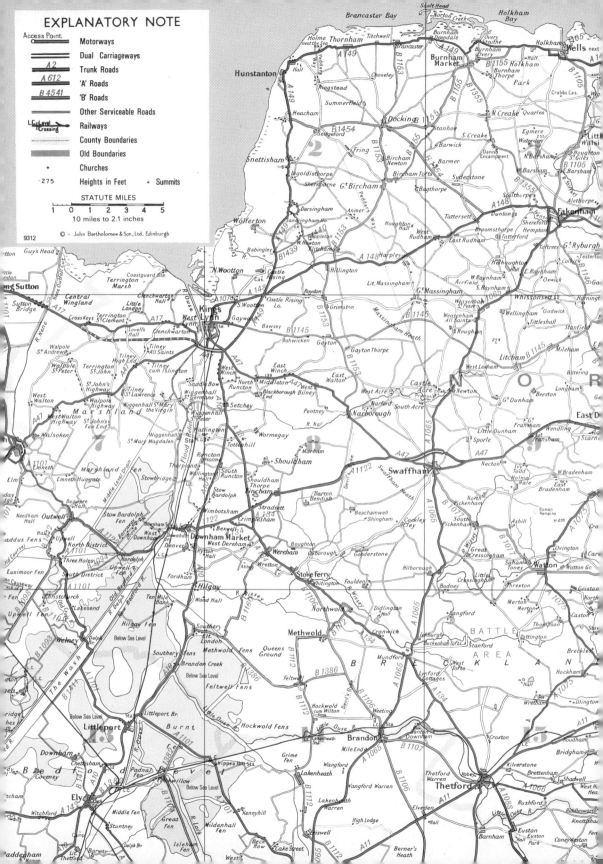